CAMBRIDGE STUDIES IN
MEDIEVAL LIFE AND THOUGHT

Edited by M. D. KNOWLES, Litt.D., F.B.A.
*Fellow of Peterhouse and Regius Professor of Modern History
in the University of Cambridge*

NEW SERIES VOL. 5

BRADWARDINE AND
THE PELAGIANS

NEW SERIES

Other volumes in preparation

BRADWARDINE AND THE PELAGIANS

A STUDY OF HIS 'DE CAUSA DEI' AND ITS OPPONENTS

BY

GORDON LEFF

Fellow of King's College, Cambridge

CAMBRIDGE

AT THE UNIVERSITY PRESS

1957

CAMBRIDGE UNIVERSITY PRESS
Cambridge, New York, Melbourne, Madrid, Cape Town, Singapore, São Paulo

Cambridge University Press
The Edinburgh Building, Cambridge CB2 8RU, UK

Published in the United States of America by Cambridge University Press, New York

www.cambridge.org
Information on this title: www.cambridge.org/9780521055369

First published 1957
This digitally printed version 2008

A catalogue record for this publication is available from the British Library

ISBN 978-0-521-05536-9 hardback
ISBN 978-0-521-08162-7 paperback

To my
MOTHER *and* FATHER

CONTENTS

PREFACE

ALTHOUGH this work originated as a study of Thomas Bradwardine's *De causa Dei*, it soon became plain that, even for the
barest understanding of it, his opponents would have to be considered. This has meant dividing the subject into two parts, the
first exposing Bradwardine's system, the second relating it to the
climate of thought of the time. Inevitably, therefore, much of the
second part has taken on a more general character. In particular,
I have found it necessary to treat, at some length, of scepticism
and of the main philosophical issues in the earlier fourteenth
century. I have not, however, attempted to bring science, as
practised by Bradwardine or his contemporaries, within the
scope of the present book. So far, no authoritative account of
fourteenth-century thought exists. Michalski's series of articles
still remain the boldest attempt at comprehending the period,
but they were never intended to provide full answers. I have
relied mainly upon the primary sources listed in the bibliography,
and I am well aware of the provisional and limited nature of my
findings.

In producing this study, I am deeply indebted, above all, to
Professor Knowles, both for introducing me to the subject and
for his unfailing aid and guidance as supervisor and editor. I offer
grateful thanks also to Professor E. F. Jacob, for his consideration
and attention at all times, and to Fr D. Callus and Miss Beryl
Smalley, for their criticisms and comments. My wife, by her
devoted help with proofs and index, has spared me from many
errors. For those that remain I am alone responsible.

30 June 1956 G. L.

INTRODUCTION

A STUDY of Thomas Bradwardine has been long overdue. Not only is it necessary in itself, for he was a thinker of a very high order; it has become imperative for an understanding of his age, and, indeed, of the fourteenth century. At present, the intellectual life of the period is everywhere still largely veiled in mists; but in England the obscurity is nearer to fog: the few gleams of knowledge that there are, as for example in the cases of Ockham and Wyclif, tend only to emphasize its prevailing density. We lack means of assessing its thinkers and we have no clear knowledge of the currents in which they moved.

Bradwardine has suffered in the same way: while his importance has long been recognized, little that is definite or consistent has been said about him. Apart from the mid-nineteenth century commentary by Lechler,[1] and two articles, by Hahn[2] and Laun respectively,[3] a few pages at most have been allotted to him in any work. In consequence, his reputation rests almost as much upon myth as upon fact. At one extreme he is traditionally regarded as an Augustinian, with insufficient attention paid to his own contribution; at the other, de Wulf,[4] for example, sees him as strongly influenced by Ockham's method and scepticism. Between these there is a variety of differing judgements: Rashdall calls Bradwardine 'the Mertonian Realist',[5] while the *Enciclopedia Italiana*[6] gives St Thomas Aquinas the greatest measure of control over him. Even the *Dictionnaire de théologie catholique*[7] in its recognition of his many sides fails to do justice to his individual role. Clearly, Bradwardine stands in need of attention; and for this

---

[1] G. Lechler, *De Thoma Bradwardino commentatio*.

[2] S. Hahn, *Thomas Bradwardinus und seine Lehre von der menschlichen Willensfreiheit*, in Beiträge zur Gesch. der Philos. des Mittelalters (1905).

[3] J. F. Laun, 'Recherches sur Thomas de Bradwardine, précurseur de Wyclif', in *Revue d'histoire et de philosophie religieuses*, IX (1929).

[4] M. de Wulf, *Histoire de la philosophie médiévale*, III, pp. 171–3 etc.

[5] H. Rashdall, *Medieval Universities* (ed. Powicke and Emden), III, pp. 268–9.

[6] *Enciclopedia Italiana*, VII (1930), p. 665.

[7] *Dictionnaire de théologie catholique*, XV, cols. 765–73.

B

a full exposition of both his thought and his place is needed.

Thomas Bradwardine was born c.1290.[1] His birth place is not certain, though Hertfield or Heathfield in Sussex is generally suggested. He himself makes a single reference in De causa Dei to Chichester as his home.[2] He entered Merton College, Oxford, and in 1323 his name appears on the college register as Master of Theology. His career was, above all, that of a thinker, scientist and teacher at Oxford; only later did he become a man of affairs and move to the court at London. In his combination of pursuits Bradwardine followed closely in the wake of Grosseteste, his great forerunner at Oxford.[3] Like Grosseteste, Bradwardine combined science and theology in the Oxford tradition; he did not belong to any of the religious orders, and he ended his life in high ecclesiastical office, indeed the highest in the land, that of archbishop of Canterbury.

From 1325–7, Bradwardine was proctor of the university; and to the best of our knowledge he remained at Oxford until 1335. He must, however, have visited Avignon once at least during this period, for in De causa Dei he mentions a dispute that he heard there in which a famous philosopher from Toulouse (almost certainly Pierre Aureole)[4] was involved. No doubt, too, Bradwardine took part in the general intercourse between Oxford and Paris, where he is cited by Thomas of Cracow as having engaged in disputation with Thomas Buckingham.[5]

In September 1335, Bradwardine was summoned to London by Richard de Bury, bishop of Durham, adviser to Edward III, well-known bibliophile and friend of Petrarch. Bradwardine, as one of the great minds of the age, had been attracted into the circle of learned men and clerics which Richard de Bury had gathered about him; and he now became one of Bury's chaplains and chancellor of St Paul's. This was followed in 1339 by his appointment as chaplain and confessor to Edward III. In this office, Bradwardine accompanied the king on his journeys and

---

[1] I have taken this account of Bradwardine's life mainly from Dictionnaire de théologie catholique and also from H. B. Workman's John Wyclif, I, pp. 120–2.

[2] Ed. Savile, p. 559.

[3] Robert Grosseteste, 1175–1253; first chancellor of the University of Oxford and bishop of Lincoln.

[4] De causa Dei, p. 693 (ed. Savile).   [5] See p. 235 below.

campaigns abroad. The year 1346 found him with the expedition to France which culminated in Edward's victory at Crécy, his dispatches being one of the immediate sources of news of its progress; and in the same year he delivered an impressive sermon on this battle and that of Neville's Cross.

In 1348, Bradwardine was elected by the monks of Canterbury to be their archbishop; but their haste offended the king, who demanded the appointment of John Ufford in his stead. Ufford, however, died shortly afterwards from the Black Death, and this time Edward consented to Bradwardine's election. He was consecrated at Avignon on 19 July 1349, but one month later on 26 August he was himself dead from the plague in Lambeth Palace.

Bradwardine, in his own day, seems to have enjoyed a great reputation for his learning and the power of his thought. This can be seen in his title of *Doctor Profundus* and the reverence with which Wyclif was later to regard him. Moreover, that his name continued to be spoken down the fourteenth century is evident from Chaucer's allusion to 'Bishop Bradwardine' and the coupling of his name with St Augustine in the 'Nun's Priest's Tale'.[1] As yet, however, his full place cannot be clearly assessed. Although definite traces of his influence are to be found in such thinkers as Nicholas d'Autrecourt, Jean de Mirecourt and Gregory di Rimini, we have, so far, insufficient knowledge to draw any final conclusions.

The period in which Bradwardine lived and worked is in marked contrast to the thirteenth century. It was one of disturbance and sharp change in every aspect of life; and in thought the quest of the preceding century for harmony between faith and reason was now replaced by an atmosphere of doubt. It was a time of regrouping: as E. Gilson has said, the marriage between theology and philosophy was being dissolved[2] and each party was making claim upon the other. The height of their union had been reached in the synthesis of St Thomas Aquinas (d. 1274). With him both faith and reason had become defined and given a common meeting-point: he saw one as complementing the other and together uniting into a single outlook. St Thomas's system may well be called the culmination of almost two centuries of

---

[1] Line 422. [2] E. Gilson, *La Philosophie au moyen âge*, p. 605.

thought since St Anselm (d. 1109), in which the supernatural and the natural had each gradually come to be treated in its own right.

This harmony, however, was short-lived; and from the first there had been a strain upon their common bond. It had never been easy to sustain, meeting as it did the attacks of the orthodox Augustinians giving primacy to faith, on the one hand, and of the Averroists, who implicitly accepted natural standards for their speculation, on the other. The former, as the representatives of tradition and ecclesiastical authority, gave Thomism a severe setback when in 1277 Etienne Tempier, bishop of Paris, condemned 219 theses as heretical.[1] These varied from denying God's existence to making Him an impersonal and indirect mover; and although the censures were directed primarily against the Latin Averroists (Siger of Brabant and Boethius of Dacia), they included several Thomist opinions bearing upon the relation of form to matter, such as the assignment of one, not several, forms to each being.

The chief importance of the condemnation, however, lies more in its ultimate repercussions than in the immediate details. It marked a turning-point in the use of Aristotle to support theology, expressing the hostility felt towards associating God and His ways with physical operations in this world. Bishop Tempier's action, in effect, constituted the revolt of those holding to the traditional concepts of Augustine against the Aristotelian hierarchy of cause and effect from God on high to His creatures on earth. It gave a new impetus to the Augustinians' more personal and immediate view of God. For them the illumination which came from God was independent of the material and sensory world. They opposed the Thomist view of analogy by which the created offered an approximation, dim though it was, to its source in God; they refused to accept the Aristotelian relation of causes as evidence of God's existence as the first uncaused cause; they rejected the Thomist method of abstraction whereby perception of material objects by the senses provided the intellect

[1] See Gilson, *op. cit.* pp. 550–70; also E. Bréhier, *La Philosophie du moyen âge*, Paris, 1949, pp. 341–3. The following brief account of the respective views of the Augustinians and Thomists makes no claim to be, in any way, comprehensive, and readers are referred to the two works just quoted for a fuller exposition.

with its true immaterial form. The Augustinians, on the contrary, disregarded the senses as in any way acting upon the intellect: true knowledge was to be found in the mind illumined by God. Similarly over questions such as the relation of essence to existence, of form to matter, of potency to act, the thinkers, in the era following the deaths of St Thomas, St Bonaventure and Albert the Great, were opposed to the innovations of Thomism. The last quarter of the thirteenth century was deeply impregnated with the new atmosphere of distrust of Aristotle created by the Paris condemnations. Both secular thinkers and Franciscans united against Thomism; and such men as Henry of Ghent (d. 1293), Giles of Rome (d. 1316), Matthew of Aquasparta (d. 1302), general of the Franciscan order in 1287, John Pecham (d. 1292), archbishop of Canterbury in 1279, William de la Mare (d. ?), Roger Marston (d. 1292), all took up the position of the Augustinians mentioned above.

Thus it is only in retrospect that we can talk about a synthesis in the thirteenth century. At the time, the immediate effect of the application of Aristotle to Christian belief had been the varying condemnations culminating in 1277.[1] St Thomas himself had owed much to Averroes in his separation of what belonged to reason and what belonged to faith; and while he had made the distinction the better to do justice to each, his system was regarded with suspicion by his opponents. Its immediate effect was not one of acceptance at all, but of the strongest opposition. Numerous treatises were written to disprove one or other of the Thomist tenets, and William de la Mare's *Correctorium fratris Thomae* was expressly directed against St Thomas's views.

Fundamentally, the great difference between the Thomists and the Augustinians was one of priority. St Thomas, following Aristotle, and in this sense Averroes, restricted reason to what was intelligible; it was his awareness of its limits that made him take the material world as the source of human knowledge. But unlike Averroes he did not stop there: far from regarding this world as complete in itself he recognized it to be the effect which derived from God as first cause. Accordingly, the natural was of value in leading man to an awareness of the supernatural. St Thomas's system was essentially to work from effect to cause as the only

[1] E.g. those of 1210, 1231 and 1270.

natural means of approaching God. This gave reason and the senses an essential but limited part to play, and at a certain stage they had to give way to revelation of truths which came from faith alone.

The Augustinians, on the other hand, in keeping with their Platonic origin, started with the cause, and refused any independent value to the effect. For them, only the true archetype, or idea, from God counted; every individual, therefore, as subsequent to the idea, could not be the means of its true understanding or real in itself. In this way, the Augustinians saw existence as belonging to the idea; it had to come before the object. As St Augustine had said, everything had to be known in the light of God, as first truth, and not as it derived from an object.[1] True to this tradition, given expression in St Anselm's ontological proof of God, that which was real in the mind was also real in reality, and knowledge of truth could only come about through the ideas in the soul. This enabled the Augustinians to extend reason equally to fact and to matters of faith, for in each case it depended not upon objects but upon illumination. St Bonaventure's outlook had given the fullest expression to this, and it was taken up by his followers as the main challenge to Thomism.

Up to a point Augustinianism assigned a definite role to reason; even though it was from divine illumination, and not through abstraction, it had a part to play in discerning God. Though, as Bréhier has said, it was a meditation upon faith, it yet allowed for discussion; indeed, in one sense, it did not limit its extent enough, for it recognized no natural bounds to its efficacy. Nevertheless its very denial of any validity to effects made it ever liable to rule out practical experience altogether; it made the tangible links between God and His creatures so tenuous that they could at the slightest pressure be snapped.

This, in effect, was what Duns Scotus (d. 1308) did. True to the Augustinian tradition of the Franciscans he took up the growing opposition to Thomism, but with an added impetus which paved the way for the separation of faith from reason in the fourteenth century. Duns was preoccupied with the impossibility of reaching a cause through its effects; his proofs for the existence of God, his denial of analogy and causality between the divine

[1] Bréhier, op. cit. p. 312.

and the created, all expressed his rejection of St Thomas's methods. In particular, in his desire to show the impossibility of correlating God's actions with those of His creatures, Duns reverted to the Augustinian emphasis upon God's will as the measure of all that He did. God was so infinitely free that there was no means of attributing any mode to His operations; far from being the first cause in the manner of Aristotle, God acted so freely that His ways could not be calculated by human reason and no relation could be established between Him and His creatures.

Duns's outlook was of the greatest importance for the future. In the first place, it put God beyond the reach of His creatures by breaking any direct link between Him and their knowledge of Him. To say that God was so infinitely free that nothing could be said about Him was to make Him virtually unknowable. Although Duns allowed God all the traditional attributes such as omniscience, justice, mercy, and so on, he offered no means of tracing them in His creatures. Moreover, even while substituting a common (univocal) being shared by God and His creatures, this brought man no nearer to Him. Secondly, then, Duns took a stage further the division between faith and reason in his refusal to allow natural knowledge to support revealed truth: there was not even the illumination of the Augustinians to give man a sign of God. Thirdly, and perhaps most significant, Duns's rejection of any ascertainable connexion between the created and the divine was to turn philosophy and practical knowledge loose; there could be no simple reversion to the pre-Anselmian era where reason did not yet stand in its own right but was the expression of faith founded on authority. In contrast there now stood a powerful corpus of metaphysics, logic and dialectic, able, together with a growing body of scientific knowledge, to discard guidance from revelation. To follow Duns was to concede the natural standards of the Averroists.

With William of Ockham (d. 1349) and his followers, these consequences came to pass. In his 'Commentary on the Sentences' in 1318, Ockham gave effect to this new division between faith and reason, the supernatural and the natural. As we shall examine in Part II below, he limited knowledge in such a way that everything outside man's practical experience was beyond its reach. Revealed truth and all that was extra-sensory were, accordingly, not amenable to reason. God's existence or His goodness, for example, could be believed as a matter of faith but could not be proved by reason: they were not within the realm of rational demonstration. If subjected to reason they became at best probable; and hence arose the attitude of scepticism which Ockham's outlook generated. Reason and faith were so separate and distinct that the gap between them could not be bridged: reason could not enlighten belief nor faith increase man's natural knowledge.

Now it was this very union between reason and faith which had formed the main foundation of scholasticism. Differently as it might be interpreted, practically every scholastic thinker from St Anselm onwards had accepted the validity of reason in matters of faith; it had been at the heart of Augustinianism no less than Thomism and from it the syntheses of the thirteenth century had been built. Now, however, the break between the two spheres which Duns's outlook had portended was given open expression by Ockham.

The effects of Ockham's rejection of the extra-sensory, and with it the traditional metaphysical concepts, were soon apparent. In the first place, with the breach between faith and reason there was no longer room for the traditional outlooks. There was a change in direction and aim among the fourteenth-century thinkers as compared with those of the thirteenth century.[1] No longer was the quest for the divine the main motive; instead the natural and the supernatural tended to become separate areas without apparent connexion. As a result the climate was very different from that of the classical systems of the thirteenth century; the comprehensive nature of these disappeared and in their place came, to use Michalski's words, an attitude of criticism and scepticism.[2] Where the thirteenth century looked for an ordered hierarchy between God and man, whether through the divine emanations of the Neoplatonists or through Aristotle's system of causes, the fourteenth thought in terms of definition:

[1] The following remarks apply especially to Robert Holcot, Thomas Buckingham and Adam of Woodham, all examined here (Part II below).

[2] See Michalski's articles listed in the bibliography below, p. 272, especially 'Le criticisme et le scepticisme' (in *Bulletin de l'Académie polonaise des sciences et des lettres*, 1925), 'Les courants critiques et sceptiques' (*ibid.* 1927), and 'Les sources du criticisme et du scepticisme (*ibid.* 1928).

Ockham and his followers refused, either explicitly or implicitly, to pretend to look beyond human experience; thought, for them, became an exercise in logic, the ordering of concepts and their reduction to conform to experience. Anything outside its range, such as universals, proofs for God's existence, theories of value, were rejected as without reality.

In the second place, the questions discussed underwent a marked change both in number and in content. This was especially apparent in the Commentary on the Sentences, for a hundred and fifty years the main introduction to the study of theology.[1] The four books of the original Sentences by Peter the Lombard had comprised 182 distinctions and over 600 chapters.[2] Each book had dealt with a different aspect of theology: the first with God; the second with His creatures; the third with Christ; and the fourth with the sacraments. Within these all the fundamental questions of belief had been comprehended. Until the time of Ockham the Commentary on the Sentences had followed these main lines of the original.[3] Each question had been divided into three parts: the 'Divisio textus', 'Expositio textus' and 'Dubia circa litteram', in which the question was examined, the arguments *pro* and *contra* put and the objections answered.

So soon, however, as the new limitations of Ockham's theory of knowledge were imposed, the Commentary shrank in size and hardly bore any relation to the classical Commentaries of, say, St Thomas, St Bonaventure or even Duns Scotus. Where Ockham had openly ruled out the possibility of proving God's existence, his successors such as Buckingham, Holcot and Woodham did not mention it; or if they did, as in the case of Buckingham and

---

[1] See P. Glorieux, *Dictionnaire de théologie catholique*, XIV (art. Sentences), cols. 1860–84.

[2] Each book was divided into distinctions under which the separate topics were discussed; and these were further subdivided into chapters, with often five or six chapters to each distinction.

[3] Ockham's commentary was divided into his *ordinatio* and *reportatio*. The *Ordinatio* (covering bk. I) was the personal exposition by the bachelor. The *Reportatio* consisted of notes by his hearers, taken either freely or from dictation. They were therefore *résumés* or extracts of a larger work. It is in this form that the last three books of Ockham's Commentary are known to us. While the first book followed the Lombard's method of distinctions, the others were in *quaestiones*.

Woodham, it was to Anselm's ontological proof that they appealed, thus referring to the one proof which started and finished as a mental concept not requiring the support of practical experience. Similarly, little or no attention was paid to the nature of being, the existence of universals, or the relation of form to matter. Instead, in the Commentaries of those thinkers under discussion here, there are three new features: the first is the very small number of questions involved, varying from a mere six in Buckingham's case to ninety in Woodham's, and often not following the original four books of the Sentences at all. The second is the virtual replacement of the classical *distinctio*, into which the main questions were divided, by the *quaestio*, so that frequently one *quaestio* comprised two or more distinctions. Thirdly the questions themselves revolve, in greater part, around four main themes: one, the relation between the various attributes in God, such as omnipotence, will and knowledge; two, correspondingly, the relation of the faculties in the human soul, e.g. will, knowledge and love; three, the place of grace and the resources of free will; four, the sacraments.[1] The first two groups usually resolved themselves into subsuming God's attributes under His will and, likewise, regarding man's faculties as expressed by his will. This then cleared the way for the central part of these Commentaries, the relation of divine will to free will over the question of grace and future contingents; finally, as a corollary, the sacraments were usually examined, both for themselves and in relation to free will, as in the case, say, of repentance and contrition.

What is so striking about these questions is that they were virtually reduced to those concerning the relation of free will to divine will, in which grace and predestination, for the first time since the Pelagian controversy of the fourth century, became the central problems. It is evidence of the breakdown in the old harmony between the divine and the created that, instead of ascertaining God through His traces in this world, His existence had to be reconciled with man's. The unity between the divine and the created which formed the starting-point of the thirteenth-

[1] E.g. Adam of Woodham's Commentary. In bk. I the first 26 questions deal with the Godhead and with the faculties in the human soul; the remainder of the first book is taken up with the need for grace. Bk. II discusses the increase and decrease of grace; bk. III is concerned with future contingents; and bk. IV with the sacraments.

century systems had given place to a one-sided attitude in which the two were not apprehended as part of one another.

This led to the third main change in the outlooks of the fourteenth-century thinkers: their eclecticism. Because they were no longer asking the same questions they could not turn to the traditional systems for support. In consequence, although Holcot was a Dominican, Buckingham a secular and Woodham a Franciscan, their outlooks can in no way be distinguished according to their orders; indeed, to take one case, Holcot had far more in common with the other two thinkers mentioned above than with Durandus of St Pourçain, a member of his own order. In this connexion the Commentary of Robert Halifax is illuminating: although not a sceptic like the other thinkers mentioned here, he followed the same choice of questions as they[1] and he was equally eclectic in his views. Thus by the time these thinkers had combined concepts taken from St Augustine, St Thomas and Duns Scotus there is no means of designating them in traditional terms.

Such were the circumstances of Bradwardine's time, and his own importance derives from his opposition to the views put forward by Ockham and his followers. Faced with the first full blast of the icy winds of Ockham's scepticism, he did not hesitate to seek protection in the folds of theology. De causa Dei was essentially the response of faith to scepticism; it was from one for whom theology came first above all. It was concerned to cut, root and branch, at that outlook which started from men, not from God. Its aim was to rebut the consequences which followed from such a wrong attitude and to win back all attention to God. If in the divorce between philosophy and theology, Ockham and the sceptics took the side of philosophy, Bradwardine was the protagonist of theology. He was the other party to the conflict, which followed Duns Scotus, and, like his opponents, he was not prepared to rest content with less than all. The stand that he took in De causa Dei was the first counterblast to the challenge of scepticism; and in the extremity of its views it went far towards

[1] Robert Halifax (d. ?1357) is still virtually unknown. There is no printed edition of his Commentary, but three manuscript copies of it exist in the Bibliothèque Nationale, Paris (F.L. 14,514, F.L. 15,880 and F.L. 15,888). 14,514 and 15,888 cover bk. 1, and 15,880 covers bk. 1 and two questions in bk. 11.

the positions to be taken by Luther and Calvin in the sixteenth century.

Although it would be misleading to see this division between faith and scepticism as hard and fast and full-throated, it forms the dominant *motif* around which the main questions of the day were arrayed. Each side was struggling to redefine the relation between the divine and the created; neither was willing, or able, to return to the balance achieved by St Thomas Aquinas in the thirteenth century. Both Bradwardine and the sceptics shared in the common reaction against an analogy between God's deeds and His creatures' actions; each equally refused to accept reason and metaphysics to describe God; both were agreed that the point of contact between God and His creatures lay in His acting directly through His will. They both, therefore, started from a common predicament: in their refusal to accept the seeming in-exorability of the Arab systems, they had to find a new balance be-tween theology and philosophy, faith and reason. Because the two parts as added together in the thirteenth century did not give the full answer, a new solution must be found. Either the figures could be rearranged or an unknown factor postulated.

Ockham and his followers tended towards the second of these; they refused to move beyond that which could be verified: God, as outside these terms of reference, was essentially a shadowy figure whose relation to His creatures was unknowable. He was virtually excluded from their system, and, as the Masters at Avignon themselves recognized,[1] Ockham could equally have dispensed with God in expressing his views on grace. One can-not but feel that God would have no real place at all with Ockham and his followers were it not for the need to safeguard themselves. Bradwardine, on the other hand, regarded the differing claims of faith and reason as a false problem. In his system, faith was the supreme and overwhelming consideration: reason existed only to translate the truths that came from revelation alone; it could add nothing; it met no intrinsic need, but rather expressed the weakness of God's creatures in that they could not, like God, dwell amidst the supernatural alone. With Bradwardine, then, reason became the merest fraction, incomplete in itself as the ex-pression of a greater value. These differences in approach had to

[1] See pp. 189–92 below.

lead to opposite goals: ultimately the one used faith to the exclusion of reason, and the other made reason the primary consideration.

This was the setting to Bradwardine's dispute with those whom, throughout *De causa Dei*, he calls the modern Pelagians. His treatise was essentially an answer to the current scepticism. We shall examine below[1] the precise forms that it took; here it suffices to say that, through their refusal to allow God to be proved and discussed by reason, the sceptics made man the centre of their attention; their exclusion of theological truth forced them back upon a rational and logical explanation which applied only to the natural order and omitted God. Thus they saw man where Bradwardine insisted that they should see God; free will for them came before grace; they measured the nature of the future and of contingency in human not divine terms. The emphasis, therefore, of scepticism could not but be upon men and free will. These came within practical knowledge, whereas God did not. There was no room for the traditional theology with them.

It is this that Bradwardine called Pelagianism: although it had its roots in an outlook very different from Pelagius's, it gave rise to many similar features: man was exalted; God was virtually ignored; the limitations of the former were not made the basis for the omnipotence of the latter. Thus, though the problem involved far more than man's powers after the fall, the place of grace and merit played a very large part in the disputes between Bradwardine and the sceptics. Pelagianism, for Bradwardine, was concerned with the full range of the divine and created wills, including the concept of God, His will, grace, sin, the power and the scope of free will, the nature of the future and the problem of necessity and freedom. Each of these concepts was related to the central one of the place where God's actions ended and those of His creatures began. In every case Bradwardine was determined to assert God's dominion to the exclusion of all other powers, and to put His cause beyond question.

Bradwardine, in the preface to *De causa Dei*, tells of the origin of the work: it lay in his revulsion against the emphasis upon free will and the disregard for God's grace which he had heard preached as a student in the schools.

[1] See pp. 127–39 below.

I rarely heard anything of grace said in the lectures of the philosophers . . . but every day I heard them teach that we are masters of our
own free acts, and that it stands in our power to do either good or
evil, to be either virtuous or vicious, and such like. And when I heard
now and then in Church a passage read from the apostle which exalted
grace and humbled free will, such as, for instance, that word in
Romans IX, 16, 'Therefore it is not in him that willeth, nor in him that
runneth, but in God that sheweth mercy,' I had no liking for such
teaching, for towards grace I was still graceless . . . . But afterwards,
and before I had become a student of theology, the truth before mentioned struck upon me like a beam of grace. It seemed to me as if I be-
held in the distance, under a transparent image of truth, the grace of
God as it is prevenient both in time and nature to all good works—
that is to say, the gracious will of God which precedently wills that he
who merits salvation shall be saved, and precedently works this merit
in him—God in truth, being in all movements the primary Mover . . . .[1]

De causa Dei first started as a course of lectures in opposition
to such views.[2] He consented to their publication, he says, in
response to repeated requests and in the hope that they might
help in a return to the established faith.[3] The whole tenor of the
work is polemical: far from being an exercise in theology or the
simple reassertion of St Augustine, it is first and foremost an
answer to the ills of the time. Bradwardine shows in his preface
how he regarded the work as part of the crusade against the new
Pelagians:

I burn with ardour for God's cause, knowing that I thrust my
hand into a terrible flame, for I am not unaware how the pestilential
Pelagians are wont to harass an agitated mind with tumult and abuse,
and how they will strive to tear this small treatise with their savage
teeth.[4]

His frame of mind here bears witness to the strength of contemporary scepticism: for he clearly regarded himself as going
against the stream and taking up an unpopular stand. This, however, seemed only to make him more determined, for he sees himself in company with those of the past, such as the prophets and

---

[1] Taken from H. B. Workman's *John Wyclif*, I, p. 121.
[2] On the question of its date, see Appendix I below.
[3] *De causa Dei* (ed. Savile), Preface (i). The figure in parentheses represents my page-numbering as there is none in the preface of Savile's edition.
[4] *Ibid.* (v).

St Paul and St Augustine, who also struggled to uphold belief in God.[1]

The overriding charge which he makes against the modern Pelagians is that they are subverting God's will by free will: today, he continues, a multitude support Pelagius and free will against God's grace freely given; they consider free will alone to suffice for salvation, whilst even those who employ grace do so perfunctorily or make it conditional upon free will, so that it is not grace at all.[2] In any case, they deny God's omnipotence and act with impiety towards Him. The Pelagians' assertion of free will makes God its servant not its master;[3] they allow it such liberty that even over the future they are ready to confound the voices of the prophets in its interests.[4]

Bradwardine's reply was to reassert God's grace to the exclusion of all merit. His intention was to win back for God all power which he considered to have been usurped by men. His whole system was designed to establish God as the senior partner in all that concerned His creatures. This allowed no independent area of freedom to them at all; and it is the essence of his system. The importance of this divine control, which I have called the 'principle of divine participation',[5] cannot be overrated: by making God the most immediate cause of all that they do, men were left with no autonomy; they became dependent upon Him for their being, movement and worth; they had no positive qualities or powers to call their own. In this way the whole world became, in effect, nothing more than the extension of God's will, with no part of it capable of acting but by His immutable decree.

This was Bradwardine's reply to scepticism, and its novelty and extremity are striking: he rejected not only all claims for the independent existence of free will, but denied any other form of determinism in the interests of God's. Thus, although the sovereignty of free will was his main target, he could only answer it effectively by denying any power to natural necessity, the power of the stars or the planets or any form of psychological pressure which might detract from God's omnipotence. Hence, throughout *De causa Dei*, Bradwardine, in his defence of God's

[1] *Ibid.* (v).   [2] *Ibid.* (i).   [3] *Ibid.* (ii).   [4] *Ibid.*
[5] See pp. 50–2 below.

cause, waged a twofold battle: the main one was directed against free will, but he was ever ready to crush any signs of a rival determinism to God's, and in this he was always mindful of the theses condemned at Paris in 1277. He was as much an opponent, though for different reasons, of the Greco-Arab determinism of the thirteenth century as the sceptics were.

Bradwardine's method, no less than his system, was his own and of his century. Like the other thinkers mentioned above, he eschewed the diversity of subjects to be found in the systems of the thirteenth century. We have already suggested that after Ockham there was a great change both in the climate of thought and the treatises themselves. Bradwardine, no less, bears ample witness to it. So far as his outlook is concerned, he too lacked the comprehensive interest of his predecessors. He took for his subject those questions raised by the sceptics, namely, the relation of God to man; and, in effect, *De causa Dei* was moulded to the twin topics of grace and future contingents. Everything in the work was directed to asserting God's pre-eminence and denying the claims of reason and free will.

When he does refer to matters outside his immediate theme, he does so incidentally, and his opinion on them is rather to be gleaned than found fully expressed. His theory of human knowledge, his views on matter, the nature of the angels, for example, are all confined to references which usually issue from other arguments: indeed, in the case of the angels, there is not enough evidence on which to venture an opinion.

Similarly, in his mode of argument, Bradwardine eschewed philosophy and metaphysics. He was not primarily concerned with problems of being or its nature, nor with the scope of human knowledge. In this, of course, he had much in common with his opponents; and like them he used logic and fact as the arbiters of his discussion. Once having asserted a proposition, Bradwardine is more concerned with its inner consistency than with a discussion of possible alternatives taken from quite other premises. Where he differed from them was in the theological terms of his propositions; for him theology was the only truth; the place of logic and fact, when available, was to support it for those unable to feel it. Thirdly, Bradwardine, too, was eclectic in his antecedents. For the comparatively narrow foundation of his system he was quite prepared to employ those materials ready furnished which were to hand. Thus his view of God is made up from concepts taken from St Anselm, St Thomas and Duns Scotus; his theory of matter and the relation of causes is from Aristotle; while his over-all outlook on God and man comes primarily from St Paul and St Augustine. As with his contemporaries, it is hard to describe Bradwardine in traditional terms, for he was arguing on different grounds from his predecessors. Their respective aims and circumstances were too different for their systems and methods to be the same.

Bradwardine's originality of method may be seen as flowing from these general tendencies. Firstly, as a closely reasoned, powerfully argued treatise on a particular topic and with a set purpose, *De causa Dei* may be claimed as unique during this period. The central argument is never lost, and, allowing for what in our eyes is the inherent medieval *penchant* to excessive repetition, it is without any real digression. The argument is not to be seized indirectly through a maze of discursive allusion, but according to a plan which, while often overlapping, is never disordered. Each of the three books is in logical sequence: the first establishes God's existence and attributes; the second deals with the nature of free will; the third seeks the meeting-place between them. Although it has not been possible to work through *De causa Dei* in such direct order, these broad divisions stand; and for all the repetitions, the listing of authorities and the different nuances of meaning, the work possesses a unity compelling enough to preserve the argument throughout.

This, in a sense, is Bradwardine's most notable feat; its originality lies in the way in which he builds his system around a central theme and disciplines the width of his references and authorities to this end. He allows no room for idle speculation nor, normally, for equivocation: a point is included not for its own interest but for its relevance to the argument.

The second way in which Bradwardine leaves his personal stamp is in his mode of discussion. This is moulded to a mathematical plan in which he moves from one position to another with geometrical precision. As in geometry, each argument consists of a general proposition, its proof and objections, with the

C

conclusions and corollaries drawn. In this way Bradwardine is able, by the weight of a growing body of established axioms, to give momentum to his argument. It is by this means, above all, that he is carried so effectively to his extreme views: the ground has always been carefully prepared beforehand. His manner of argument gives an effect superficially similar to that used later by Spinoza and Leibniz, and its influence upon the seventeenth century may well be greater than is at present realized. But in Bradwardine's case it is founded on the syllogism of the medieval schools, and it is based upon the authority of the Scriptures, the Fathers, particularly St Augustine, and the arguments of the main medieval schoolmen. In all this it is essentially a work of the period.

While it is no part of the present work to discuss Bradwardine as a scientist, it is not hard to see the influence of science upon his thought in general. Apart from the current use of Aristotelian logic, Bradwardine adopts Aristotle's view of matter and form, with its divisions into potency and act, and also his view of causes. From these he derives one of his two proofs for God's existence. In consequence, his opinion of God's relation to His creatures moves on Aristotelian lines, and his extreme determinism can be seen as deriving from St Thomas's use of Aristotle. This, in turn, influences Bradwardine's view of free will and contingency; and in this sense the whole of his system must be said to have its origin in Aristotelian principles. Bradwardine lived at a time when not only the laws of logic, but those of science, were derived from Aristotle, and in their application to *De causa Dei* Bradwardine is able to reinforce his own assertion of theology. By his knowledge of mathematics and of physics, Bradwardine the scientist was able to confirm and support Bradwardine the theologian, and this combination was one of the main sources of his strength.

What kind of man was Bradwardine? Like so many medieval thinkers, it is hard to conjure up any living picture of the individual behind such a massive work. If to some extent it is true that the work reveals the man, Bradwardine emerges as an inhumane genius. He undoubtedly was a man of parts, being a member of Richard de Bury's circle and one of the King's entourage, to say nothing of his standing as scientist and theologian at Oxford. His was the stature of one who had sufficient trust in his own powers and independence of judgement to plough his own furrow. He was quite prepared to go against the prevailing tides and winds in following his own course. He was concerned with his view of the truth to the exclusion of everything else, as *De causa Dei* clearly shows. Yet, as seen through its pages, he can hardly be called lovable. His system is built to disprove human worth; he so succeeds in depressing man that one is tempted to ask why so perfect a creator should have willed such creatures. Though his God is moved by love, Bradwardine allowed none to enter man's nature. In his intentness to vindicate God's cause Bradwardine forgot the obligation to His creatures; by his doctrines the sufferings of Christ Himself lost any meaning: for man had no justification.

The importance of the disputes between Bradwardine and his opponents lies in the change wrought upon scholasticism. Each side, in starting from either faith or reason to the exclusion of the other, made them virtually separate pursuits. Since Ockham and his followers refused to see the supernatural through the natural, they put faith beyond reason's bounds. Because Bradwardine allowed reason no autonomy it lost any validity, and faith became the only law. This meant that, on the one hand, reason, philosophy and science tended to become autonomous disciplines without reference to theology; while, on the other, faith and theology became increasingly a regime for worship, independent of ratiocination. The effect of this break was plain to see: for philosophy and reason it meant the virtual self-sufficiency preached by the Averroists; it could choose to discuss man in its own terms without more than passing reference to God. At the hands of Ockham and his followers, it recognized no more than a nominal obligation to be at the disposal of faith, while in its attention only to practical knowledge it in fact rejected such a role. On the part of theology, the effect of this division was no less far-reaching: through the withdrawal of reason's support, faith came increasingly to rely upon dogmatic assertion and personal experience. If belief were to be challenged by logic and scepticism, the answer was to show its truth in Scripture: if God's existence were dismissed as only possible or His goodness counted as unproven, personal experience of Him was the reply. Where the head could not be convinced, the heart could know; where scepticism questioned, authority could assert. Such was the twofold response by theology which culminated in the Reformation with Calvin and Luther: Calvin was prepared to build upon the dogmatic certainty of God's eternal ordinances without regard to the niceties of dispute; Luther put all trust and knowledge in personal belief and the authority of the Bible. Different though they were, neither had need of reasoning or proof, Catholic tradition or ceremonial. They each transferred the argument to a theological plane.

It is in this light that we must measure both Bradwardine's *De causa Dei* and his opponents' scepticism. They were not simply ceasing to argue along traditional lines; they were disputing the very existence of traditional concepts. The questions over grace and free will which constituted the central theme of their quarrels arose from these new circumstances. To follow the natural laws of the sceptics could only mean that grace was questioned, for its existence was too intangible to be asserted. Similarly, Bradwardine, who made the divine his touchstone in everything, could only regard free will in terms of faith, for alone it lacked *raison d'être*. Theirs was a conflict in which the speculations of reason were countered by the assertions of dogma, involving assumptions, methods and topics radically different from the preceding era. Only if we recognize these changes can we do justice to the views of Bradwardine and his opponents. While in no way to be identified with the thinkers of the sixteenth century, neither can they be regarded as the simple continuators of those of the thirteenth century. Both Bradwardine and the sceptics, despite superficial similarities with the past, as in maintaining the mode of disputation and their use of traditional sources, had largely turned away from tradition. Each side, though from an opposite pole, was refusing to combine the natural with the supernatural, and, as a result, scholasticism was in the melting-pot. Until we can identify the new moulds in which its concepts were being reshaped we shall not be able fully to comprehend their products in the succeeding centuries.

PART I
'DE CAUSA DEI'

CHAPTER I

THE DIVINE NATURE (I): DIVINE BEING AND ITS ATTRIBUTES

THE DIVINE BEING

THE starting-point of Christian thought, as opposed to that of Neoplatonism, has always been God's existence. God is above everything else. Before we can talk of His goodness, mercy or justice, we must know that He exists; for it is upon God's being that all His other attributes and virtues are founded. They are the particular expressions of a simple and indivisible essence.

Bradwardine is no exception to this. *De causa Dei*[1] begins with the proofs for God's existence, and throughout the work these constitute the source both of God's nature and His actions, governing His relations with His creatures. Despite the great significance which God's will has for Bradwardine, and his principle of divine participation,[2] his God remains rooted in His own existence. He never disintegrates into a series of transcendental qualities, as in the case of Neoplatonism; nor, in Bradwardine's own view at least, is God's being merged with that of His creatures, as in pantheism. Bradwardine's intention, whatever the ultimate results, is to preserve God as the Supreme Being, distinct in Himself. For him *Sum qui sum* is the first truth.

There are, he says, two different aspects in discussing God: the superior and the inferior. The superior deals with His own simple and intrinsic nature and the attributes which belong to Him; the inferior with the divine nature in relation to created things. Together they constitute two different kinds of what Bradwardine calls 'complex knowledge'. This differs from uncomplex or simple knowledge in being analytical. While simple knowledge is simple affirmation of God, an intuitive awareness which avoids all discourse and reasoning, complex knowledge

---

[1] Ed. Savile used throughout.   [2] See pp. 50–2 below.

describes and explains, affirms and denies, with the result that God is distinguished in His different aspects.[1] Both types of truth derive from God; for He is the first cause of all being.[2]

To describe God, then, is to exercise superior complex understanding, that is, that part of it which deals with His own nature and not with created things.[3]

His existence, as the first principle of all things and therefore of all knowledge, is both the foundation of His own nature and of all creation. It comes first in the order of truths about God. Before He can will, He must know, and before He can know He must be omnipotent, and, to be omnipotent, He must be. This is the logical sequence of truths concerning the divine nature.[4]

The first step in discussing God, therefore, is to prove His existence; and Bradwardine opens his *De causa Dei* with a twofold proof of God. The first comes from Anselm's ontological proof, the simple assertion that the highest perfection and good, than which nothing greater can be envisaged, is God.[5] The second is based upon the Aristotelian and Thomist theory of an unmoved mover. This Bradwardine expresses when he says that there is not an infinite process in things, but one first cause for everything.[6]

Now these two quite different approaches not only illustrate the difficulty of giving Bradwardine a label, but also explain his

[1] 'Quod primum principium necessarium et verum incomplexum est Deus; et quod principium complexum primum simpliciter est de Deo: puta Deus est, Deus scit omnia, Deus vult omnia, vel aliquid simile' (cap. 11, p. 198).

[2] 'Primum ens omnium entium, et prima causa essendi quodcunque' (*ibid.*).

[3] 'Apparet ergo quod Deus est, vel Deus est Deus, sit primum principium complexorum. . . . Sunt autem vera duplicia, superiora scilicet, et inferiora: inferiora sunt omnia dicta de creabilibus, vel creaturis; et universaliter de quocunque quod non est Deus, vel etiam de Deo per respectum ad aliud, ut Deus est Dominus omnium, vel Creator: Vera superiora, quae in solo Deo consistunt; ut Deus est potens, sapiens atque bonus. Horum autem haec quidem sunt, quodammodo posteriora naturaliter, haec priora . . .' (p. 201).

[4] 'Est enim aliud verum naturaliter prius isto, scilicet Deum esse, Deum esse cognitivum, Deum esse omnipotentem, cum similibus suis, distinguendo et multiplicando ista in Deo' (p. 200).

[5] 'Credimus, inquit Deo, te esse aliquid quo nihil melius excogitari possit' (p. 1).

[6] 'Nullus est processus infinitus in entibus, sed est in quolibet genere unum primum' (*ibid.*).

double attack in combining the near-mystical evocation of St
Anselm with the physics of Aristotle. They serve to emphasize
God from both the divine and created aspects: on the one hand,
God as the sovereign good; on the other, God as the source of all
that is created, the uncaused cause. Naturally this means that, in
practice, the second (Aristotelian) approach will play a far more
active role; it establishes God's infinite goodness and omnipotence, where the Anselmian proof can only assert, and it is on
Aristotelian lines that the relation of God to His creatures is developed. But the influence of Anselm's view of God must not be
neglected; for, although we know Him through our own mental
experience, this is real enough to be described when we say that
God is the highest good. It is from this view of God as pure goodness and love that all that He does will be judged. In a certain
sense, then, we may say that Bradwardine takes from St Anselm
the spirit by which God may be perceived, while from St Thomas
and Aristotle he takes the method by which He can be distinguished. Both are important; for they are both different aspects
of a single conception: to have an unmoved mover, devoid of infinite worth, would be as futile as to have this infinite worth without infinite powers. Anselm provides the first, Aristotle the
second.

Bradwardine's development of the second proof starts with the
physical distinction between causes. It follows the Aristotelian
principle of an unmoved mover: this holds that, since there cannot be an infinite series of cause and effect, without beginning,
there must be a first cause, which, uncaused itself, is the ultimate
cause of everything else. It is this argument for a first cause which
Bradwardine employs to establish God's existence; for He must
be this first cause.[1] In support of this Bradwardine distinguishes
between necessary and possible being.[2] God, he says, could either
be necessary or possible; it is far better and more worthy to be
necessary of Himself than through the agency of another. For, if
He were not the cause of Himself, there would then be a cause

---

[1] See p. 2.

[2] 'Illud quod est per se, non dependens ab alio, prius natura, perfectiusque
est illo, quod non est per se, sed aliunde dependens: id quod est necesse esse
necesse esse est huiusmodi, respectu illius quod est possibile. Hunc et
Averroes sequitur in Comment . . . quod necesse esse secundum se non habet
causam et quod possibile esse, per se habet causam' (*ibid.*).

greater than He; and He could not be the first cause. But God, as the highest good than which nothing is better or more perfect, can have no superior cause. Therefore, God is necessary being of Himself; He is His own *raison d'être*. Moreover, what is once necessary of itself always will be, while all that is only possible, to become actual, needs to be moved from without. The possible cannot, therefore, be self-sufficient. Only God, then, as the first cause of everything, is necessary. This is another way of making the Aristotelian distinction between act and potency: it means that only God, as necessary, is by His nature: He cannot not be. Everything other than God, as potential and dependent on a superior cause, could as well not be as be; it could for ever remain a possibility, of itself incapable of becoming actual.[1]

Although Bradwardine never defines God in the way St Thomas does, as the identity of essence and existence, this is, in fact, where his doctrine leads. God as necessary and completely realized, in His own nature, is without anything potential; for, if He did not have every virtue developed to infinite perfection, He could be neither the highest good than which nothing is greater, nor self-sufficient. Only if God is recognized as pure act—in the Aristotelian sense of a quality fully realized—can He be necessary; if some quality were undeveloped within Him, His sovereignty would be impaired. He would be incomplete in Himself and He could not be self-moving; for part of His own nature would be beyond His grasp, and, to reach this, He would have need of some other aid outside Himself. God, therefore, as necessary being and infinite in perfection, must also possess complete identity of essence (His nature) and existence (the realization of His nature). In Him the two are one. Conversely, what defines a creature is the distinction between essence and existence; the essence is possible by nature, that is, it has no capacity or need to come into existence, as in the case of, say, Socrates, there is nothing in his own nature which makes Socrates exist; his essence does not of itself imply his existence as a living person.

God, then, can be defined in two ways. First, in His own terms,

[1] 'Nihil enim per se possibile esse et non esse habet esse, nisi ab aliquo per se necesse esse; a quo semper dependeat in essendo. . . .

'Omne autem existens per se possibile esse, et non esse, est existens huius-modi; ergo per aliud. Solus vero Deus per se necesse est' (p. 146).

as the highest perfection. Secondly, in terms of this world, through relation, physics and logic. Together they unite to show us that God is necessarily perfect; that He is pure act, self-sufficient, the *primum movens immobile*.

What is interesting in Bradwardine's theory of God's existence is not the assertion of the actual proofs, which are well established, but their combination. They are the harbingers of the method and outlook of *De causa Dei* in two important ways. In the first place, they illustrate the use he makes of Aristotelian method to establish theological assertion, without giving away anything to philosophy and metaphysics as an independent science of inquiry. God's existence is asserted; it is confirmed, not by speculation, but by physical fact and common sense: there is a hierarchy of cause and effect, which must have a first cause; and this is God. Similarly, the distinction between act and potency comes from a scientist who lived at a time when science was based upon Aristotelian categories. Thus theological assertion is reinforced by scientific evidence; there is no intermediate sphere of speculation. In the second place, from the distinction between God as necessary being, and His creatures, as contingent and possible, without *raison d'être* in themselves, Bradwardine builds his system of the extreme dependence of man upon God: for him necessity alone means value, thus depriving man of all inherent worth. In consequence, Bradwardine sees God's hand everywhere, actively directing all that His creatures do; without Him they are incapable of existing or of acting.

THE DIVINE ATTRIBUTES

Bradwardine, having established God's existence, elaborates His nature and powers over forty corollaries, framed as answers to the most frequent assertions by heretics or infidels. These may be considered as developing the proofs that he has already applied to God's being. On the one hand, God, by definition, is the highest good, infinitely perfect; on the other, His mode of existence is distinguished from everything else as necessary, where every quality in Him is realized to its infinite perfection. These are the twin points, of perfection and infinity, which Bradwardine elaborates. They in no way imply, however, a division of God's nature into these attributes. Bradwardine frequently asserts God's simple, indivisible nature.[1] He is unique; divine in His own, not human, terms, without parts or magnitude.[2] If this were not so, He would be a whole whose parts were dependent upon one another; and this would mean that their unity would come before God himself, a position which would negate God as already defined.[3] In the same way, Bradwardine attacks[4] the Arians for separating the Divine Persons into individual substances, and the Donatists for holding that, while the Divine Persons are of the same substance, they are unequal, the Son less than the Father, and the Holy Spirit less than both.

God, indeed, is so unique and infinitely perfect that it is an affront to worship any idol as His image. Bradwardine attacks[5] equally worshippers of the sky, the sun, the stars, the planets, the elements, nature, animals or men. Nor will he, of course, allow the slightest qualification to God's supreme position, above everything else, in the shape of equally powerful Gods or several Gods in different relations to one another. For, he says, He is not God who is not the highest perfection.[6] In this regard, he also attacks the Neoplatonists,[7] Plotinus, Iamblicus, Porphyry, Apuleius 'et Platonici caeteri', for their denial that He need be simple, one, and not several, together with those who place many first principles together, not reducing them to a common source.[8]

Bradwardine employs a similar argument against idolaters,[9] for God's infinite perfection allows of no comparison. To make idols represent God is to make a new God, passive, corruptible, destructible, finite. To suppose, moreover, that this idol were God would be equally sacrilegious: it would make the idol equal to Him; and man, as the creator of the idol, would, by this token, be

[1] Corollaries 8, 22, 23.

[2] 'Contra fingentes Deum ex membris humanis, vel aliis, seu quibuscunque diversis componi, negantesque ipsum esse substantiam simplicissimam, impartibilissimam, nullam compositionem, partibilitatem, magnitudinem habentem, magnitudinem scilicet corporalem' (cor. 10, p. 7).

[3] Quomodo insuper esset Deus summe perfectus, sive sufficiens et beatus . . . si necessario dependeret ab aliis, et aliis necessariis indigeret? Actualius etiam atque potentius videtur ex se, et per se sufficienter existere, quam alieno fulcimento et adminiculo supportari. Deus autem est summe actualis et potens, ita quod nihil actualius et potentius esse posset. . .' (*ibid.* pp. 10–11).

[4] Cor. 22 and 23.   [5] Cor. 12, 13, 14, 15 and 16, pp. 8–12.

[6] 'Non enim est Deus, quid non est summe perfectus. . .' (cor. 16, p. 12).

[7] Cor. 17, p. 12.   [8] Cor. 18, p. 13.   [9] Cor. 21, p. 15.

superior to God by his power to create similarity. Idolatry cannot, then, be the way to worship God.[1]

When we talk of God we must always remember His infinite simplicity and unity which sets Him above everything else. It is our discourse which divides and describes Him, not His own nature; and all that we can say about Him is to be understood in this light. It is, however, necessary to us, as fallible mortals, to distinguish qualities in God, in order to combat his detractors. Bradwardine attacks those who fail to do so, and who simply assert His infinite virtues.[2] There must, he says, be a distinction between the good and the bad, in order to show God's infinite goodness. This, as we shall see,[3] is the opposite of the position held by Ockham and his followers. Similarly, His infinite perfection can only be asserted by dismissing slackness or insensibility from His nature. By His infinite power, infinite virtue, and so on, we can gain three meanings: first, as in the case of an active power such as heat, which could, say, generate so much potential power beyond its own temperature; that is, increase its own power twice or four times beyond its present state. Now God can do this to infinity; and, as pure act, He realizes everything to its infinite intensity. This then is the degree of His power. Second, the way God does this is from Himself; He creates from His own power out of nothing, since He is the first cause. Thirdly, the measurement by which God creates is outside time; He does in one eternal instant that which every other cause does in time.

Every quality in God, then, may be said to be omnipotent, as infinite in intensity, immutable, as coming from Him alone, and eternal, as being outside time. To this must be added omniscience, as the foundation of His actions; for as the height of perfection, He knows and knows perfectly.[4] He knows actually and on account of knowing Himself.[5] Moreover, as there is nothing prior to God, or superior to Him, or better or more perfect, in any way, there is nothing which He does not know distinctly and

[1] 'Idolum etiam est factibile, et corruptibile: Deus vero necesse esse. . .' (*ibid.*).
[2] 'Contra non distinguentes, sed concedentes simpliciter Deum esse infinitae virtutis et potentiae infinitae. . .' (cor. 25, p. 19).
[3] See Part II below.   [4] Cor. 9, p. 6.
[5] 'Deus cognoscit actualiter, et si aliquid cognoscit, maxime videtur quod seipsum cognoscat' (*ibid.*).

directly. It would be absurd to imagine that God, as the cause of all things, did not know His own creatures; to carry out any act He must know what He does.[1]

All that God does, He does of His own accord;[2] He is self-sufficient, and subject to no passions which make Him change. As pure act, He cannot be passively moved by anything. As outside time, He is immutable and His actions universally efficacious. His will can in no way be impeded or its course changed. This can be seen in the creation of the world. Bradwardine attacks Aristotle and the Arab philosophers, mainly Averroes, for denying, first, the possibility of creation, and secondly the creation of the world in time.[3] These can be disproved from the powers we have seen to exist in God. He is omnipotent, and so can do anything; thus He can both create and destroy what He has created.[4]

In the case of the world, Bradwardine distinguishes between God's logical and temporal priority. He is not prior to the world in time; but He is by nature, as coming first, logically, to His creatures.[5] This is not due to God's sudden appearance from nowhere; for then He would not be eternal. It is that God exists outside space and time; space and time are categories that belong to the created world. This distinction between priority in time and priority in logical order means that, in a certain sense, the world can be called eternal; that is to say, from a purely temporal standpoint, the world is co-eternal with time, and thus eternal. God then, in this way, is not older than the world, temporally.[6] But this is not the same as saying that, in divine terms, the world or matter is eternal, or that God did not exist before they were

[1] 'Scit ergo posse facere, destruere et mouere aliquid extra ipsum. Quod si ponatur, tunc illud cognoscit; operatur non temere sed scienter et non nouit aliquid nouiter . . . et quia prius sciuit se posse et velle sic facere, et ita se facturum: aeternaliter ergo illud nouit, quare et quodlibet aliud simile ratione. . . . Necessario ergo aeternaliter omnia vera nouit' (cor. 9, p. 6).
'Ipse [Deus] ergo omnia perfecte et distincte cognoscit' (*ibid.*)
[2] Cor. 5, 6, 7, 8, pp. 4–6.   [3] Cor. 33, 34, 37, 40, pp. 65–145.
[4] 'Deus habet voluntatem uniuersaliter efficacem . . . quis ergo non faciliter videat, Deum cum sit necesse est, et omnipotens simpliciter, omniquaque de sua potentia absoluta posse annihilare quodlibet aliud' (p. 65).
[5] 'Voluntas enim Dei aeterna qua fecit mundum, non est antiquior mundo antiquitate seu proprietate temporis, sed naturae: nec mundus ea nouior aut posterior tempore sed natura' (cor. 33, p. 66).
[6] 'Concedo vobis quod Deus non est antiquior mundo antiquitate temporalis actualis' (*ibid.*).

created.[1] Bradwardine, accordingly, refuses to accept that time existed before the world began: both spring jointly from God's act of creation.[2] That he creates the world at a certain instant A in no way means a change in Him, but simply the appearance in time and space of powers which in Him are ever present.[3] In the same way, that He did not once exist according to time means that time did not exist, not that He lacked what was outside time.[4] God made time, as He made everything else; and it is our weakness which confuses the physical measurements of the created world with the eternity of His nature.

In the creation of the world, we see the full demonstration of the divine powers, which Bradwardine mentioned in corollary 21. From His omnipotence, omniscience, immutability, in fine, from the infinite perfection of the divine nature, all creation derives. Now the significance of Bradwardine's discussion of creation is twofold: first, through it, the full range of God's powers is demonstrated; as we have seen, this involves attributes which God alone possesses. His power and self-sufficiency have to be so overriding that neither time nor the actions of anything outside Him can alter His course. The simple perfection of His own nature is quite beyond anything that we can comprehend in the physical terms of time or space. Second, in creation we have evidence of God's goodness; for, since there can be no compulsion or obligation which in any way urges God to an act, this must come from His own nature. This can only mean that God, as the highest good, acts from pure, disinterested love: there would be

[1] 'Nihil aliud a Deo fuerat ante mundum. . . . Deus est immutabilis omnino' (p. 67).

[2] Si autem [Averroes] intelligatis non sicut caeteri homines, sed modo vestro quod est per omne tempus actuale, potest concedi quod mundus est aeternus, sicut tu Aristoteles videris definire aeternum' (ibid.).

'. . . dico tunc, quod in A instanti successionis illius Deus voluntarie produxit mundum, et quod tunc incoepit B prima mutatio noua, seu primus motus nouus, quem nulla mutatio noua praecedebat, nisi forte partes illius successionis aeternae per vos positae' (p. 67).

[3] 'Dico igitur quod quaerens quare etc. quaerit causam; causa autem efficiens est illa potentia libera; quia igitur est actiua potentia rationalis et libera, libere tunc producit' (ibid.).

[4] 'Deus tamen qui nihil facit casualiter, quouismodo sed per suam sapientiam infinitam . . . nunquam fecit, facit, aut faciet aliquid in aliquo tempore vel instanti, cum ab aeterno disposuit illud tunc facere, ideoque ab aeterno disposuit facere mundum in A instanti, et fecit illum in A sine transmutatione aliqua praecedente . . .' (p. 69).

nothing that He could gain from what can only be inferior to Him; nor, as self-sufficient and perfect, is there anything that can be added to His nature: He is already complete.

The assertion and defence of God's overriding goodness is the second main aspect of the divine attributes with which Bradwardine deals in the corollaries to chapter 1. As the initial thesis of chapter 1 says, God is by definition the highest good than which nothing can be more perfect. He is so necessarily,[1] and this means that He is in no way subject to changes of mood, at one time irascible and at another good-tempered. That He can in no way be considered in human terms applies as much to His passions as to His powers: Bradwardine condemns those who conceive of God,[2] or gods, as the ancients did, as being lustful, drunken, amusing or mischievous or as portraying any other similarity to mortals. God's goodness is an essential of His being; there can be no such things as accidents in His nature.[3] He cannot therefore change for the better, since He is perfectly good, nor, for the same reason, can He change for the worse. Two consequences follow from this. In the first place, everything God does He does for the best; therefore the Manichean view, which says that there are good and bad equally in everything, is false.[4] God, as the first principle of all that exists, acts from love; and everything which comes from Him is good. In the second place, as the highest good, His mercy is infinite.[5] God, then, as the highest good can admit any sinner to grace and reconciliation without any merit on the sinner's part.[6] Conversely, God in no way gives grace as a reward in proportion to precedent merit.[7] Would He as the highest good exchange or sell rather than give? All must have faith in Him, for He is good and He can do anything.[8] He wants only the good of His creatures; and all that He does is from goodness. His justice is part of His goodness; He will neither let good go unrewarded, nor sin unpunished. His actions must come from Him alone, for the distance between our poor, finite selves and God is too great

---

[1] Cor. 6, p. 5.   [2] Cor. 18 and 19, pp. 13–14.   [3] Cor. 26, p. 20.
[4] Cor. 31, p. 25.
[5] 'Si namque Deus est summe bonus, ita quod nihil melius esse possit: est et summe misericors, ita quod nihil misericordius possit esse, aut etiam cogitari, est et simili modo summe pius et clemens, summe diues et potens, summe liberalis, summe largus. . .' (cor. 27, p. 21).
[6] Cor. 28, p. 22.   [7] Cor. 29, p. 23.   [8] *Ibid.*

for any proportion between our deeds and His.[1] God's attributes may thus be summarized as constituting the highest good to an infinite capacity, with love as His only motive.[2]

With the help of these two faculties, Bradwardine is able to establish God's primacy in everything. Since God alone is necessary and uncaused, He must be present in everything caused. In five corollaries to chapter 5 Bradwardine reaches a position which makes God essential and necessary everywhere, both in the world and outside it.[3] Besides His being infinitely perfect and powerful, He is omnipresent and, without Him, there could be nothing. Although this conception of God is in keeping with tradition, it is Bradwardine's application of it which distinguishes him from previous thinkers. This, as we shall see,[4] involves the virtual denial of a separate existence to God's creatures. For the present, however, our concern is with Bradwardine's method.

Throughout his discussion of creation he has been applying theological truths to all with which he has dealt; these, rather than any independent reasoning, have been his instruments. From the theological premise of God's infinite resources Bradwardine makes everything else follow: once these are established, he feels that he can give a definite answer to every question. Unlike St Thomas Aquinas, he need never pause between what can be proved metaphysically and what can be only from revelation: he regards all truth as coming from theology and the Scriptures. It is, therefore, absolute in its own right without the need for metaphysics. Thus, in the case of the world's creation, while St Thomas held that its eternity was an open question philosophically, and Duns Scotus said that it could only be asserted by theology, Bradwardine *proves* it theologically: he makes it follow logically from the theological truth of God's omnipotence. Bradwardine's position, therefore, is important in two respects. In the

[1] 'Ipse autem est superexcellentissime generosus et superabundantissime liberalis. . .' (p. 21).
[2] 'Non est ergo aliquod maximum quod potest, nec minimum quod non potest, quare veraciter dici potentiae infinitae' (cor. 25, p. 20).
'Contra indoctos artis amandi, nescientes Deum esse propter seipsum amandum, et caetera propter Deum, omnesque actus humanos ad ipsum propter se finaliter ordinandos, ipsumque super omnia diligendum. . .' (cor. 30, p. 23).
[3] *De causa Dei*, p. 175.   [4] See pp. 50–2 below.

D

first place, he rejects metaphysics and philosophy, as independent means of arriving at the truth, in favour of the vigorous application of logic to theology. In the second place, this leads him to disregard the value of the human intellect in its search for knowledge. God is the source of truth, and, since our finite selves cannot reach His infinite nature, we can never know Him through our own powers.[1] Truth, therefore, lies beyond the bounds of reason: it belongs alone to theology and the Scriptures.

These are the rules which govern *De causa Dei*: they ask for, and give, only definite answers; they allow for no independent realm of possibility. Harnessed to Bradwardine's inflexible aim of upholding God's cause above all else, they give the work its startling character.

[1] Cor. 32, p. 26.

CHAPTER II

THE DIVINE NATURE (II): INTELLECT AND WILL

As we have seen in Chapter I, God's omnipotence equally implies omniscience and a sovereign will which is completely irresistible. To the power to create and move there must be added both the knowledge and the will to do so. Now it is in his theory of divine will that Bradwardine fashions the motor of his system. This makes God's knowledge an active force in the same way as it was with Duns Scotus; and once established, Bradwardine has but a short step to the heart and soul of his system—God as the senior partner in every one of his creatures' actions.

GENERAL NATURE OF DIVINE KNOWLEDGE

Now before discussing the different aspects and types of divine knowledge there are certain general qualities which are common to the whole of it.

In the first place, God knows everything actually and distinctly and perfectly, not discursively, as we have already seen.[1] In the second place, His knowledge comes from His own intellect and not from outside agencies.[2] If it came not from Him, He would not be infinitely perfect. As we only see the shadows through the light, so it is through Him that all things are intelligible and can be known: things known are the effect, not the cause, of God's knowledge.[3] Aristotle and Avicenna, says Bradwardine, were right when they said that God's knowledge is perfect and cannot be improved by anything known. So, too, was Duns Scotus, when he said that no truths move the divine intellect, but that it knows from its own power.[4] There is no place in God's

[1] Cor. 9, p. 6.   [2] Cor. 6, p. 4.

[3] 'Semet igitur, divina sapientia cognoscens, cognoscit et omnia, immaterialiter matarialia, et non partite partiter. . . . Et sequitur, Ipso uno omnia et cognoscens et adducens' (p. 216).

[4] 'Item Johannes. . . adhaerens rationi Averrois praetactae dicit quod vera

intellect for receiving knowledge from objects themselves. Simi-larly, Bradwardine opposes the suggestion that things known,[1] although not the cause of God's knowing, are a prerequisite for it.[2] These would then become an essential part of His knowledge, without which He could not know, and thus limit God's sover-eignty. In the third place, God's knowledge is eternal and im-mutable.[3] As we have seen, the past, present and future are in Him the ever-present instant. That which, in the created world, happens temporally, in Him happens constantly. This is the other aspect of God's self-sufficiency; not only is He immutable but He is eternal, and in both cases immune to outside interfer-ence.[4] As there can be no stages in God's knowledge, there is no room for amendment, and this excludes all actions upon the part of things known from helping Him to know.[5]

God's knowledge is therefore perfect, eternal, and uncaused, and extends to everything. These qualities apply to everything He knows regardless of the type of knowledge.

TYPES OF KNOWLEDGE

Now, just as there are two different kinds of truth, the simple and the complex, with its division into superior and inferior, so there are two different types of divine knowledge with a corresponding division. There is, first, God's simple knowledge; this (like simple truth) is an intuitive understanding of His essence in

non mouent intellectum diuinum ad apprehendendum talem veritatem, quia tunc intellectus diuinus vilesceret, quia pateretur ab alio ab essentia sua' (p. 216).

[1] Cap. 16, p. 218.

[2] 'Contra quosdam dicentes, quod res scitae sunt causa sine qua non diuinae scientiae, sed non causa' (*ibid.*).

[3] 'Necessario ergo aeternaliter omnia vera nouit' (cor. 9, p. 7).

[4] 'Quod Deus habet distinctam scientiam omnium' (cap. 6, p. 181).

'Ex his igitur patet, quod Deus scit omnia nunc praesentia, et eisdem rationibus similiter ostendetur, quod semper sciuit, et sciet omnia praesentia quae tunc erant, aut erunt praesentia' (p. 183).

Again: '. . . quod Deus habet distinctam scientiam omnium, nedum praesentium, praeteritorum et futurorum: verum et omnium possibilium et impossibilium, imaginabilium et cognoscibilium quouismodo, unde et omnisciens, sicut veraciter dici potest' (cor. to cap. 6, p. 184).

[5] 'Deus enim scit omnia simul et semper, non per vices temporum; sicut ipsa scita incipiunt esse, vel desinunt more humano, quoniam apud ipsum non est transmutatio, nec vicissitudinis obumbratio' (p. 189).

which He knows without analysis or discussion. Second, there is His complex knowledge in which He distinguishes in the same way as with complex truth. Like complex truth, God's complex knowledge is divided into those truths which concern Himself and those which are outside Him; that is, in His creatures. The first aspect is superior truth, the second, inferior truth.[1]

The great dividing line in God's knowledge is not so much the difference between simple and complex as in the different methods by which He knows; and it is of supreme importance in Bradwardine's system. Firstly, everything that concerns Himself God knows through His essence. Whether this knowledge is simple and intuitive, or composite and analytical, it all comes within the province of His intellect, and concerns all those faculties in God which come before His will in order of priority. His will, coming after His essence, omnipotence and intellect, has no jurisdiction over them: as Bradwardine says: 'This is so not because God wills it to be, but, on the contrary, because it is, He wills it.'[2] Before God is in a position to will, He must be; He must have infinite power; and He must have perfect knowledge of everything. Secondly, on the other side of His will, there is everything outside God's essence, no matter how much these may refer to Him, as for example God as creator of the world. This is the inferior order of complex truths, and they are governed in quite a different way. God knows them through His will, and it is the sovereign law of their existence. He knows them, therefore,

[1] 'Ostenso igitur quod Deus scit omnia scibilia scientia complexa, non per scita posteriora, sed per claram essentiam, sibi omnia distinctissime praesentantem, nunc restat consequenter quomodo Deus scit omnia scibilia complexa. Pro quo est primo sciendum, quod scibilia complexa et vera sunt duplicia: quaedam enim naturaliter praecedunt voluntatem diuinam, et quaedam eam naturaliter subsequuntur. Praecedit eam naturaliter Deum esse, Deum esse aeternum, Deum esse omnipotentem et similia: Non enim quia Deus vult sic esse, ideo sic esse; sed potius e contrario. Sequuntur autem eam mundum esse, quamlibet creaturam esse, et universaliter omnia illa vera complexa quorum veritas causatur et pendet ab ipsa. Illa igitur vera complexa quae voluntatem diuinam praecedunt, scit Deus per suam solam essentiam, sicut alia vera incomplexa. . . . Illa vero quae voluntatem eius sequuntur, non scit Deus per illa complexa neque per aliquid aliud voluntate eius semota, sed per suam voluntatem, vel per suam substantiam cum sua voluntate, ita quod ad scientiam suam complexam est sua voluntas necessario prius naturaliter requisita' (p. 221).

[2] *Ibid.*

through a faculty which, of its very nature, is active and directing. In relation to His creatures, then, for God to know is also to will. It is this identity which, as we shall see, enables Bradwardine to make God's control over His subjects so far-reaching and intense.

Thus in spite of Bradwardine's initial division between God's complex and simple knowledge, the real distinction lies in His self-knowledge on the one hand, and His knowledge of His creatures on the other. These are regulated by two different laws, and each must be examined in greater detail. While the divine intellect knows, without acting, the divine will knows actively and approbatively; that is to say, to will (even when this is the same as to know) must mean to want and *ipso facto* to approve.[1] As a result, there is a very fundamental division between the knowledge of the divine intellect and that of the divine will.

THE DIVINE INTELLECT

Through His intellect God's knowledge extends to everything. This must be understood quite literally; for it includes not only those things which are actual and possible but also all that is non-existent and impossible. His omniscience, like His omnipotence, compasses everything; for, as the corollary 7 to chapter 13 says, the necessary cannot be limited by the possible or the impossible.[2] Just as God is the first cause of whatever is, He is also the first cause of whatever is not,[3] and this includes negative truth.[4] Since He alone is the judge of what is to be or not to be,[5] it is He who decides what is impossible or contradictory.[6] He must, therefore, know everything; but this is not the same as saying

[1] 'Quintum vero per hoc soluetur, quod diuina scientia cognitionis solius, seu simplicis notitiae non est sufficiens causa rerum, sed cum ea requiritur etiam scientia approbationis, et beneplacitum voluntatis, vel aliquis talis actus in voluntate diuina. . . . Pro octauo est sciendum quod intellectus diuinus prius quodammodo naturaliter suo velle, et ideo necessario simpliciter et penitus absolute cognoscit simplici notitia veluti incomplexa, omnia complexa cogitabilia, vera vel falsa, possibilia vel impossibilia; non tamen notitia complexa adhaesiua, quae scientiae nostrae complexae et compositiuae superius comparatur' (pp. 225–6).

[2] 'Quod necessarium nequaquam recte per possibile vel per impossibile definitur' (p. 204).

[3] Cor. 11, p. 204.   [4] Cor. 10, p. 304.   [5] Cor. 11, p. 204.
[6] Cor. 12, p. 204.

that everything that He knows He wants. Far from impairing the authority of His will, this gulf between what God knows and what He wills is its foundation: for it is the omniscience of God's intellect which creates the special role for His will.

Omniscience, in the sense that Bradwardine uses it, equals neutrality and indifference. Thus the choice of what to select and what to leave uncreated must lie elsewhere—in His will. While God's intellect sees, His will acts. His intellect accepts equally the impossible and the possible; His will rejects the one and realizes the other.[1] God's intellect, as omniscient and indifferent, plays no active part in creation. It knows everything through the divine essence, and is not concerned with which of the possible is made actual and which not; its part is to present everything to be known, possible and impossible, to His will; from there His will takes control. Thus God's intellect knows everything in its pure, immaterial essence. It is the efficient cause of His understanding and action, and through His intellect God manifests this knowledge eternally in the Word.[2]

This raises the problem of how God's knowledge of Himself is related to His knowledge of everything outside Himself: in short, the place of divine ideas. Bradwardine discusses the general opinion of the Fathers about divine ideas; but he does not agree with their view, which would seem to suggest that these ideas are different or distinguished from the divine essence. Rather, he says, they are the same, as part of a completely simple unity in God: as we have seen in Chapter I above, nothing in Him is diverse.[3] Bradwardine compares the divine essence to a self-

[1] 'Item cognitio Diuina de se videtur indifferens ad faciendum, vel non faciendum; imo ipsa per sola non apparet factiua; ergo nihil potest efficere nisi per aliquid determinans limitetur; hoc autem poni non potest nisi Diuina volutio actualis' (p. 190).

[2] 'Item potentia intellectiua, siue intellectus producit, sicut causa efficiens, omnemque suam intellectionem, et quemlibet suum actum; ergo Intellectus diuinus est causa cuiuslibet suae intellectionis, et scientiae cuiuscunque. Sic enim Deus producit et causat aeternaliter suum verbum. . .' (p. 219).

[3] 'Reliqua vero intelligibilia, quae non sunt Deus, habent secundum Patrum sententiam duplex esse; scilicet intelligibile, et existentiae, seu reale, id est sunt intelligibilia priusquam existant in actu completo. Primum esse istorum praecedit quodammodo intellectionem diuinam; Prius enim quodammodo sunt intelligibilia, quam intelligantur a Deo, non per se (cum enim nihil sint omnino, nullam aptitudinem seu potentiam per se habent, ut

reflecting light. This is, of course, only a dim approximation to God; but it helps if we try to imagine a light of dazzling clarity, seeing everything, and completely unmoved by outside objects: from its own infinite illumination it actively receives and reflects everything to be known, revealing itself and the forms of all things. Such is the light by which the divine intellect sees all things and which it receives from God's essence. God by knowing Himself knows the ideas of all intelligible objects; this knowledge is all one in Him, with its source in His being.[1]

There are, then, two aspects to God's knowledge through His intellect. While His being is its source both for knowledge of Himself and of everything else, He knows the latter through divine ideas. These provide the pure immaterial form of every species: thus, for the individual Socrates, God possesses the pure idea, Man, the true archetype of all men. Every idea in God is part of His own essence; there can be no real distinction between Him and them but only one of logic in which they can be formally separated. This comes very near to the *distinctio formalis* of Duns Scotus, though Bradwardine never uses this expression, nor gives it his widespread application. It is enough to notice here that it is by this means that God's unity is preserved.

With the divine intellect as the cause of all God's knowledge it is *ipso facto* superior to His will. Indeed, His intellect is the efficient cause of every action which He wills. Were it not for the knowledge which His intellect provides, God's will would be blind. In this sense God's intellect must be the true cause of

constat ex prioribus), sed per Deum, et sic quodammodo sunt causae intellectionis diuinae, non autem vere ipsa (cum nihil sunt omnino), sed sola essentia diuina, ex se primo omnium intelligibilium ideis et rationibus propriis grauida et foecunda praeuenit intellectum diuinum' (p. 219).

[1] 'Videtur enim mihi quod essentia diuina sit velut quoddam speculum intelligibile, clarissimum, infinitum, nihil ab obiectis patiens, recipiens aut reflectens, sed actiue ex sua infinitissima claritate distincte non confuse vultus proferens, et ideas omnium intelligibilium obiectorum; in quod speculum oculus intellectus diuini prospiciens, haec omnia speculatur. Non autem opinor quod rationes huiusmodi seu ideae in diuina essentia ab ipsa essentialiter, et realiter distinguantur sicut verba patrum videntur sonare in auribus aliquorum, sed quod hae omnes sint realiter idem quod diuina essentia, imo quod haec essentia unissima, et simplicissima ex se sola omnia intelligibilia repraesentet. . . . Omnia Dei unum sunt in Deo, excepto quod ad relationem pertinet. Nam sapientia Dei, et veritas, et aeternitas, non sunt diuersa inter se, sed unum sunt. . .' (*ibid.*).

whatever is created.[1] The act of creation therefore has a twofold aspect: first, the intellect presents to God every possibility and impossibility; next, God's will decides to carry out a particular action on the basis of this knowledge.[2] It is in this light that Bradwardine's voluntarism, like that of Duns Scotus, must be seen. There is no question of His will running riot in God; for every faculty in God comes before it in logical order of priority. Nor is there any question of its being blind and wilful, in the literal sense. Its role, as we shall now examine in more detail, is to choose from the knowledge presented by the intellect, and to give effect to its choice. Without the direction of God's intellect, His will could not act as it does.

THE DIVINE WILL

Now if the principle of the divine intellect is omniscience and, with it, indifference, the principle of God's will is love, and, with it, unfettered activity. Where the intellect observes, the will chooses and acts.

God's will is doubly free: free from any internal necessity within God's nature, and immune from any external pressure. Internally, His will is the means by which God can act freely; had He no will, God would be acting of necessity, for He would then be following, without free choice, whatever was known to His essence.[3] Moreover, if the first cause did not act freely this would mean the destruction of all liberty and contingency among His creatures, which, Bradwardine holds, is not the case. Both of these states would strike against the nature of God, for they would destroy His goodness and His omnipotence.[4] Freedom therefore

[1] 'Et habet corollarium, quod diuina scientia, quae est notitia eius simplex, est vere causa cuiuslibet rei factae, non solum causa sine qua non' (cor. to cap. 17, p. 220).

[2] 'Item intellectio et cognitio actualis mouet voluntatem, et est causa volutionis illius . . . diuina volutio actualis est causa cuiuslibet rei factae' (*ibid.*).

[3] 'Maxime quia si quid fiat ab essentia eius sola sine aliqua voluntate, illud fit per modum naturae et necessitatis, sicut effectus causarum naturalium, cum libertas in sola voluntate ponatur' (p. 191).

[4] '. . . quare cum omnes causae inferiores siue secundae in causatione sua quacunque subdantur necessario primae causae, omnes causationes earum, sicut et quaelibet causatio primae causae proueniunt de necessitate naturae, et penitus absoluta: quare uniuersaliter omnis libertas et contingentia, ac meritum destruetur' (pp. 190–1).

must reside in God's will, and all that He does He does freely.[1]

So far as external forces are concerned, His will, as the first principle of freedom, must be equally free and unmoved as it is free in Him. It is universally efficacious, irresistible, eternal and immutable, the first cause of everything created.[2] As the source of all things, it is the expression of God's omnipotence.[3] From this Bradwardine advances a stage further, and emphasizes the supremacy of God's will, when he says that everything that God wills and creates must be in the way He decrees. Not only is it the cause of everything in general, but also of the particular ways in which His creatures act.[4]

Now a very important consequence follows from this; for God's will alone is the criterion of what is possible and impossible, and how, and when all that is to be is. Moreover, as He is immutable, exempt from space and time, everything that He wills and does must be outside space and time. His will is eternal, allowing of no alteration or appeal;[5] everything He wills is already happening in Him; His willing makes it eternal law.[6]

Before we can discuss the effects of this view of God's will upon His creatures, we must ask if His will is arbitrary and without principle. The answer is No, both from its motives and from its nature.

The motive for any act on the part of God is love; and His will, when it moves, only gives effect to God's nature, which, by definition, is infinitely good. Goodness alone, then, prompts Him. God has two ends in view when He wills: one is Himself, the

---

[1] 'Libertas ergo est in sola voluntate ponenda, et prima simpliciter in prima simpliciter, quae est Dei' (p. 197).
[2] 'Habet corollarium per omnia quae facta fuerunt, facta fuerunt a voluntate diuina, et quae facta erunt, facta erunt ab ea' (cap. 10, p. 195).
[3] 'Quod diuina voluntas est causa cuiuslibet futuri atque praeteriti. . .' (cap. 14, p. 208).
[4] '. . . quod ad Deum velle facere, seu fieri quippiam per se, vel per aliud quodlibet quouismodo, necessario sequitur illud fieri illo modo, nec modo nostro conando alias vires apponit' (cor. to cap. 10, p. 197).
[5] 'Fiet si Deus voluerit, non quia Deus nouam voluntatem quam non habet, tunc habebit; sed quia id, quod ex aeternitate in eius immutabili praeparatum est voluntate, tunc erit' (p. 208).
[6] 'Si Deus esse desineret, nihil esset praeteritum nec futurum, verum nec falsum, possibile vel impossibile, necessarium vel contingens, nec etiam posset esse; ex quo et oppositum sequitur euidenter, videlicet ipsum Deum, et sic aliquid praefuisse, esse, et fore. . .' (cor. to cap. 14, p. 209).

ultimate end; the other, the immediate end, is man as first among His creatures on earth. Thus every act of God's will has love for man as its object, which itself derives from God's self-love.

The nature of God's will is inseparable from His essence; it is both the expression of His goodness and the means by which His goodness is realized: as last in the hierarchy of God's attributes, its actions must be coloured by them, even though its choice is its own. In this sense God's will is directed by the love and reason in His nature. Moreover, as we have already seen,[1] the starting point for the actions of God's will lies in the knowledge provided by His intellect. His will must, therefore, act rationally in everything that it does.[2] There can be no question of regarding God's will as a power unto itself; it can have no separate identity from His nature, nor any desires which would contradict it.[3] They are indivisible.

Bradwardine goes into some detail to establish the precise relationship between God's will and His reason. There are, he says, three possible types of reason: obligatory, preponderant, congruent and concomitant, each of which he discusses in turn.

Obligatory reason ordains whatever should, or should not, be done. It is so overwhelming and imperative that whoever, among mortals, receives it, and ignores it, sins. God's will is not governed in this manner; for if it were, it would be subject to necessity and He would not act freely, which He does. Preponderant reason is not so overwhelming as in the first case, though it is still the dominating influence in relation to the will. It is the reason which says that to do this is better than to do that, or not to act at all. As with obligatory reason, preponderant reason has no place

[1] See p. 37 above.

[2] 'Sufficere nobis debet ad rationem voluntas Dei cum aliquid facit, licet non videamus cur velit. Voluntas namque Dei nunquam est irrationalis: Ergo ratio mouet voluntatem diuinam, et efficit eius velle' (p. 230).

[3] 'Est enim aliqua prima ratio in Deo necessaria absolute, prior naturaliter voluntate sua, sicut forsitan Deus esse, vel Deum esse veracem seu veritatem, ex qua multa alia necessario consequuntur; et sunt ut aestimo, omnia illa quae sunt necessaria absolute; Ex antecedente enim necessario tantum necessarium necessario consequetur, et omne necessarium absolute est primum necessarium, vel necessario reducitur ad illud, et necessario sequitur ex illo. Si enim sequatur ex illo, et non necessario, hoc est per aliquod medium contingens, puta per voluntatem diuinam; sed nihil dependens a causa contingenti et libera est necessarium absolute; haec igitur omnia necessario absolute sunt similiter rationabilia absolute' (p. 231).

in God's will. If it had, God would then be able always to do better than He does. Congruent and concomitant reason, on the
other hand, are in proportion to the will; they in no way super-
sede it, but as part of the will, are inherent in what it is and does.
Such reason asserts that which it is fitting to do. This is the mode
of reason by which God's will is guided, in all that refers to His
creatures. He is not obliged to act in a certain way; it is enough
that reason informs all His deeds. God is thus always able to act
freely and rationally. This is the ideal in man also, but, whereas in
God congruent reason suffices, for man it is far safer to follow
either obligatory or preponderant reason, when he has them.[1]

What has been said of the relation between reason and God's
will applies equally to justice and the other virtues by which
He acts. In every case these inform God's will, since in every
case God's will starts from their full array. They are given in
everything He does. An act is not just because God wills it,
but because the principle of justice inheres in it; justice is
part of the eternal law which neither God's will nor man can
alter.[2]

From this we can conclude that God's will has no authority in
ordaining what is true and what is false. The principles of truth
and justice exist in God as part of His nature, and it is beyond the
power of His will to alter them. In fact, however, we do the divine
will a wrong ever to consider it in such a light. It is sovereign
alone in regard to God's creatures; it is only arbitrary in the
general sense that it acts of its own volition, not in the sense that
it is ever capricious, contradictory or unjust. God does not newly
love or hate; nor does He vary the degree in which He does so.
Nothing can change what He has willed from eternity; He is
guided solely by the virtues in His own nature.[3]

[1] See pp. 231–2.
[2] 'Quod etiam aliquid sit per se iniustum, non solum quia prohibitum,
patet per Augustinum I de libero arbitrio 6. . . . Et infra eodem, Lex aeterna
est, quia iustum est, ut omnia sint ordinatissima; et haec lex, ut videtur, non
dependet a voluntate diuina, sed est immutabiliter per se iusta' (p. 232).
'Hoc autem principium proprium videtur infallibilis veritas diuinae
essentiae, qui velut immobile fundamento omnia iudicia iustitiae innituntur.
. . . Haec autem prima iustitia est iustitia per se, et primo, necessario, et
penitus absolute, nullo modo dependens a voluntate diuina, sed naturaliter
prior ea' (p. 233).
[3] Cor. to cap. 23, p. 240.

When we consider that the divine will is the means by which God knows the created world, we can see how important a part it plays in Bradwardine's system. It makes His knowledge active, formative and causative; as such, it has nothing in common with ordinary simple understanding. Where the intellect can know without being committed to action, the will, by its act of knowing, moves and determines. Bradwardine is at pains to emphasize this distinction, for, by this, he can release in full flood the reservoir of God's power over His creatures. Knowledge *qua* knowledge, he says, can at best only influence indirectly through memory, image and intention; to know does not imply to do, as for example to know about Phoenicia or India is not the same as to be there.[1]

In the created sphere, therefore, everything that God knows He actively moves. Moreover, He knows eternally all that will happen because He knows His own will. Bradwardine here follows Duns Scotus, from whom he quotes the opinion that, if God did not know His own will, He would be dependent for His knowledge of the future upon His creatures.[2] In that case, God would not be infinitely perfect; His dependence upon His creatures for knowledge would mean that they could exist independently of Him. In fact, says Bradwardine, still following Duns Scotus, God's knowledge of the future comes from His will. God by knowing the future must also will it. Thus He does not predestine an individual because He foresees that he will make good use of his free will, for this would make God's knowledge passive and His actions subsequent to those of His creatures. On the contrary, because God foresees through His will, He decides that a certain person will make good use of his free will and a soul is

---

[1] 'Proprie ergo loquendo non est verum, quod omne intellectum mouet intelligentem: Multa enim intelligo, quae omnino non sunt, quare et omnino proprie mouere non possum. Multa etiam existentia intelligo, quae proprie non me mouent: intelligo enim Phoenicem Arabiae, et mirabilia Indiae, et quomodo mouerent haec proprie me existentem Oxoniae. . . . Haec autem nec immediate mouent, nec sufficient totum medium alterare' (p. 225).

[2] 'Qui [Johannes] . . . reprobans opinionem dicentem ideo Deum quenquam praedestinare ad vitam, quia praeuidet ipsum bene usurum libero arbitrio scribit: Sed contra istud arguitur, Primo quod Deus non praeuidet ipsum bene usurum libero arbitrio, nisi quia vult et praeordinat istum bene usurum eo quod sicut dictum est dist. 39. Certa praeuisio futurorum contingentium, est ex determinatione voluntatis suae' (p. 223).

predestined to that end.[1] That God's knowledge of the future comes through His will can be illustrated in the case of Judas and Lucifer. It would not be enough for God to permit them to do wrong, for His will is active, and regulates all that happens among His creatures. God sees beforehand that He will co-operate in the actions of Lucifer which will lead to sin. When He foresees a sin of commission this means that He wills the action leading to this; and, similarly, for Him to foresee a sin of omission means that He has willed not to co-operate in the act of His creature who so sins. In either case God foresees by His will, and, as we have seen, His will acts rationally and freely, without compulsion.

We can sum up God's knowledge of the created world as follows: God knows everything created eternally, no matter how infinitesimal or minute this knowledge may appear. He knows all that is, past, present and future. God's knowledge, moreover, is active knowledge and comes through His will. Thus nothing can come into being, or change, without His willing. In the third place, His knowledge cannot be determined, impeded or frustrated: as part of God's nature it contains all His infinite virtues. All that can be said is that its motive is love. Where the intellect (that is, God's simple knowledge) understands, the will (God's knowledge of His creatures) loves. The Word, by which the divine intellect is explained, corresponds in His will to the love expressed in the Divine Persons.

The importance of this view of God's will is plain to see. It means that knowing and doing are the same in God *vis-à-vis* His creatures. Because God can never permit without participating, He must be included in every human action. This is the instrument by which Bradwardine extends divine power and control, literally, to all that exists; God is involved in all that is created, and involved actively. By means of His will, Bradwardine eliminates any autonomous activity on the part of God's creatures; the divine and the created become merged; the barrier between the

[1] 'Item Deus recte scit futura contingentia, ergo per aliquid quod realiter est certum; sed hoc non est per aliquod futurum contingens, cum illud non sit certum, nec aliqua causa inferior sufficiens ad productionem illius in causatione eius est certa, sed contingens similiter ut effectus: Alias enim ille effectus esset certe et determinate futurus. Relinquitur ergo quod Deus ista sciat per suam voluntatem sibi certissimam, qua vult omnia illa fore' (p. 223).

natural and the supernatural is overlaid by the sheer physical presence of divine power amidst His creatures. Duns Scotus, through this theory of God's will as knowledge, drew a more exalted picture of man, as a consequence. Bradwardine, on the other hand, uses this concept to depress the merits and powers of His creatures: God's presence everywhere, far from exalting them, is a measure of their dependence upon Him. They have nothing in their own right; God alone is their *raison d'être*.

At this point, Bradwardine's view of God breaks off sharply from the traditional theories. So far, what has been most striking in his treatment of the divine nature is, first, the extreme rigour of the method, and, second, the combination of his antecedents. If God's spirit is that of Anselm, and His mode of existence mainly Thomist and Aristotelian, His knowledge and activity are based upon Scotus. His God, if original, is also traditional; He evinces nothing strikingly new in His nature, existence or the extent of His powers. The application, however, to which Bradwardine is now to put these attributes is both novel and extreme, and the instrument he employs is the Scotist view of God's will.

CHAPTER III

CREATION: ITS LAWS, ITS NATURE AND THE PLACE OF SIN

THE SOURCE

ONE truth alone informs the Universe—this is God. By Him it was created; by Him it is governed and sustained. In starting from this basic assumption, Bradwardine develops a theory of divine control so extreme that the created world is left with nothing to hold in its own right.

It is evident from creation that there must be a creator. This is God. He is both the first principle of all that is created and the source of all truth. As such, He is positive not negative.[1] He alone decides what is possible and impossible, limited only by contradiction, as this would frustrate His will. That which God wills, He does; and it is through His will, acting freely and from love, that everything else comes about.[2]

Although He alone gives existence and value and is the governing principle in everything, He yet remains infinite and distinct from His creatures.[3] Bradwardine compares God to an architect, who through His Word brings into being that which He sees in His mind. His will gives realization to the idea, just as the stonemason makes real that which comes from the architect's mind. Here the comparison must end, for God is the very principle of existence. He is its triple cause, formal, efficient and final. In God all forms, which in matter are only potential, are real and

---

[1] 'Primum ergo principium complexorum nullatenus negatiuum, sed affirmatiuum firmiter arbitrandum' (p. 200). See also corollaries to cap. 5, pp. 203–5.

[2] '. . . omnia quaecunque sunt et fiunt per bonum et optimum sunt et fiunt, et ad hoc omnia videt, et ab ipso mouentur et continentur, et propter ipsum et per ipsum in ipso omne principium exemplatiuum, consummatiuum, intellectuale, speciale, formale, et simpliciter omne principium. . .' (p. 150).

[3] 'Quoniam nulla creatura ab eo condita per se subsistere valet nisi ab eo sustineatur quia eam creauit, extra omnia sed non exclusus; intra omnia sed conclusus' (p. 147).

actual.[1] Every quality which appears in the material world is an
extension of its true nature as it exists fully and perfectly in
God. A good deed, a just man, a true friend, are aspects of goodness, justice, truth, virtues whose forms come from God.[2]

This argument of archetypes, although going back to Plato, is
used in a different sense both by St Anselm and St Thomas as
evidence for God's existence. While Plato regarded Ideas as complete in themselves, Christian thinkers took them as evidence of
the divine nature: they were, for them, expressions, or emanations, of the perfect principles in God. Thus by this view goodness, justice, truth and the other virtues sprang from the same
source, in God, where they united in His indivisible essence.
Similarly, for Bradwardine, these principles are further evidence
of a perfect being; and he concludes from this that everything,
however diverse, springs from one source, quoting a wide list
of authorities, which includes Aristotle, Avicebrol, Plato, Proclus,
Dionysius, and in the case of the last named using his expression
monad.[3] God is thus the source of the forms which give the created world shape and meaning; there is for everything an idea in
God.[4] Thus in the beginning was the Word, and the Word was
with God and God was the Word; without Him there would be
nothing.[5]

[1] '. . . et ideo dicitur quod omnes proportiones et formae, quae sunt in
potentia in prima materia, sunt in actu in primo motore' (p. 155).

[2] 'Certissimum quidem et omnibus est volentibus aduertere perspicuum,
quia quaecunque dicuntur aliquid, ita ut inuicem magis vel minus, aut
aequaliter dicantur, per aliquid dicuntur quod non aliud et aliud, sed idem
intelligitur in diuersis, siue in illis aequaliter, siue inaequaliter consideretur:
Nam quaecunque iusta dicuntur ad inuicem, siue pariter, siue magis vel
minus, non possunt intelligi iusta nisi per iustitiam, quae non est aliud et
aliud in diuersis. Et item dicit de omnibus bonis diuersis, quod sunt bona per
aliquid unum bonum existens idem in diuersis, et quod ipsum solum est
bonum per seipsum; et nullum aliud bonum est illi aequale vel maius, quare
ipsum est summum' (p. 158).

[3] 'Omnis numerus unitur quidem in Monade. . .' (p. 159).

[4] 'Huiusmodi autem numeri unitates propriae sunt rationes in mente
diuina omnium creatrices, nutrices, et continuae seruatrices. . .' (p. 160).

And: '[Lincolniensis] dicit quod Uniuersalia sunt cognitiones rerum
creandarum, quae fuerunt in prima causa aeternaliter, et sunt rationes
earum et causae formales, et exemplares, et ipsae sunt etiam creatrices;
et hae sunt quas vocauit Plato ideas et mundum Archetypum; et hae sunt
secundum ipsum genera, et species et principia tam essendi quam cogno-
scendi' (pp. 160–1).

[5] *Ibid.* p. 156.

E

THE GOVERNING PRINCIPLES: DIVINE PARTICIPATION

So far Bradwardine has been preparing the ground. He has made God the source of all creation and His will its law. In this he has kept within the bounds of tradition; it is when he comes to discuss God's relation to His creatures that the break is made. Bradwardine now puts into operation all three aspects of God's nature which he has developed previously. First, Anselm's view of God's infinite perfection provides the *raison d'être* for all that He does. Love of Himself and His creatures is His sole motive, complete in itself. Secondly, the Aristotelian-Thomist principle of God as first cause is transformed by Bradwardine to mean not simply a hierarchy of cause and effect dependent upon an unmoved mover; but the subjection of everything caused to the active and immediate control of the first cause. The latter no longer acts, as it were, from above, moving everything below it in a certain direction; it is now directly engaged in everything, inseparable from it. Bradwardine, to use his own terminology, makes God the co-efficient in all that concerns His creatures. He is the senior partner in all that they do.[1] For want of a better expression, we shall call this concept the Principle of Divine Participation. It is the heart of Bradwardine's system: from it flows the extreme power which he assigns to God's actions, and the worthlessness of His creatures, including man. Similarly, it confronts Bradwardine with his one insoluble problem—the cause of evil and sin. Thirdly, this theory of divine participation is built upon the role that Bradwardine, following Duns Scotus, has assigned to God's will.[2] With this as the source of God's knowledge of His creatures, Bradwardine is able to make Him participate in all that happens in the universe.

This emphasis upon God's knowledge and will as essentially active accordingly affects the whole of creation; it involves God immediately and directly in its affairs; the line between the divine and created wills becomes blurred beyond recognition; and nothing remains unmoved by their union. This is the direction

---

[1] 'Quod cuiuslibet actus voluntatis creatae Deus est necessarius coeffector' (bk. II, cap. 20, p. 540).

And: 'Quod in omni actione communi voluntatum increatae et creatae, increata creatam naturaliter antecedit' (bk. II, cap. 30, p. 578).

[2] See Ch. II above.

that Bradwardine gives to his combination of St Thomas and
Duns Scotus: from one he takes the elements of his determinism;
from the other, the instrument which transforms it from an impersonal hierarchy into God's direct control. Together they make
up his principle of divine participation where everything is
determined by God as its most immediate cause. Bradwardine's
method here is to apply each part in turn. He starts by asserting
that God, as creator, is the necessary conservator of everything
created.[1]

Nothing could remain in being for an instant without His
immediate and constant participation. From this Bradwardine
draws three conclusions: first, that no created being alone suffices
to conserve anything else; this can only be through God. Second,
that God is both necessary in Himself, and necessary to conserve, immediately, whatever is created.[2] Thirdly, it follows that,
for anything created to be conserved, God as first cause has to do
this Himself. Next, Bradwardine turns to God's will. It was one
of Duns Scotus's emphatic arguments against the determinism
of the Arab philosophers that God always carries out His actions
directly. Bradwardine, too, takes up this cry. Throughout *De
causa Dei* he refers for support to the 1277 Paris condemnations
of those theses which regarded God as a remote cause. Unlike
Duns, however, Bradwardine takes up the same cry the better to
assert God's active participation; for if He were not the immediate and direct cause of His creatures' actions, He could not be the
coadjutor in them. This is the main reason for Bradwardine's
strenuous assertion of God as an immediate cause.

He then goes on to draw three conclusions from God's active
participation in creation. The first is that nothing can be done, or
move, without God. The second is that only God can be the immediate mover. If He did not direct a creature in every action
which it performed, then there would be no action from a created
will. The third is that there can only be an action by a created will
at all if God moves it more immediately than anything else.[3] It
is not possible, then, to describe anything created as entirely the

[1] Cap. 2, p. 146.
[2] 'Omne namque de potentiale, si debeat actuari hoc necessario erit per
aliquem actum' (p. 162).
[3] Corollaries to caps. 3 and 4, pp. 171 and 174.

immediate cause of its own actions; for, in every case, God will be more immediately the cause than any creature.[1]

Bradwardine, having established that God is not only the immediate cause of everything done in the created world, but also the most immediate cause, has gained the full field for determinism. God has a triple relation to His creatures, as their cause (efficient, formal and final), as their conservator, and as the senior co-actor in all that they do. Bradwardine has by these tenets fashioned so strong an instrument of divine power that its application leaves no room for the slightest freedom in the actions of His creatures. God's activity, by the principle of divine participation, has been extended into the whole of creation. This is the great leap that Bradwardine has made, as its consequences clearly show.

On the part of God it means that there can be no separation between divine and created actions. It comes perilously near to pantheism in so far as God is made to participate in every detail of the universe; indeed, logically, it is hard to see that Bradwardine has any valid means of safeguarding his system from such a charge. Theologically, on the contrary, the whole spirit and purpose of *De causa Dei* is only too concerned with emphasizing the infinite chasm between God and His creatures. On the part of God's creatures, the effect of the principle of divine participation has been to deprive them of all independent powers. They can make no claim to any intrinsic activity of their own. Their position may be likened to bubbles in a pipe; they cease to exist the instant the blowing ceases: and, conversely, they move only under its impact. Thus equipped, God's power, always irresistible, has, in Bradwardine's hands, become irresistibly active. From such a position, all claims to merit or independence on the part of men can be crushed.

Bradwardine considers it necessary to devote some space to discussing fate. Whether he feels that his view of God's will forces him to explain his attitude to fate, lest, like St. Augustine, he be

[1] 'Prima, Quod nihil potest quicquam mouere sine Deo idem per se et proprie commouente. Secunda, Quod nihil potest quicquam mouere sine Deo immediate idem mouente. Tertia, Quod nihil potest quicquam mouere sine Deo idem mouente immediatius alio motore quocunque. Quarta, Quod nulla propositio tribuens quodcunque creatum cuicunque causae secundae, est immediata simpliciter' (p. 174).

accused of introducing it, or whether he wishes to remove any possible rival to his view of providence, cannot be said. In the event, the outcome is not altered, for the conclusions he reaches could apply equally to both suppositions.

God's will, says Bradwardine, is the cause of all that is created. It is, therefore, the power by which the universe is governed and directed;[1] and he repudiates the idea of fate as contrary to the interests of faith.[2]

There are, he says, two views of fate: one as inevitable necessity, in general, due to the heavenly bodies; and, more specifically due to individual stars, ruling those born within their orbit. The other view, from the word *fando*, is taken to mean a certain disposition, a guidance from above. Now the first view, which regards fate as astral coercion, cannot be accepted by Christians at all, and is unanimously condemned by them. If, however, the necessity which dominates this view is withdrawn, and the fate of the stars is seen rather as a disposition and inclination in men, it need not be completely rejected; for divine fate must be recognized.[3] Is it not written: 'He spake and it was done'?[4]

Thus, in the sense of fate as derived from *fando* or *fiat*, we can talk of divine fate. With St Augustine, Bradwardine regards divine fate as a branch of divine will; and all the divers descriptions of an omnipotent power over men are really alike in describing God alone.[5]

Our wills, therefore, have just so much power as God's wills, and fate, as the temporal application of God's wishes, is the means by which His will influences ours.[6]

Bradwardine treats of fortune and cause in much the same way.[7] These, too, like fate, are to be considered as the workings

[1] Cap. 27, p. 261.

[2] 'Quod Fatum est a sanitate Fidei respuendum' (p. 264).

[3] 'Fatum vero diuinum est proculdubio concedendum' (p. 265).

[4] 'Nonne scriptum est in exordio creaturae; Dixit Deus, Fiat Lux, et facta est lux? et ita de caeteris creaturis? et alibi; Ipse dixit et facta sunt? Omnia enim quaecunque voluit, fecit, quia voluntas eius perfecta; istud autem fatum diuinum est maxima voluntatis diuinae, quae est efficax rerum causa' (*ibid.*).

[5] 'Sunt autem haec omnia nihil aliud nisi Deus. . . . Nam prouidentia est ipsa diuina ratio, in summo omnium Principe constituta, quae cuncta disponit; Fatum vero inhaerens rebus mobilibus dispositio, per quam prouidentia suis quaeque nectit ordinibus' (p. 266).

[6] Cap. 29, p. 267.   [7] Cap. 29, p. 268.

of some power beyond the reach of men. There are two ways of looking at this preternatural quality: as either the intention of some general agent, so that it cannot be given a cause; or as the specific intention of a particular agent or of an inferior cause. The first view can simply be called fortune; the second implies that nothing can be entirely uncaused and accidental: for this reason, Bradwardine holds, the second is the correct view.[1]

We only call things fortuitous when we do not know their cause: in fact, as in the case of fate, the cause of everything is in God. In this sense, therefore, it is through the limitations of men that God's workings are invested with names such as fate, fortune and so on. All things, in reality, are governed by the laws of divine providence,[2] from our fears and joys to the power of popes and kings. Far from being God's benevolent assent to what we do, it is the active dispensation of His will. Accordingly, there is no room for God's passive permission through providence. As with everything that comes from His will, to permit is to act.[3] Providence, then, is God's active governance of creation: it has nothing in common with fate or chance or the stars.

THE NATURE OF THE UNIVERSE

Bradwardine, having discussed the source and the principle of the universe, now turns to its nature. Since, he says, the whole of creation is governed by divine providence, it is actively regulated by God's love. Everything created, therefore, as coming from God, is good; and nothing created is, by nature, bad.[4] We can, Bradwardine says, see this principle of goodness in everything

---

[1] 'Sciendum quod omnes qui loquuntur de Casu, et Fortuna, dicunt haec esse, quando aliquid accidit praeter intentionem agentis. . . . Aliquid ergo contingere praeter intentionem agentis dupliciter cogitari; vel praeter intentionem cuiuslibet agentis omnino, ita quod a nullo simpliciter intendatur, vel praeter intentionem alicuius causae particularis, vel cuiuslibet causae inferioris: Primum potest vocari simpliciter casuale aut fortuitum; Secundum vero secundum quid; Nihil igitur est casuale simpliciter neque fortuitum, sed secundum quid tantum. . .' (p. 268).

[2] 'Quod res voluntariae diuinae prouidentiae legibus gubernantur' (cap. 30, p. 271).

[3] 'Quod omnia proueniant a Dei prouidentia actualiter disponente, non solummodo permittente' (cap. 32, p. 282).

[4] 'Quod tota universitas rerum est bona, et nulla res per se mala' (cap. 26, p. 251).

which exists. All things desire an end to which they can direct themselves. Now God as their necessary first principle and source must be this end.[1] He must also be positive; for as pure negation, He could neither exist nor be the first principle of all things.[2]

Accordingly, everything that tries to follow its true nature, as created and conserved by God, is good, since goodness is inherent in it. Only when this nature is impaired does evil arise; for it then ceases to be a complete entity.[3]

Now Bradwardine, with characteristic vigour, presses this meaning to cover every act which can be recognized as having an individual nature and existence. Thus all that exists in its own right, possessing a positive nature, such as, say, an apple, and is not a parasite on the positive, such as the canker in an apple, is by nature good. In this sense we can include such *actions* as homicide and adultery; they cannot be bad, according to Bradwardine, because they represent actions from which, by nature, value derives. If we condemned the *acts* by which homicide and adultery were achieved, we should condemn the positive results which are achieved by these same actions. Not only do these acts lend themselves to homicide and adultery; they are also responsible for death (in its natural sense) and marriage.[4]

The nature of anything must not be confused with the purposes to which it is put: an apple as an apple is a positive nature, and good; if it is worm-eaten instead of healthy, its nature as an apple is still good. Being alone is pure goodness.[5] Evil, on the other hand, has no essence or positive nature; it is lack of goodness, and so negative, without a positive cause; it cannot therefore be regarded as part of the natural order of creation. Moreover as parasitic on the good, which alone is positive, evil is always associated with good, as for example in the case of

[1] Cap. 11, p. 198.
[2] 'Est enim causa illius quia enim bonum est bonum, ideo non est malum, et non e contra; quia non esse malum, penitus nihil ponit, et per consequens nihil causat. Primum ergo principium complexorum nullatenus negatiuum, sed affirmatiuum firmiter arbitrandum' (p. 200).
[3] 'Nihil ergo est quod naturam conseruans Deo contrarie conetur' (p. 253).
[4] 'Item homicidium, adulterium, non sunt per se mala, nec aliqui actus exteriores, quia non in pueris, morionibus, dormientibus, seu etiam furiosis, cum careant arbitrio libero voluntatis causalis' (p. 255).
[5] 'Esse est bonitas pura et perfectio pura' (p. 259).

homicide and adultery which represent the distortion of death and marriage. Evil can thus never exist on its own, for pure evil is the equivalent of pure deficiency, that is, nothing.[1] Indeed, it is only because the created world is by nature good that evil comes about, being conditional upon it. Hence the presence of evil is simply further evidence for the existence of good.

Bradwardine's view of the nature of matter is to be gained more by gleaning stray remarks than from any full and sustained discussion. As with so much else in his system, it is too removed from his central theme to deserve specific attention. Yet a closer examination of his scattered references will show it to have a definite place in the assumptions on which his arguments are based.

Broadly speaking, there are three main ways of looking at matter: first, as devoid of any kind of form or existence in itself; the mere wax, as it were, upon which the seal of form can make its imprint. In this view—the view of Aristotle—matter is mere potency: only a form can give it being and shape. Matter, in turn, is the means by which the universal is expressed in the individual: thus the form of man is his reason, or rational soul; to become a particular man, the individual, Socrates, this form must be embodied. The second way of looking at matter is that of Duns Scotus, where there is a common being before any individual beings. In this sense, matter has form in its own right: before there is the particular form, which distinguishes an individual, there is the common form which belongs to all matter. The third view of matter is that in which form and matter are united in one combination (hylomorphism). This unity constitutes the stuff of which everything is composed as the primal source. Within these broad divisions there are, further, aspects such as seminal forms, but what concerns us here is whether matter is entirely subject to form or whether it has tendencies of its own.

Bradwardine's view is that of Aristotle and St Thomas Aquinas. Matter itself is formless and only potential. To be realized

[1] 'Malitia vero non habet essentiam, sed est priuatio substantiae, et utilitatis dispositionis suae . . . ita malum non est aliud quam absentia debiti boni' (p. 259).
'. . . quod bonum et per se malum, seu bonitas et pura malitia non sunt contraria propria, sed opposita priuatiue' (cor. to cap. 21, p. 260).

into actual being, a form must be imposed upon it.[1] If the form is withdrawn, the matter by which it was governed will again recede into potency. Thus without the form embodied in matter we could not understand the matter.[2]

Bradwardine's theory of matter can be called Aristotelian, first, in that he uses the Aristotelian distinction between potency and act, and applies these to proving God's existence as St Thomas does.[3] Second, because matter, alone, is incapable of realizing its potentialities. From this, in the third place, it follows that existence is superior to essence; a quality of itself cannot become actual unless it is given a form which transforms it from potency to act. Hence an essence, as such, in opposition to the view of Duns Scotus, is without meaning unless the special state of existence is added to it. Finally, there comes the vital corollary that only through matter can a form, or universal, become individual; it is only when the form Man is embodied in matter that it becomes the individual man, Socrates.

While Bradwardine does not explicitly and fully discuss these aspects together, these conclusions may fairly be drawn from what has here been said; from his application of the distinction between essence and existence to God; and from his theory of man,[4] as a being with a rational soul for its form.

THE PLACE OF SIN

Perhaps the most striking paradox in any Christian system of thought is that while God the creator is the highest good, His creatures are sinful. To reconcile the cruelty and wickedness of the created world with an infinitely perfect creator has been one of the central preoccupations of all Christian thought. The traditional explanation derived from considering sin as a negative concept, which we have already seen Bradwardine employ in the

---

[1] 'Omnis autem mutabilis etiam formabilis sit necesse est' (p. 153).
'Nulla autem res formare seipsum potest quia nulla res potest dare sibi quod non habet; et utique habeat formam, formatur aliquid' (*ibid.*).

[2] 'Si quicquid mutabile aspexeris vel sensu corporis, vel animi consideratione capere non potes nisi aliqua numerorum forma teneatur, qua detracta in nihilum recedat necesse esse' (*ibid.*).

[3] See pp. 24–7 above.

[4] *De causa Dei*, pp. 78–9; and pp. 87–9 below.

case of evil.[1] God alone is completely good; His creatures are sinful because they are less than completely good. Sin, then, is the measure of the distance between God's infinite perfection and the finite, imperfect natures of His creatures.

This general concept of sin, despite differences of emphasis, is one which fitted the traditional systems of thought. For Bradwardine, however, this is not possible, try as he does to give sin its place as a purely negative factor. His God is not only the highest good and the first cause of everything in nature; but He is the *active* and most immediate cause. In addition, everything that God knows about His creatures He also wills. This prevents God's influence from ever being merely to conserve that which He wills. When God permits He also acts.[2] God, then, would seem to be Himself implicated in every act of sin by virtue of sin existing at all. Now this is inconceivable: for how can the highest good be also the source of evil? The dilemma is apparent: either to admit that God causes sin; or to reduce the extent of God's active participation in His creatures' actions, and allow them a measure of independence. Now, since Bradwardine's whole system stands or falls by his principle of divine participation, the second is ruled out at once. This means modifying the first in such a way that God is not the cause of sin but still remains in active control. The effect on Duns Scotus of making God's will knowledge was that he adopted a very much more favourable attitude towards men. The heinousness of the fall was minimized and a more exalted view taken of man's natural powers. This, in turn, moderated the ill effects of sin; the Incarnation was considered as a divine act which would have occurred in any event, even had there been no fall.

For Bradwardine this way is barred; his use of the Scotist theory of God's will does not extend to Duns's view of man and sin. Instead, Bradwardine allies God's active will to St Augustine's concept of man, as worthless and powerless to do good of his own resources. This is not, however, as with St Augustine, directed to man specifically as having fallen from his originally righteous state; it lies in the very nature of God's power that His creatures are inherently weak and dependent upon Him. It is this, and not so much the fall, which has the effect of denying any

[1] See pp. 54–6 above.　　[2] See p. 54 above.

independent worth to man; in this sense, men, whatever their condition, would, if left to themselves, sin continually. For it is Bradwardine's emphatic opinion that nothing can exist or do anything unless God actively uses His will to direct it. The two pieces fit so tightly that there can be no chink or loophole through which sin can escape. On the one hand, God is the motive force in everything His creatures do; on the other hand, as perfect in Himself, He cannot want sin. Bradwardine has so firmly nailed his colours to the masthead that they can only be lowered by cutting down the mast. Rather than weaken any part of his purpose, of vindicating the overwhelming power of God's grace and opposing the claims of human merit, Bradwardine tries to evade a clear-cut solution to the problem of sin. It is a measure of his intentness in building up his position that he is prepared to risk being outflanked rather than withdraw an inch. It is a measure also of its extremity.

Bradwardine, in dealing with sin, takes two approaches: one is to regard it as part of the pattern of the universe. It is the means by which the good stands out in comparison with the bad. The other approach is to dissociate God as the cause of sin by asserting that sin, as negative, cannot have a positive cause. These in themselves illustrate the almost contradictory way in which Bradwardine deals with sin. They represent his twofold responsibility to his view that God is infinitely active as well as infinitely good, attributes which between them allow no room for sin.

Chapter 34,[1] 'If and how God wills, and does not will, sin', sets a tone of ambiguity so different from the directness of Bradwardine's arguments elsewhere. In a certain way, he says, it seems that God wants sin, for its presence shows that He permits it.[2]

God is both the cause of all that exists and all that does not exist; that which is positive comes before the negative, and so sin can only be the result of goodness, not an end in itself. This

---

[1] *De causa Dei*, p. 294.

[2] 'Et videtur quod aliquo modo velit; Deus namque permittit peccatum' (*ibid.*).

'Item Deus voluntarie prouidet et facit omnia opera voluntaria tam mala quam bona cum omnibus suis circumstantiis positiuis. . . . Item peccatum esse est verum, et non est primum verum, sicut ex duodecimo huius patet. . . Primum autem verum est Deus, ut patet ibidem. Deus ergo est causa huius veritatis, et non nisi voluntarie. Vult ergo Deus hanc esse veram, Peccatum est' (*ibid.*).

involves God in sin; but, because all that He does is good, He wants it as a means of achieving good.[1] It is through contrast to the good that the good is made the more apparent. In music, for example, harmony is the result of discords.[2] The blending of opposites is a principle of the universe: from diversity comes unity, and from contrast, harmony. It can be seen in everything we care to examine;[3] from the heat and the cold, the wet and the dry, and so on, there emerges an over-all balance. In the case of the stars, for example; by the darkness of their setting, their own brightness is intensified: from the union of the contrasts of light and dark comes a heightened illumination.

Now this principle of unity through opposites applies no less to good and bad than to light and dark. The bad, as deficiency, does not exist in its own right: it is there to do the bidding of the good: to establish its transcendence as the night establishes that of the stars. We cannot, therefore, judge sin in isolation. Bradwardine follows St Augustine in saying that the beauty of the universe is not to be considered from its individual parts, but, as with a picture, our judgement must come from its over-all aspect. As the black in a picture is, in relation to the rest of it, a means of enhancing its beauty, so sin must be regarded as enhancing the good in the universe.[4] Everything, moreover, as coming from God is just.[5]

So far, then, the general principles are clear. Sin is not to be regarded in its own right; its place in the universe is to augment the existence of the good, not to detract from it. Within these general terms no violence is done either to God's powers or to His goodness. But it is when we ask the cause of sin in particular

---

[1] 'Item omne quod facit ad pulchritudinem universi, Deus totius pulchritudinis pulcher Autor vult esse: Peccatum est huiusmodi . . .' (p. 295).

[2] '. . . in vocibus diuersis unam harmoniam perfecit' (ibid.).

[3] 'Sic igitur et omnium constitutionem, Coeli dico, et terrae undique totius permixtam, maxime contrariorum principiorum una decorauit harmonia, siccum humido, calidum frigido, graue leui, rectum circulato decorauit' (pp. 295–6).

[4] '[Augustinus] dicit, quod pulchritudo uniuersi non est consideranda in una parte tantum sed in omnibus, et in toto. Error quoque noster parti adhaerens per se foedus est: sed sicut niger color in pictura cum toto fit pulcher, sic totum istum agonem decenter edit ex contrariis incommutabilis diuina prouidentia' (p. 296).

[5] 'Item omne iustum a primo iusto, scilicet Deo, est iustum: et Deus vult illud esse iustum et esse' (ibid.).

that the difficulties arise. Someone has to begin the process: is it God, as infinitely good, or is it His creatures as infinitely power- less? As we have already seen there are, logically, insuperable difficulties which attend either reply. Accordingly, Bradwardine never attempts to meet the problem fully from either end. What he does is to follow three main lines of argument. The first is in reality the extension of his general vindication of sin's existence. It is God's means of asserting justice. He punishes sin by sin. The second is that sin comes from men and angels alone, when they try to follow their own free will, and not God. Bradwardine here approaches St Augustine's solution of sin as caused by human free will; but in Bradwardine's case this cannot occupy the same central position because of his principle of divine participation. The third argument, and one that recurs spasmodically through- out the rest of *De causa Dei*, is that God, in so far as sin is the deprivation of good, is the negative cause of sin.

That sin is God's means of punishing a sin already committed is an argument strongly pressed by Bradwardine. He quotes St Isidore to this effect: 'A preceding sin is the cause of the sin which follows.'[1] In this way, God only makes those sin who will sin in any event. Their sins therefore are the working out of His justice.[2] There is no need in this case to try to absolve God, as the Lombard does, when he says that the sins by which God pun- ishes previous sins are not sins, from His point of view, but a penalty. Bradwardine holds such a distinction to be false; for this would mean that God could not see the effect of His action, which is sin, but only the cause, as penalty. In carrying out any action God foresees every possible effect.[3]

God always knows and wants the consequences of everything

[1] *Ibid.* p. 297.

[2] '. . . sicut dicit Apostolus. . . . Facit ego Deus quosdam peccare, sed in quibus iam talia peccata praecesserunt, ut iusto iudicio eius mereantur in desideriis ire' (*ibid.*).

[3] 'Si quis autem dixerit cum Lumbardo, quod Deus vult peccatum sub ratione, qua est poena, non sub ratione qua est peccatum, potest sic argui contra eum: Ista poena et peccatum per se, scilicet sub ratione qua est peccatum necessario et inseparabiliter coniunguntur, et illa necessitas et inseparabilitas est a Deo, sicut ex praecedentibus patet: Ipse enim est prima necessitas, et primum necesse esse. Vult ergo illa sic coniungi et esse con- iuncta, et esse; ergo vult peccatum esse' (p. 298).

'Deus autem scit et vult ista duo taliter copulari, et scienter et rationaliter vult unum, scilicet poenam peccati; ergo et peccatum' (pp. 298–9).

that He wills. The effect must always follow the cause, except
through some deficiency; and this can never apply to God's acts
or to His knowledge.[1] Far from His not knowing the effects of all
that He wills, God ensures that these follow from His actions and
are not contradicted. He wants sin in the same way as a doctor
knowingly purges a patient to cure him. It has no other application than the reassertion of the good.[2] Sin, then, comes last in
God's will: He first wills Himself; then that which is outside
Him; and finally evil: goodness is the constant aim, and evil is
only invoked to this end.[3]

That God wants sin as a means of healing is not the same as
making God its author. This is Bradwardine's second argument.
The reasons for this are, first, that sin is a deficiency and has no
efficient cause.[4] It therefore cannot come from God's will as the
first cause, for God as the highest good is the cause of good, not
deficiency. Moreover, to quote St Augustine again, sin is an
act, not a substance in its own right. It does not subsist as some
permanent quality, but is continually in flux. St Augustine
concluded from this that sin, as an act, devoid of stability or
substance, is by nature non-existent.[5]

Moreover, as St John says, He who sins is the slave of sin. Thus
if God willed sin, He would thereby create it; and this would
make God the author of sin and so its servant. Accordingly, God
cannot be the first cause of sin, and by this token He cannot create
it. This, as it stands, is in complete opposition to the first argu-

[1] 'Quicumque vult aliquid, necessario vult ea quae necessario requiruntur
ad illud, nisi sit ex parte eius defectus, vel propter ignorantiam, vel quia a
recta electione eius quod est ad finem intentum abducitur per aliquam
passionem, quae de Deo dici non possunt' (p. 299).

[2] 'Non enim vult peccatum nisi forsan sicut Medicus in medicaminibus
suis [vult] venenum, in quantum scilicet valet ad exercitium bonorum, ad
punitionem malorum . . .' (p. 301).

[3] 'Deus vult seipsum primo, secundo quodammodo vult bona alia extra
ipsum, tertio vero mala, quatenus videlicet ex malis proueniunt quaedam
bona, ipsius prouidentia omnia suauiter disponente; sicque vult Deus bonum
prius quodammodo et antecedenter, malum vero posterius et consequenter,
quia finaliter propter bonum' (p. 600).

[4] '[Augustinus] probat quod Deus non est autor mali, quia non est causa
deficiendi nec tenendi ad non esse quod fit peccando, cum ipse sit summum
bonum et causa essendi' (p. 300).

[5] 'Intelligit enim, quod non est substantia proprie dicta, quia non per se
subsistit, vel magis communiter, quod non est essentia permanens, sed
consistens semper in fieri, aut in fluxu' (p. 540).

ment. But Bradwardine does not leave it to stand there. That sin exists is a fact. Must we then conclude that it is part of the nature of the universe? This is not, he replies, capable of a simple reply. Sin exists, but it does not apply to the first cause of all creation. As he has already shown, God is both the cause and the criterion of goodness. This means that sin must arise from disorder among secondary causes; it cannot appear as something absolute in itself, but comes from some maladjustment, however slight, among created things.[1]

This is the farthest point that Bradwardine reaches in making secondary causes the starting-point of sin. Their deficiency prevents the full realization of their natures; it is through this lack in His creatures that God wills them to sin. Bradwardine further absolves God from sin when he switches from God's will to His intellect as His means of knowing created things.[2] This change enables God to know without causing what He knows; and Bradwardine justifies it on the grounds that God is the cause only of the good and the positive.[3]

The link between these first two arguments is provided by the third. We have noted that at no time does Bradwardine make a full affirmation either of God as the cause of sin or as completely remote from it, without soon qualifying each. This is most clearly seen in his assertion that,[4] though secondary causes themselves are responsible for the lack which is sin, God wills this indirectly, as their first cause. This is the position to which Bradwardine seems most firmly to hold in subsequent references to sin. Sins are privation which cannot be understood in themselves, but

[1] 'Videtur ergo quod non sit aliqua inordinatio, deformitas, aut peccatum simpliciter in toto uniuerso, sed secundum quid tantummodo, respectu videlicet inferiorum causarum, ordinationem superioris causae volentium, licet non valentium perturbare' (p. 301).

[2] 'Ita Deus omnia quorum autor est, praescit, nec tamen omnium, quae praescit, ipse autor est: quorum autem non est malus autor, iustus est ultor' (p. 302).

[3] 'Verum est tamen et aliter, et veraciter dici posse quod videlicet, Deus non est autor peccati, sicut recte facti; huius enim sic est autor, quod ipse solus supernaturaliter creat, et dat recte facienti fidem, spem et charitatem, et forsitan alios habitus ad meritum inclinantes, et omnem meritum facientes, non sic autem ex parte peccati' (pp. 301–2).

[4] 'Quapropter non potest improbabiliter aestimari, quod Deus saltem secundum quid vult peccatum, licet non simpliciter, quia non seipsum' (p. 301).

come from the natures they defile. In this sense, since sin comes from the good, and the good from God, it comes indirectly from Him. Sin is a negative result of His will.[1]

Bradwardine's final summing-up, as expressed in later parts of *Decausa Dei*, tends to regard sin as a negative effect of God's will. This, in fact, results in making God an indirect cause of sin; and for all his qualifications, Bradwardine leaves the impression that sin, as firmly rooted in the universe, cannot be separated from God's will.[2] It makes God the efficient, formal and final cause of sin, but not the material cause;[3] and it is in this light that Bradwardine attacks the view as false[4] that God alone performs every good act, but has no connexion with the bad. The bad, Bradwardine replies, is based upon a substance, which, by nature, is essentially good. God, therefore, in so far as the bad derives from the good, effects a bad action.[5]

Bradwardine seems finally to be caught in his own system. The delicate balance established between sin and God's will is too precarious to maintain. As the work proceeds, sin comes more and more within the area of God's will, so that in these later references God is *causa actus peccati*. The route to this position is hesitant and (almost) illicit. From the first, the conflicting tenets allow of

[1] 'Vel potest dici in his omnibus, sicut dicitur a nonnullis, quod sicut peccatum et omnis priuatio non intelligitur per se, sed in comparatione ad suum habitum et non proprie positiue, sed quodammodo priuatiue, sicut 26um tradit; sic etiam peccatum est a Deo volutum priuatiue; quilibet tamen actus secundum id quod est; quia, ut sic, bonus est, volutus a Deo proprie positiue . . .' (p. 307).

[2] 'Manifestum est autem quod actio peccati quoddam ens, et in praedicamento entis positum unde necesse est dicere, quod sit a Deo. Secundo autem idem patet ratione speciali: Necesse est enim omnes motus secundarum causarum causari a primo mouente: Deus autem est primum mouens respectu omnium motuum et spiritualium et corporalium; unde cum actus peccati sit quidem motus liberi arbitrii, necesse est dicere quod actus peccati in quantum est actus, sit a Deo. Hoc idem et plane testatur Johannes Scotus. . . . Ex praemissis, ut arbitror, satis claret, quod ad hoc quod voluntas creata efficiat suum actum quemcunque bonum vel malum, diuina coefficientia necessario requisita' (p. 554).

[3] '. . . quod concedimus dicentes, quod Deus est causa efficiens, formalis, finalis malae actionis, sed non materialis' (*ibid.*).

[4] Cap. 21, p. 555, opinion no. 6.

[5] 'Omnis ergo actus malus secundum substantiam actus aequaliter efficitur, sicut bonus, quare et aequaliter habet causam efficientem, quae necessario coefficientia Dei eget. Deus ergo vere et proprie efficit quemlibet actum malum secundum substantiam seu essentiam puram actus' (p. 567).

no satisfactory explanation; and Bradwardine turns now to one door, now to another, like a man who has become imprisoned in his own house. We miss the incisive progress from position to position; and the final words of chapter 34 seem almost a relieved admission that he has tried his best and that he can say no more: 'I would prefer on so important a question to hear the great rather than, as one so small, reply.'[1]

[1] *Ibid.* p. 307.

CHAPTER IV

GRACE[1]

THE *Dictionary of National Biography* in summarizing Bradwardine's views as given by Dean Milner in his *History of the Church of Christ*,[2] remarks that Bradwardine's 'doctrine of Grace and God's foreknowledge are linked together'.[3] Now, so far as it goes, this statement is true; but, as we have seen, God's foreknowledge of His creatures is through His will: and, through His will, God participates in their every action. It is more accurate, therefore, to say that Bradwardine's doctrine of grace is governed by the principle of divine participation. Through this Bradwardine is able to show, first, the completely gratuitous nature of grace; secondly, its necessity in any good act on the part of man; thirdly, that merit or good works by man have no influence whatever in gaining grace, but are themselves the result of grace having already been given; finally, that every disposition to good on the part of God's creatures is the result of preceding grace. Such a doctrine resurrects all the inexorability of St Augustine; it also anticipated Luther and Calvin in its denial of merit to any consideration.

Bradwardine considers that he has much in common with St Augustine; and to a certain point this is so. Like St Augustine, he says, he used to believe that faith was not the gift of God but could be obtained by our own powers. But he, too, came to realize his mistake as a victim of the mischievous Pelagians.[4] Again, as with St Augustine, he was fighting the encroachment of free will upon God's grace. Thus the similarity of their cause must be recognized. Yet their differences are almost as great. First, there is the extremity of Bradwardine's doctrine which will allow of no worth in man; there is none of the concern that Augustine felt for the *massa damnata*: man's worthlessness is one of the eternal verities and the more readily it is grasped the better.

[1] Throughout this chapter the reader is referred to Appendix II below.
[2] Dean Milner's *History of the Church of Christ* contains the longest account (III, pp. 218–42) of Bradwardine to be found in any general work.
[3] *D.N.B.* II, p. 1097. [4] See Introduction, pp. 13–14 above.

Second, there are Bradwardine's opponents: as we shall discuss in Part II below, they raise questions which go beyond the simple problem of grace and free will, important though these are; and for this reason alone, neither they nor Bradwardine afford a direct comparison with the struggle between St Augustine and Pelagius.

THE NATURE AND DIVISIONS OF GRACE

For Bradwardine every gift which any creature possesses comes under the heading of grace. Unless the powers by which men and beasts alike live were freely given to them by God, they could not exist. In this sense everything is indebted to God for His grace.[1]

Now the broad division is between uncreated grace and created grace.[2] Uncreated grace (*gratia gratificans*) is God's will itself, by whose love He gives Himself and all that is good to man.[3] It is the source of all created grace, and being moved only by love, is oblivious of either merit or reprobation and free from any other motive. It can be regarded, says Bradwardine, as two different aspects of uncreated charity: generally as the Trinity and specifically as the Holy Spirit.[4] In each case, therefore, it represents God's will. Its main features are, firstly, that as an attribute of God, it resides in Him alone and is the fount of all goodness; secondly, that, unlike created grace, which in its broadest sense applies to all creatures, it is not known to all men;[5] thirdly, that it is by its agency alone that the elect are predestined to glory and

---

[1] 'Quapropter et quodlibet donum Dei potest non incongrue, gratia Dei dici, gratia scilicet gratis data: Haec autem gratia est omnibus creaturis irrationalibus et rationalibus, gratis pariter et ingratis' (*De causa Dei*, p. 307).

[2] 'Gratia vero potest similiter accipi, ut videtur; Est enim gratia increata, et creata, siue gratia gratificans seu gratis dans, et gratia gratis data' (p. 247).

[3] 'Gratia increata et gratificans est diuina voluntas non propter aliquid meritum antecedens, nec propter aliquam retributionem, aut utilitatem propriam subsequentem, sed gratis volens aeternaliter bonum alicui, temporaliter dans sibi' (*ibid.*).

[4] 'Haec etiam gratia increata gratificans seu gratis dans quae est divina voluntas, potest accipi dupliciter, sicut charitas: Communiter et essentialiter sic competit toti Trinitati et cuilibet personarum; ac specialiter ac personaliter et sic appropriatur spiritui sancto' (*ibid.*).

[5] 'Gratia vero creata, seu gratia data est effectus huius gratiae increatae. Secundum membrum huius est omnibus satis notum, sed primum gratia increata non est omnibus notum' (*ibid.*).

sinners redeemed. Its presence divides the saved from the damned and, without it, no degree of created grace is efficacious.[1]

Created grace, as applied to man, is the supernatural gift which comes from uncreated grace,[2] and he possesses it in its highest form. It is God's special gift by which a man is rendered dear to Him; it sanctifies him whom it informs and, in turn, disposes him to love God. By its means, a man becomes God's adopted son in this world and shares in His glory in the next.[3] Like uncreated grace, created grace cannot be earned on account of merit. It has to be freely given by God. It is here that Bradwardine crosses swords most fiercely with the Pelagians; they assert that this first grace can be won from God. He, on the contrary, says that sanctifying grace is the precondition for all merit.

Now, before examining created grace in its details, it is of the utmost importance for Bradwardine's controversies with the 'Pelagiani moderni' to emphasize his attitude to created grace. Although he sees it as coming through uncreated grace, and therefore as secondary, he nevertheless makes it an essential milestone *en route* to glory. While his opponents[4] employ uncreated grace as the justification for dispensing with created grace, he makes one the inseparable concomitant of the other. This flows from the principle of divine participation: for God's creatures, dependent upon Him at every turn, need also to carry His spirit in them as a habit, if they are to stay free from sin or to have the faintest impulse to good. As to its nature, created grace, too, can be understood both generally and specifically:[5] as habitual grace (*gratia gratis dans et volens*) it causes its recipients to want good generally; it is in this broad aspect that created grace sanctifies him who possesses it. Specifically, created grace (*gratia gratis data*) is the special gift by which he who receives it can achieve good in leading another person to salvation.[6] This was the

---

[1] 'Sed sola charitas increata, quae hos habet charos ad regnum, et hos non habet, diuidit inter filios regni, et perditionis, sicut in principio lucem a tenebris diuidebat' (p. 247).

[2] *Ibid.*   [3] *Ibid.* p. 307.   [4] See Part II below.

[5] 'Est etiam gratia gratis dans bonum, quia redemptionem et remissionem peccatorum, ubi similiter patet effectus gratiae gratis dantis' (p. 247).

[6] 'Potest enim dici gratia gratis volens et dans generaliter quodcumque bonum, vel specialiter volens alicui bonum iustitiae et gloriae sempiternae, et dans sibi aliquam specialem virtutem, qua posset consequi tale bonum, et correspondenter per omnia dicitur gratia gratis data' (*ibid.*).

accepted division of created grace in Bradwardine's time: while
gratia gratis dans is sanctifying or habitual grace, a supernatural
gift from God, *gratia gratis data*, as a more specific supernatural
gift for the purpose of saving a soul, comes under what is now
called actual grace; it is a more transitory gift from God and not
necessarily *inherent* in the soul.[1]

Since created grace is itself the result of uncreated grace, and
Bradwardine has already said that uncreated grace can be understood in its specific form as the Holy Spirit, the Holy Spirit is
inseparable from created, sanctifying grace. To possess created
grace, then, is to participate in the divine nature; it is a supernatural quality infused by God.[2]

God and the Holy Spirit, Bradwardine concludes, are in this
sense said to constitute charity and grace; by grace God not only
loves Himself and man, but man similarly loves God.[3]

Through the supernatural *habitus* of grace alone, therefore, is
man capable of wanting and doing good.

THE CAUSE OF GRACE

Bradwardine is so concerned to show the wholly gratuitous
nature of grace that he refuses to recognize goodness apart from
it. All our gifts come by God's mercy; and all that we do is secondary to this.[4] Thus the cause of grace lies in God; and man is
utterly dependent upon it. God must be ever and immediately
with him in his simplest actions. This involves both the movement of His spirit (uncreated grace) and its presence in His creatures as a habit (created grace); and every good act must com-
prise both.

Bradwardine asserts the essentially arbitrary character of
grace in the manner of St Augustine and St Paul. The saying of
the latter from Romans[5] has an almost mystical significance for

[1] See Appendix II.
[2] '. . . ulterius ostendendum quod Deus et Spiritus Sanctus Dei primo
naturaliter efficit quemlibet talem actum, quam gratia eius dicta' (p. 374).
[3] 'Quod Deus et Spiritus Sanctus dicuntur quoquomodo charitas et
gratia, qua chare et gratis nedum Deus diligit se et hominem, verum etiam
qua homo similiter diligit Deum et proximum' (cor. to cap. 42, p. 375).
[4] *Ibid.* p. 373.
[5] 'Non volentis, neque currentis, sed miserentis est Dei' (Rom. ix. 16).

him. Like St Augustine, Bradwardine regards grace as the saving will of God, whatever the particular mode by which it is imparted;[1] it cannot have any other cause than God's love and mercy. Accordingly, Bradwardine rejects in turn Cassian's solution that God gives grace to some without preceding merit and to others only if they have merited it;[2] the semi-Pelagian plea of making merit the grounds for grace;[3] the theory that men can prepare themselves for grace and that then God will freely award them grace;[4] and finally that consent by man to God's grace is the cause of His conferring grace.[5]

All of these positions in greater or lesser degree give men some part to play in the award of grace, impairing the infinite freedom, and love, of God's action.[6] Such dispositions in men towards good can come only as the result of grace: they are its signs, not its cause,[7] though Bradwardine does not deny the value of natural feelings such as fear of evil.[8]

We must conclude with St Augustine, then, that our merits are God's gifts, and when he rewards them, He crowns them not us.[9]

THE NECESSITY OF GRACE

If grace is the means by which a man can love God, it must also be the direct cause of every good act; and its necessity must be absolute for any good wish or deed.[10]

[1] 'Omne autem bonum quod in nobis operatur Dei bona voluntas, ut dictum est, gratia gratis data dicitur, sed sola conformitas voluntatis nostrae voluntati diuinae est gratia data, quae nos reddit gratos Deo' (p. 376).

[2] *Ibid.* p. 313.   [3] *Ibid.* p. 314.   [4] *Ibid.* p. 316.   [5] *Ibid.* p. 319.

[6] 'Licet credere vel non credere sit in arbitrio voluntatis humanae, tamen in electis praeparatur voluntas a Domino' (p. 317).

[7] 'Item homo non potest aperire, nec consentire in talibus ex seipso, sed ex voluntate divina . . . . Nemo potest venire ad me nisi Pater meus traxerit illum' (p. 319).

[8] 'Verum licet ista ita se habeant, non est tamen intentionis meae negare omnem praeparationem et dispositionem praeuiam charitati, et gratiae in adultis: Scio enim quod timor seruilis, timor poenae, timor incommodi, amor commodi, et virtutes morales multum retrahunt a peccato, inclinant ad opera bona, et sic ad charitatem et gratiam, et ad opera vere grata praeparent et disponunt, sicut satis ostendunt autoritates . . .' (p. 318).

[9] 'Cum, inquit Augustinus, Deus coronat merita nostra nihil aliud coronat quam munera sua' (p. 324).

[10] 'Quod gratia, quae est habitus gratis datus a Deo una cum voluntate

This follows from the principle of divine participation by which nothing created, angel or man, can exist or move of its own accord. Only by following God's will can man be, or do, good; and for this he must be informed by His grace.[1]

Bradwardine, in dealing with the necessity for grace, is concerned to show the inherent weakness of the human will; so that, by its very nature, it is inconceivable that, alone, it could *ever* have remained free from sin. In its present state, therefore, it is doubly handicapped: its own original nature, which was itself too weak to transcend its desires, has, since the fall, become weighed down and weakened by the burden of sin.[2] Thus the need for grace forms an essential part of Bradwardine's view that God must participate in everything which concerns His creatures, if they or their actions are to exist. Now it is significant that this dependence upon grace in no way arises from the fall. Had man remained in his original state, grace would still have been necessary. It is in the nature of man, like every creature, to need God's participation. Both Bradwardine and Scotus, because of the role they assign to divine will, react in this emphatic manner towards man's relation to God: each, though from opposite poles, is concerned to show that, had man not sinned, his present state would have been substantially the same. While Duns interprets this state in a manner favourable to man, Bradwardine makes it serve only to emphasize the dependent nature of any creature upon God. It is vain, he says, to think in terms of man's ever having been able to act of his own resources; he has always been as dependent upon God's grace as the angels are still. Alone, man is incapable of serving God; if his own powers sufficed to do so then the supernatural virtues of faith, hope and charity would be in vain and without meaning. On the contrary, their presence is the sign of man's dependence upon them.[3]

humana est causa efficiens proprie cuiuslibet boni et meritorii actus sui' (cap. 40, p. 364).

[1] 'Ostenso quidem quod gratia cum voluntate efficit bonos actus. Puto autem quod gratia gratis infusa prius naturaliter voluntate, faciat actus bonos' (p. 371).

[2] *Ibid.*

[3] 'Frustra ergo ponuntur hi tres habitus, scilicet fides, spes et charitas supernaturaliter nobis infusi, cum sine his naturalia nostra nobis sufficiant ad faciendum et servandum omnia divina mandata sicut pelagius asserebat. . . Et hoc nedum nos in statu praesentis miseriae, sed etiam Angeli et primi

There are two stages in a good deed, both dependent on grace. A man can want the good only after having received the impulse from grace. With God's further help he can then co-operate in doing good. In either wanting or doing good he is dependent upon grace. This is the sense in which Bradwardine uses 'operating' and 'co-operating' grace,[1] quoting Augustine that 'co-operating grace perfects that which has been started by operating grace'.[2] This means that there has to be a special action on the part of God to ensure any good action by man.[3]

Now Bradwardine makes a vital distinction between the grace which enables a man to want good (sufficient) and the grace which can transform this desire into practice (efficacious). Although not himself using these terms he leaves no doubt that the difference between potentiality and act is the difference between created and uncreated grace. No one, he says, however great his created grace, can overcome temptation[4] or avoid sin[5] without God's special help, and this special help he defines as God's will.[6] Thus God's will is the means by which the good inclinations deriving from created grace are realized; without God's special aid sin and final reprobation will result. This gift of uncreated grace, moreover, is not restricted to Christians, but reserved for the elect whose number is immutable, decided from eternity.[7]

We shall discuss below the way in which Bradwardine's views over both co-operating and operating, sufficient and efficacious grace differ from tradition.[8] Here it is enough to note the way

parentes in statu primae innocentiae similiter indigebant, quando nullum obicem posuerunt mortalem, nec minimum venialem' (p. 326).

[1] 'Operans enim gratia praeparat hominis voluntatem ut velit bonum, gratia cooperans adiuuat ne frustra velit' (p. 366).

See Appendix II below.

[2] 'Co-operando Deus in nobis perficit, quod operando incipit, quia ipse ut velimus operatur incipiens, qui volentibus cooperatur perficiens' (p. 366).

[3] 'Nullus tamen aliquid horum potest nec se quouismodo disponere sine Deo specialiter id agente . . .' (p. 318).

[4] 'Quod liberum arbitrium quantacunque gratia creata suffultum sine alio Dei auxilio speciali non potest temptationem aliquam superare' (bk. II, cap. 5, p. 477).

[5] 'Quod nullus non tentatus, solius liberi arbitrii viribus, sine gratia quantacunque creata, absque alio Dei auxilio potest peccatum aliquod euitare' (bk. II, cap. 7, p. 490).

[6] 'Quod illud Dei auxilium speciale est voluntas eius inuicta' (bk. II, cap. 6, p. 489).

[7] *Ibid.* p. 203.   [8] pp. 149–50. See also Appendix II below.

in which God's will is asserted to the virtual exclusion of anything that can be called the actions of free will.

It is in this sense that Bradwardine regards the special aid of final perseverance. It is, he says, following St Augustine and St Thomas, the means by which the saved may resist all temptation, and sin, until they reach final glory.[1] Accordingly it is from God's will, no degree of created grace enabling a man to do good or abjure evil for an hour without it.[2] It has two aspects: to overcome the desires of the flesh and to maintain virtue. Thus, in effect, it is synonymous with God's uncreated grace, which, as we saw above, enables the elect to persevere in goodness to the end.

To question why such grace is given to some and not to others is to question God Himself; all that can be said is that no one can follow this path of righteousness unless he is prepared to do so; but for the soul to want this, it must already have received this special gift of grace: free will of itself could never serve the good. God's will, therefore, as first inciting the human will to desire good (*praeueniens*) and then moving it to do good (*subsequens*), alone causes a man to persevere. The cycle is complete: there can be no grace of perseverance unless a man wants to persevere; and for a man to want to persevere, he must already be in grace.[3]

In this connexion Bradwardine very strongly opposes the view of Lombard for having held that man's free will was self-sufficing

[1] 'Perseuerare est in eo quod est detinere, et pro differentia illius ad continere, subiungit: Continentia autem in eo quod est superare, quemadmodum et non vinci in vincere, propter quod et elegibilius continentia perseuerantia' (p. 491).

[2] 'Item si quis posset perseverare per unam horam, cum in fine illius horae esset ita fortis spiritualiter sicut prius, vel forsitan potius fortior, posset adhuc aeque faciliter vel facilius perseuerare, similiter per aliam horam sequentem, et sic per omnes, et ita finaliter contra capitulum iam praemissum' (p. 497).

[3] 'Nemo certe seruat rectitudinem hanc acceptam nisi volendo, velle autem illam aliquis nequit non habendo, habere autem illam nullatenus valet nisi per gratiam.... Nempe quamuis illa seruetur per liberum arbitrium, non tamen est tantum imputandum libero arbitrio quantum gratiae, cum haec rectitudo seruatur, quoniam illam liberum arbitrium non nisi per gratiam praeuenientem et subsequentem habet et seruat; sic autem gratia subsequitur donum suum, ut nunquam, siue magnum, siue paruum sit, illud dare deficiat nisi liberum arbitrium volendo aliud, rectitudinem quam accepit deferat' (*ibid.*).

before the fall; though, at the same time, Bradwardine is careful to emphasize that he does not regard him in the same way as the Pelagians. Bradwardine, like St Augustine, has only evil to say of free will when unattended by grace: it is capable only of doing wrong; to do good, it must follow God's will. Thus the first man fell through the inability of his will to remain good;[1] and human nature, in righteousness or in sin, cannot stand without God's aid.[2] The need for grace, then, in whatever form, is overwhelming. It supports man and moves him: if it is withdrawn, even for an instant, he will fall like any cripple whose crutch is taken from under him.

THE EFFECTS OF GRACE: MERIT AND JUSTIFICATION

As we have seen, the nature, and necessity, of grace arise from God's goodness and man's weakness. The award is so unconditional on God's part and the need so indispensable on man's, that the latter can play no part whatever in its bestowal. Merit and justification therefore owe nothing to human inclinations or deeds; they are gifts for which man can take no credit.

In the case of merit, this view leads to Bradwardine's complete rejection of merit *de congruo*. This doctrine held that while absolute merit (*de condigno*) could not exist in men naturally, but was a supernatural quality which came from grace, men, through a disposition to do good, had a certain moral claim to grace, though not possessing it (*de congruo*). Thus merit *de condigno* as strict merit does not depend upon any comparative standard; merit *de congruo*, on the other hand, is proportional and relative without any fixed and absolute value. It relies upon God's liberality and mercy, for it does not suppose a state of grace. This view of grace had been accepted by the great scholastics such as St Bonaventure, St Thomas Aquinas and Duns Scotus. But in Bradwardine's time it was becoming the most specious form of semi-Pelagianism: it was even being extended so far as to mean that

[1] Bradwardine is not so explicit here as he might be. It is not clear whether he means that man fell because he did not possess final perseverance. If so, he does not discuss the possible reason for its absence.

[2] 'Istam gratiam non habuerat homo primus, qua nunquam vellet esse malus; sed sane habuit, in qua si permanere vellet, nunquam malus esset, et sine qua etiam cum libero arbitrio bonus esse non posset; ergo illa gratia a libero arbitrio differebat . . .' (p. 504).

sinners could perform good works.[1] In Bradwardine's eyes, this doctrine was tantamount to asserting that grace could be gained by man; it was at the very centre of all that he was opposing in *De causa Dei*. Hence, having asserted the completely free and un-caused nature of grace, he brings down the axe on merit *de congruo* itself.[2]

This support of merit *de congruo*, by his contemporaries, was to Bradwardine the greatest error of the times and one of the main ways in which they were led into Pelagian beliefs.[3] In his deter-mination to destroy it, he ends by denying that anything good can come through men's own resources. He withdraws all value from them into God's hands. The importance which Bradwar-dine attaches to his task may be gauged by the amount of space he devotes to it: for forty pages he rebuts all claim for merit *de congruo*. To have accepted it would have been to undermine his whole system; it would, by enabling men to gain God's approval, have destroyed his principle of divine participation and wrested them from God's control. It is, accordingly, on these grounds that Bradwardine bases his arguments.

In the first place, he says, to allow that grace could come from good works and merit would be to subject God to men's influ-ence.[4] God would not then direct men; but, on the contrary, their deeds would become the cause of His actions.[5] Secondly, if a man not in charity could perform good works, this would destroy the nature of grace. Bradwardine, in common with St Augustine and St Thomas, refuses to allow of such a possibility. Once concede

[1] See *Dictionnaire de théologie catholique*, arts. 'Grace' and 'Mérite', and pp. 140–59 below.

[2] 'Contra quosdam putantes hominem ex se tantum posse mereri primam gratiam de congruo, non de condigno' (p. 325).

[3] 'Et quia ista error est famosior caeteris his diebus, et nimis multi per ipsum in Pelagianum praecipitium dilabuntur; necessarium videtur ipsum diligentiori examine perscrutari' (*ibid.*).

[4] 'Sequitur enim ex ista, quod gratia sit ex operibus et meritis, cum errore Pelagii radicali; sequitur etiam quod gratia sit ex meritis saltem, ut ex causa partiali et concausa cum primo errore sequente; et quod merita illa de congruo sint saltem causa et dispositio praeparatoria gratiae cum secundo, et quod quis possit mereri de congruo per solum, sicut tertius error ponit, quod homo possit solis propriis viribus aperire' (*ibid.*).

[5] 'Praeterea si quis de congruo primam gratiam mereatur, hoc est prius-quam habeat gratiam saltem prioritate naturae; sed priusquam habeat gratiam de qua loquor, scilicet gratificantem ad regnum, non habet charita-tem' (*ibid.*).

that good can come without a supernatural habit, and grace becomes superfluous. It would then lose its absolute nature and
could lead to the position taken by his opponents, in which created
grace does not necessarily mean to be dear to God. The whole
order between the supernatural virtues and merit would then
be destroyed. With such stakes involved, Bradwardine refuses
to conceive of goodness, either in wish or in deed, apart from
charity. To talk of a man doing good of his own accord is,
therefore, meaningless: to follow God is the only good; to follow
free will is the path to sin, for it means the illicit use of man's
powers.[1]

There can, then, be no half-way position between grace and
sin: the absence of one implies the presence of the other.[2] Bradwardine, accordingly, includes in the category of sinner all those
not in grace.[3] There is no room for any *natural* intention, or deed,
to good; its source lies in God. He provides the perfect standard
for good, from which everything else is to be measured: as a thing
does not roll in order to be round, but because it is round, so a
man is just not from his own actions, but from the justice which
comes from God. Now these virtues, such as justice and righteousness, are not, as Duns Scotus and also Ockham and his followers held, to be regarded naturally but are supernatural gifts.
There is a vast distinction between innate natural qualities, such
as an aptitude for mathematics, and supernaturally infused virtues, like grace and charity. The latter are not part of a man's
natural make-up, but reside in him as an additional, supernatural quality.[4]

Moreover, since man has no power over the bestowal of grace,
he has equally none over its quantity; God's gift cannot be

[1] 'Nam usus creaturae, si non referatur in Deum, est usus illicitus; ergo
peccatum, vel saltem non est recte factum: ergo illa intentio non est recta;
nec alicuius intentio sine charitate et gratia gratuito super omnia fertur in
Deum' (p. 326).

[2] '. . . nullum opus virtutis huiusmodi per charitatem et gratiam non
formatae; . . . quinimo et quodlibet tale opus est aliquo modo peccatum'
(p. 327).

[3] . . . quod nulla est in infidelibus vera virtus . . . imo et quod omne opus
infidelium est peccatum' (*ibid.*); see also p. 328.

[4] 'De charitate autem et gratia non possumus habere minimam scintillam a
nobis, nec ab aliqua creatura, sicut superius est ostensum; quare nec aliquid
grate facere propter Deum; quapropter nec aliquid mereri ab eo, nisi prius
eam dederit nobis gratis' (p. 333).

augmented, firstly, because it is His gift, independent of men's actions; and, secondly, because everything He does, He does infinitely and superlatively; there is no means of surpassing His acts.[1]

It is from this assertion of grace as supreme that Bradwardine proceeds to his detailed assault on merit *de congruo*. There can, he shows, be no such thing, first, because it would contradict God's sovereign goodness, omnipotence and infinite perfection in all that He does. Second, merit *de congruo* would introduce a finite relationship into God's infinite nature, which is clearly an absurdity; for this would mean that His absolute and unconditional power could be made relative and conditional. Thirdly, it would contradict God's will as the source of all that is created, and render it contingent and mutable.

It should be noted that Bradwardine's lines of argument all flow from his initial definition of God's nature and powers. As the *summum bonum* and the *movens immobile*, all perfection and power reside with Him. Once more, from the theological truth of God's existence and nature, both His attributes and those of His creatures can equally be asserted as true.

Merit *de congruo*, then, cannot exist; for all that God does, He does absolutely and unconditionally. It cannot be antecedent to God's will, for then it would move His will; it cannot be subsequent to His will, for then it would have no effect upon Him. Anything that God gives must be complete in itself, deriving no value from external comparisons and unmoved by temporal considerations. Thus whatever merit there is must be *de condigno*: for this alone fulfils these conditions; there is no room for congruity as defined. As in God everything is realized to its infinite capacity, and in Him essence and existence are one, so with merit there is a similar identity between *de condigno* and *de congruo*; for if it is fitting for Him to give merit at all, it must be *absolutely* fitting (*de condigno*).[2]

---

[1] 'Quodlibet enim opus gratiae meretur de condigno incomparabiliter maius omni tali remissione temporali, scilicet augmentum gratiae, et proportionaliter augmentum gloriae sempiternae; quodlibet ergo tale meritum de condigno, etiam pro quocunque minori sufficiet de condigno' (p. 339).

[2] 'Item si fit ita, congruum est Deum dare gratiam sic merenti, quia hoc volutum est a Deo; ergo hoc nedum congruum ut hi dicunt, sed etiam est

Bradwardine, having established that merit *de congruo* cannot be separated from merit *de condigno*, has left himself the comparatively straightforward task of showing that this cannot come from man. By rejecting the distinction between *de congruo* and *de condigno*, he is able to confront its supporters as complete Pelagians: either they withdraw and accept that merit must come from grace and so have a supernatural value, or they expose themselves to denying merit as a supernatural quality and thus set up men's natural powers on an equal footing with God's. This Bradwardine does by examining the way in which God acts; He is, he repeats, omnipotent and so everything that He does He does absolutely (*de condigno*).[1] His way of giving merit is therefore quite different from that of man. Man's case is like that of a king who, by public edict, proclaims that whosoever does a particular action, good or bad, will be fittingly rewarded. The reward is therefore conditional; it is directed to no one in particular, as the king is indifferent to which of his subjects does which particular act; and, above all, it is only when good or bad has been done that the king's will is moved either to reward or to punish. Such merit is relative and caused, in contradistinction to that of God who does everything superlatively, unconditionally, and directed by the certain foreknowledge of His will.[2] All that comes from God is therefore out of the reach of men. While merit *de congruo*, as potential merit, does not really exist,[3] merit *de condigno*, as a supernatural virtue, comes from God alone.[4]

Bradwardine's position, in fact, amounts to a complete rejection of merit as a human achievement. There can be no good act by a man which is not incited and aided by God's grace. This

condignum, quicquid Deus vult fieri dignum et iustum est fieri, sicut vigesimum primum capitulum demonstrauit' (p. 346).

'Itidem omne sic ad idem, omne sufficiens est condignum' (*ibid.*).

'Quicunque ergo meretur a Deo quicquam de congruo, meretur etiam de condigno' (p. 347).

[1] 'Deus ergo cum sit omnipotens, de condigno facit sibi tantum' (*ibid.*).
[2] *Ibid.* p. 350.
[3] 'Non quod de congruitate aliqua priori voluntate diuina sit actualiter praemiandum' (p. 362).
[4] 'Similiter quoque potest ostendi quod nullus existens in gratia potest mereri de condigno causaliter et antecedenter voluntati diuinae. . . . Alias enim qui mereretur, cogeret Deum et voluntatem diuinam necessario ad reddendum, vel ad reddere volendum mercedem, vel ad perdendum iustitiam' (p. 343).

is the ultimate conclusion that is reached, and Bradwardine does not hesitate to prosecute it to the end. One of the sharpest breaks with traditional theology has been made by Bradwardine's rejection of merit *de congruo*; for it means that sanctifying grace alone, which comes only from God, is the sole criterion of merit. As Bradwardine himself says, whatever comes from the Holy Spirit must return thereto; this might fittingly be used as the epitaph for merit. In Bradwardine's system it is only part of a rotary action, which starts and ends with grace. The logical result of this view is to remove all external forms of worship and good works. Though Bradwardine himself did not suggest such a step, these positions, which his theory had foreshadowed, were occupied at the Reformation.

Closely allied to Bradwardine's conception of merit is his view of justification. If human actions of themselves can have no relative or moral value (*de congruo*), neither can justification. He rejects all suggestions that either a disposition in a man towards good, or contrition, can help to prepare a soul to receive justification. Together with merit, contrition, repentance, and absolution are the expressions of grace and cannot nurture it of themselves.

Now the order in which God wants things is in inverse relation to the order in which they are realized. Bradwardine repeats the Aristotelian principle, that the first in intention is the last in execution, to show how God's will is the first and last cause of all human actions. As it is through Him alone that there is the impulse and power to act, it would be absurd to imagine that justification and reprobation depend upon anything temporal. His eternal willing precedes all that His creatures do, and is their cause. Thus there is a twofold aspect of predestination: temporally eternal life follows merit; logically, it precedes it. For the elect it means grace and merit in the present and glory and reward in Heaven;[1] for the damned, eternal punishment. They differ not only in having opposite effects but also in that, with sinners, the penalty, but not the sin, comes from God.[2]

[1] *Ibid.* p. 422.
[2] 'Reprobatio vero et eius effectus per horum opposita cognoscuntur. Quia vero sancti et Doctores dicunt frequenter quod Deus praedestinauit et praeparauit reprobis ignem et poenam, sed non peccata, nec eos ad peccandum' (*ibid.*).

Why then does God elect one soul and damn another? Bradwardine quotes St Paul[1] that He wants all men to be saved, but
only, he adds, if they come to Him; He does not want those who
refuse him.[2] Now it may well be asked if Bradwardine is here
giving an illicit entry to the power of human dispositions in gaining salvation. On the contrary, Bradwardine is faced with the
same problem which he met in dealing with sin: while God cannot not cause sin, men cannot move without Him. Bradwardine's
solution also is analogous to that which he applied to sin: since
God, as the highest good, cannot be the cause of a sinner's actions,
sin must come from the sinner's weakness; it is a negative quality
without an efficient cause. God foresees that the sinner will sin
and He punishes him with final reprobation. A sinner therefore is
not damned by God's own malice but by his own sins which God,
in His justice, punishes.[3]

Now there are four possible kinds of retribution: bad for bad
(as in the case of Hell fire); good for good (the Kingdom of
Heaven); good for bad (when Christ, through grace, justifies the
impious); or bad for good (Judas's betrayal and persecution of
Christ). Of these four types, the first two pertain to Justice (good
for good; bad for bad); the third belongs to Mercy (good for bad);
and the fourth is unknown to God. It is the third which is most
necessary: but for God's mercy in giving good for bad, there
could never be good for good. He is always just and always merci-
ful; these different rewards do not contradict one another, for He
always acts for the good of His creatures. Accordingly, to punish
the sinful is no less an assertion of His goodness than to reward
the good: if He were undiscriminating He could be neither merci-
ful nor just. It is in this sense that Bradwardine regards the cause
for reprobation in the eternal refusal to accept God's grace. Because grace is lacking in a person, he is unable to want to follow
God; this gives rise to resisting God (*obduratio*).[4] Thus God's
withholding of grace is the cause of man's evil acts. This both

---

[1] *Ibid.* pp. 356–7.

[2] 'Vult enim Deus homines saluos fieri, si accedant ad eum. Non enim sic
vult, ut nolentes saluentur, sed vult ipsos saluari, si et ipsi velint' (pp. 356–7).

[3] *Ibid.* p. 394.

[4] 'Reprobatio vero accipiatur pro aeterna Dei nolutione gratiae alicui [non
conferendae], et pro eius temporali effectu, scilicet gratiae priuatione seu
desertione, et haec vocatur obduratio' (p. 426).

absolves Him from sin and frees Him from dependence upon a sinner's acts.[1]

Although caused differently, predestination to glory and reprobation are both certain.[2] Ideally God wanted only glory for His creatures; man's sin introduced damnation. Bradwardine follows Scotus and Gregory in saying that, had Adam not sinned, only the elect would have been born,[3] for only the good is germane to His will. The damned are sinners whose sins have no place in Him.

The counterpart of final perseverance to good is the equally eternal perseverance to evil. This, as Bradwardine has already said, lies in obstinacy on the part of sinners. But what is its cause? Bradwardine discusses ten different replies, all of which he rejects[4] as inadequate by making God the direct cause of this obstinacy, or by making man's free will responsible for lack of grace, or by looking for the solution in terms of the nature of obstinacy itself. His own reply is, he says, twofold—positive and negative. It is negative in that a sinner cannot want the good; and this means a deficiency in such a soul through the privation of grace. In this sense, then, the privation of grace cannot be merited, for God's will is unmoved by His creatures' deeds. From this comes the positive reason for obstinacy; for had a sinner not sinned, through his lack of grace, God would not have punished his sins. God's penalty is to cut off a sinner eternally from His grace. Thus eternal obduracy is positive as coming from Him in punishment for a previous sin (which has a negative cause). The penalty of one sin is another sin.[5]

The *processus* between predestination and reprobation is reversed. While predestination to glory has the single active cause of God's will, and therefore involves no distinct action on the part

[1] Quod nullus praedestinatur aut reprobatur propter opera quae faceret si ulterius viueret, nec ullus saluatur propter opera, vel damnatur' (cor. to cap. 45, p. 427).

[2] '. . . quod omnes gradus gratiarum, meritorum, prosperitatum, aduersitatum, gloriae siue poenae, in praesenti et in futuro similiter sunt praedestinati a Deo aeternaliter et distincte' (cor. to cap. 46, p. 435).

[3] '. . . tunc secundum sententiam Gregorii 4 Moral 39° huius praemissam, nullus reproborum generatus fuisset, sed soli illi qui nunc sunt praedestinati ad vitam; nec ideo peccatum Adae est prima causa reprobationis, sed si ipse non pecasset, Deus aliter ordinasset. . .' (p. 439).

[4] *Ibid.* pp. 521–5.   [5] *Ibid.* p. 526.

G

of man, with reprobation it is both a positive and negative action, in which there is a distinction between man's action and that of God. Bradwardine elsewhere describes this as active and passive reprobation; it is active as coming from God as the first cause; it is passive as expressing a lack in the creature, which is due to the absence of grace.[1] In both cases, there cannot be any room for human actions, either good or bad, in gaining glory or damnation, and Bradwardine rejects all pleas for the recognition of human actions in justification.

There are, he says, two different points of view on grace and justification: that of the Pelagians, who assert that they can be merited, and the opinion of those who say that God infuses penitence and grace before these are possible in man. In opposition to the Pelagians, Bradwardine denies that repentance for sin can be made naturally; that, through this, grace can be obtained, and, from this, justification. Nor will he allow that repentance can come through the combined effects of the sacraments and the spirit of repentance: although it may appear reasonable *prima facie*, in fact it would mean that a sinner, having repented, would not have to make further amends. True repentance must come from a soul already in grace; only so can he be justified.[2] This excludes everyone in mortal sin.[3]

There is here the germ of the later distinction that Wyclif was to make between mortal sins as belonging to the damned and venial ones as being committed by the elect: to be in mortal sin is to be without grace and charity and in a state of *obduratio*. The penalty for this is eternally to remain in God's reprobation and so be predestined to damnation. Moreover, the full effects of Bradwardine's rejection of merit *de congruo* can also be seen here. If grace could be merited by contrition, he argues, this would mean the greatest sin could be effaced by the smallest act of repentance; in that case there could be a proportion between divine and human acts; accordingly, the more contrite a soul, the more grace he could merit, notwithstanding that he were not in God's grace

---

[1] *De causa Dei*, p. 617.

[2] 'Iustitiam enim homo non operatur nisi iustificatus' (p. 379.)
'. . . non esse fructum bonum, qui de charitatis radice non surgit' (*ibid.*).

[3] 'Omnis namque talis contritio procedit a charitate et gratia, quae omne peccatum mortale perimit et excludit' (p. 381).

in the beginning.[1] The Pelagian view would be vindicated and God's grace could be earned. Faith alone can make us justified: works have no part to play in achieving that which comes from Him alone.[2]

Bradwardine thus gives the death knell to works as of any value at all. This is yet another blow at the worth of human activity. He excludes the need for visible and natural deeds. Belief is being removed from the world of tangible activity and symbols and transferred to the realm of personal and supernatural experience. This is the distance that Bradwardine's attack upon the Pelagian view of justification has led him. He completes this progress by showing in detail how the remission of sins and justification must follow grace. Sin is a defect in a subject's nature. It can only be exorcized by a *habitus* strong enough to do so, which means God's grace. In the case of any disease, the subject to be healed must receive help from a power greater than itself. As light banishes darkness, and vision cures blindness, so goodness vanquishes evil. And whence comes this goodness if not from charity? It alone is the *habitus* of goodness, and it alone can restore a subject from sin: charity, not repentance, is the means of eliminating sin.[3]

Bradwardine, then, leaves no room for the view taken by Duns Scotus, and upheld by Ockham and his followers, that grace and

[1] 'Et quomodo remittitur culpa iuste et plene nisi per satisfactionem plenariam praecedentem, sicuti etiam omnia iura dictant? Et si quis dixerit, culpam quandoque dimitti de gratia a misericordia Domini, non iuuat Pelagianos dicentes homines mereri dimissionem et veniam peccatorum, et sic gratiam et misericordiam Domini consequenter, et non per gratiam remissionem fieri peccatorum' (p. 384).

[2] 'Sequuntur enim opera iustificatum, non praecedunt iustificandum, sed sola fide sine operibus praecedentibus sit homo iustus' (p. 394).

[3] '. . . malum seu ipsa malitia et peccatum, malitiaque peccati non est aliquid positiuum, sed tantummodo priuatiuum. Nulla autem priuatio pellitur a subiecto, nisi per positionem habitus in subiecto, et hoc naturaliter praecedentem. Inductio namque et positio habitus est causa expulsionis et remotionis priuationis oppositae. Non enim potest priuatio aliquo modo tolli, nisi per positionem habitus repugnantis manente subiecto susceptibili utriusque. Nam quomodo tollitur mors nisi per vitam, caecitas nisi per visum, tenebrae nisi per lucem . . .? Quomodo ergo tollitur malitia priuativa, nisi per positionem habitus bonitatis causaliter, et ideo naturaliter praecendentem. Sola autem charitas seu gratia est huiusmodi bonitatis, ipsumue post peccatum mortale restituens, et conseruans, sicut ex praemissis apparet' (p. 397).

sin can exist together in the same soul. The infusion of grace, as a
supernatural virtue, must mean the elimination of sin, as a deficiency which comes from natural causes.[1] Not only is contrition
not coincident with grace, but it does not need even to follow it as
the sign of grace. For this would mean that every act of contrition
signified a state of grace; and Bradwardine, like Calvin later,
strongly maintains that no *viator* knows whether he is in God's
glory or reprobation.[2]

Bradwardine applies these same arguments to confession, absolution, communion, and the other sacraments.[3] In each case
these cannot do what God can alone do. Nothing, therefore, can
precede, aid, or be substituted for, God's grace in justifying
sinners.

The absolute precedence of grace, however, does not eliminate
the need or value of these natural acts; for, although God by His
grace justifies us immediately and by His own power, these acts
of repentance and contrition are a necessary and fitting expression by us to Him.[4]

In these qualifications Bradwardine suggests an anxiety lest he
be interpreted as discarding all ecclesiastical discipline. He almost
contradicts his earlier absolutism. Nevertheless, it is abundantly
clear that his final position is one so extreme that it is but a short

[1] 'Gratia ergo infusa immediate deletur peccatum, sicut per lucem tenebrae
immediate tolluntur; vel statim gratia immediate restituit habitum oppositum
immediate peccato, qui immediate per se tollit peccatum, sicque gratia,
tantum illo habitu mediante tollit peccatum. . . . Non ergo actu dilectionis aut
contritionis causaliter et naturaliter mediante. Item gratia est prior naturaliter
contritione, et contritio non est eius effectus necessarius, nec ipsam necessario inseparabiliter consequens, quia tunc omnis recipiens et habens
gratiam semper necessario poeniteret, quod constat esse falsum de Sanctis
Angelis, de hominibus ante lapsum, de paruulis baptizatis post lapsum, de
sanctis adultis in vita habentibus gratiam Dei semper non dolentibus tamen
semper, et de Domino Iesu Christo' (p. 402).
[2] 'Nescit homo utrum amore, an odio dignus sit' (p. 338).
[3] *Ibid*. pp. 403–6.
[4] 'Solus ergo Deus hominem interius mundat a macula peccati, et a debito
aeternae poenae soluit, qui per Prophetam ait: Ego solus deleo iniquitates et
peccata populi. In iustificatione autem peccatoris adulti, quamuis iusti-
ficetur per habitum charitatis seu gratiae antecedentem naturaliter actum
dilectionis aut poenitentiae salutaris, actus tamen huiusmodi secundum
legem statutam in iustificato requiritur comitanter, velut quoddam gratuitum
consequens ex antecedente tam grato, et veluti quidam fructus sanctus ex
arbore prius mortua, sterili et maledicta, nunc autem viuificata, faecundata et
sanctificata procedens . . .' (p. 407).

step to the position that Luther was later to take up over the sacraments and Church activity in general.

Bradwardine's doctrine of grace is the most rigorous possible. It is, in the first place, based upon his principle of divine participation by which he is able to make its necessity overriding. Throughout, the most striking aspect is his complete rejection of any natural agency in its bestowal, receipt or preparation. Anything that is good cannot, by definition, come from God's creatures; they have no worth of their own. Thus God's forewilling is the cause of every good disposition and good deed; goodness is made *ipso facto* supernatural. We can see very clearly how Bradwardine's starting-point of God, as senior partner in every created act, removes any autonomy from His creatures. Hence, everything, however inconsequential, must have its starting-point in God's will. There is no realm for natural causation: it is this which makes Bradwardine's view of the necessity of grace appear so ruthless.

In the second place, predestination from eternity has decided all temporal enactments. Although from different motives, the character of predestination is twofold, for reprobation as well as for glory. This, in the third place, removes any distinction between grace and merit. The consequences of grace are so intimately involved in its cause that there is nothing that can, strictly speaking, be called merit in the whole of Bradwardine's system. Finally, as Calvin held later, there is nothing to be understood from any temporal dispositions towards justification and repentance, since no soul knows whether he is damned or elected; contrition, or any other human feeling, in no way implies the possession of grace. The rules of justification become little more than symbols of hope rather than of faith. Bradwardine, himself careful to give verbal support to these actions, in substance undermines their whole validity. Works cease to count; mortal sin is the eternal penalty for the lack of the first grace. How then can a sinner hope to be justified and reaccepted under such an inflexible judgment? Bradwardine has reached the point in his doctrine of grace where its entirely supernatural and unmerited character allows of no human action. He marks a break in kind, not merely in degree: for it is a logical extension of his own teaching either to transfer belief into a personal and emotional experience, as Luther did; or, on the other hand, to establish a theocracy on the certainty of God's predetermined will, such as Calvin was to found.

CHAPTER V

MAN

MAN is so closely entwined in God's will that it is almost impossible, and indeed artificial, to separate his own powers and actions in any positive and distinct manner. Through the principle of divine participation Bradwardine has clearly established the nature and role of man. He is, in the first place, in his very existence, and in everything that he does, subject to the overriding priority of God's will. This means, in the second place, that man is without worth, merit or *raison d'être*, in his own right. God alone gives him these qualities. Third, there has never been a time when either man or angel could be in the least degree self-sufficient or remain good: in consequence, as we have already seen,[1] the fall was only the confirmation of man's dependence and not its cause. Fourth, because predestination and grace are completely from God, there is neither purpose nor possibility in attributing grace to merits or to natural actions.

Bradwardine has thus seemingly depressed the status of human nature to the fullest extent conceivable. In one sense he has; but, for him, man remains a rational being, first in God's love among His creatures on earth, and in no way to be associated with the beasts or the brutes. It is here that Bradwardine at once confirms man's subjection to God and his superiority to all other creatures; for, if man is free from all natural determinism, and unmoved by all secondary causes, he is, by that token, subject only to God. Two themes therefore characterize Bradwardine's view of man's state: the first is his assertion of human free will and freedom as existing through God's determinism: and, second, man's complete immunity from everything natural and irrational, which alone could impair his freedom.

MAN'S NATURE

In the scattered references in which Bradwardine treats of man's nature as a rational creature, and his theory of knowledge, he

---

[1] See p. 71 above.

follows St Thomas Aquinas. It is, he says, man's rational soul that distinguishes him from other creatures.[1]

The rational soul is man's form; form and body together constitute an individual man. Moreover, because of this, there can be no place for the universal soul of Averroes; for, if there were, there could not be individuals acting singly; but, instead, each time one man moved, all men would also move. This would violate the whole principle of individuation, dispensing with degrees of individual goodness and attainment, and nullifying differences between rewards and punishments.[2]

The soul of a man must be individual to him; for it is through the conjunction of body and soul that an individual exists. This is not the same as making the soul identical in substance with the body. Where the body is material and corruptible the soul is spiritual and immaterial.[3]

Throughout his system, Bradwardine rejects any attempt at a rival determinism to that of God's power. He therefore lays great emphasis upon the individual nature of man's reason and its direct contact with the divine will. As he combats any suggestion of fate by the stars, so he will have no dealings with any power other than God, as affecting man. Man's reason suffices against natural powers. It is his form and his badge without which he could not be man, and by it he is supreme on earth.[4]

[1] 'Amplius secundum concordem Philosophorum sententiam, Naturam esse principium motus et quietis illius cuius est natura, et naturam quae est forma, esse horum principium effectiuum; animam quoque rationalem esse naturam hominis et formam' (pp. 77–8).

[2] 'Amplius autem de remuneratione seu praemitione hominum in praesenti; illud namque quo Deus praemiat virtuosos in vita praesenti, in anima potius quam in corpore est ponendum; sed si sit una tantum anima omnium, quicquid de tali proemio, vel de poena recipit unus homo, recipiunt et alii universi. Secundum hanc quoque sententiam insensatam, si unus homo haberet in anima foelicitatem perfectam, miseriamue perfectam, haberent simul et omnes, essentque omnes simul perfecti et miseri' (p. 77).

[3] 'Quare . . . dicit [Philosophus] quod hoc solum intellectum contingit separari sicut perpetuum a corruptibili. . . . Homo autem mouetur processive, loquitur, comedit, et similia operatur per animam rationalem, per voluntatem videlicet rationalem, quam potentiam quandam seu partem animae rationalis haud dubio constat esse' (p. 86).

[4] 'Quare et formam eius essentialem esse animam rationalem, inquam, non solum participatiue et improprie, sed essentialiter per se et proprie' (p. 84).

THE PROCESS OF HUMAN KNOWLEDGE

Bradwardine, besides following Aristotle and St Thomas in their view of matter and form, also takes from them his theory of knowledge.[1] The starting-point for knowledge is in the senses; through an object, impinging upon our perceptions, our intellect is moved. Once started, the intellect then abstracts from the object, brought to its understanding, its true nature; that is, its real form, purified and freed, as it were, from the matter in which it is embodied and individuated. Thus, through our senses, we perceive Socrates the individual; by our intellect we can detach from Socrates the individual our recognition of Socrates the man, as a general species of which Socrates is a member. The true form of every individual is an immaterial essence; and by the operations of our intellect we are able to regain it. In this alone lies true knowledge.

Bradwardine seems also to accept, with Aristotle and St Thomas, that all our *natural* knowledge normally comes by abstracting from singulars, and not, as Duns Scotus, that this process came with the fall.[2] He has, however, no concern specifically with the relation of individuals and species. From his Anselmian view of God's nature he upholds, as we have seen,[3] the reality of forms as the universal archetypes of all that is in being. Moreover, in his view of human knowledge he accepts their separate existence as coming before any individual. Yet this is not one of his main preoccupations; and it is stretching the term to call him a realist, above all. Rather, like St Thomas, he is quite prepared to give a place to both the universal and the individual as metaphysical, not logical, entities. Each actually exists, and the particular is the expression of the general *in fact*, not in language.

Our means of knowing these universals comes from our intellect and from us, not, as Averroes asserted, from an impersonal impulsion. Furthermore, our minds are not the *tabula rasa* that Averroes would make them. They are equipped to make actual

[1] 'Anima, inquit [Auicenna], humana iuuatur a corpore ad acquirendum principia consentiendi et intelligendi, deinde cum acquisierit, redibit ad seipsam' (p. 83).

[2] '. . . ostendit [Aristoteles] quod anima dicitur sciens seu scire in potentia duobus modis, remote videlicet et propinque, siue potentia remota seu essentiali, qualis est in homine priusquam addiscat . . .' (p. 80).

[3] See pp. 48–9 above.

(by analysis) the potential knowledge that our senses provide. If this were not so, our intellect could not be an immaterial form, but would, like matter, be corruptible and potential and passive. By the activity of the intellect in knowing, thinking and analysis, the initial impetus given by the senses is transformed. The intellect can continue to know the object first provided by the senses long after it has ceased to be present. For it is from God that this power derives, and, by this, the intellect can maintain permanently the image of the object and conjure it up whenever it so wills. In this case, it may be asked, says Bradwardine, why the intellect needs an object at all for its knowledge. The reason, he replies, is that it is not until the object has been presented to the senses that the intellect is set in motion; it has no intrinsic power of its own by which it can start to know universals without the intervention of singular objects. Their value may be compared to turning a motor which cannot, of its own accord, start; but this is only necessary initially, and, indeed, if this action were maintained while the motor was running it would become an obstacle. In the same way, Bradwardine is inclined to regard the senses as an impediment once the intellect is in action.[1]

Bradwardine gives the intellect full scope within its limitations as a secondary cause. But his view of the process of human knowledge is essentially that of his whole system. While its actual operation is Aristotelian, its movement is dependent upon God's will, and its scope, movement and reliability can only be judged in relation to His will. There is the same great distinction in Brad-

[1] 'Hoc idem et ratio clare monstrat; Ponatur enim Deum omnipotentem seruare in oculo speciem ab obiecto receptam, destructo obiecto, in qualibet specie eius in medio extra visum, habetque visus habereue potest omnimodam operationem suam intrinsicam sicut prius; videbitque videreue potest ut prius; nihil enim deficit requisitum. Obiectum enim et medium nullatenus requiruntur, nisi ad speciem in oculo generandam; vel ad genitam conseruandam. Cur ergo de potentia nobilissima intellectus non similiter sentiendum? Intellectus ergo in principio quando est totus potentialis indiget intentionibus huiusmodi extrinsicis ipsum mouentibus, informantibus, et actuantibus, sed cum plene informatus et actuatus extiterit, non indiget ipsis ultra, sed ex tunc potest per se et sua intrinsica sufficienter cognoscere universa; imo ex tunc magis videntur ei obesse, quam prodesse, eo quod distrahunt intellectum a speculatione sincera, et operatione sua perfecta' (p. 83).
'Amplius autem qui nesciat omnem potentiam cognitiuam cognoscere proprie per actum proprium instrinsicum, immanentem, non per aliquid extrinsicum proprie?' (pp. 38–4).

wardine's view of knowledge as there is throughout his thought. On the one hand, the empirical and the scientific, in which the scientist talks; on the other, the theological in which the information produced by observation is used to support faith. Bradwardine's theory of knowledge by abstraction, though Aristotelian and Thomist, does not mean that his conclusions of its value are similar to theirs. On the contrary, he sees its value in terms of his principle of divine participation; that is, knowledge, whatever its mode, is useless and unreliable on its own, and cannot give guidance or certainty in the smallest details without God's aid.[1]

PSYCHOLOGY OF THE HUMAN WILL

While Bradwardine's theory of man's form and knowledge are from St Thomas, his view of man's will is not. The former come within a scientific account of scientific fact and have their basis in his view of matter and being, both of which run on Aristotelian lines. The human will, on the other hand, is at the heart of Bradwardine's system: its impotence is the counterpart of God's omnipotence, and we are thus projected back far more to an Augustinian view.

Bradwardine opens book II of *De causa Dei* with an assertion of free will: 'That free will exists and what it is.'[2] He defines it as will guided by reason.[3] God is its first cause, for His will is both completely free and rational.[4]

Now the way in which free will acts is by the power of accepting or rejecting anything presented to it.[5] Within this freedom of choice, its object is always to seek the good and to shun the bad. This is its first and highest action. From this simple principle, however, complications arise: for free will, by its very nature, is a weak and worthless vessel alone; its very desire for good can result in its being misled into following what is evil. All things, in

[1] See pp. 119 *et seq.* below.   [2] *De causa Dei*, p. 443.
[3] 'Quod ipsum est potentia Rationalis rationaliter iudicandi et voluntarie exequendi' (p. 444).
[4] 'Quare constat Deum habere arbitrium liberum voluntatis: arbitrium, inquam, propter iudicium rationis seu intellectus: et liberum, propter potestatem spontaneam voluntatis' (p. 443).
[5] 'Actus eius velle, et nolle; diligere, et odire; Obiectum vero ipsius bonum, et malum apparens' (*ibid.*).

their true essences as coming from God, are good; they will always try to avoid evil. Even the sinners and wretches do not seek the bad: it is through their sin and misery that they are bad; and this comes from their own inadequacies and not from their original natures. The good is not wilfully or deliberately passed over for the bad: it is the weakness of all creatures that, alone, they cannot distinguish between the two. Bradwardine accordingly concludes that free will is not so much able to want or refuse anything: but rather, that it wants or refuses only that which it *can* want or refuse.[1] This means that its powers are strictly limited to its own powers of discernment: it bases its decision upon what appears to be the right course, rather than what is actually right.[2]

Moreover, its position has been still further weakened by sin; for, apart from the incidental penalties for sin, free will is weighed down and its perception made even more unstable. Nevertheless, free will exists; this can be seen in the way the soul responds to events outside it; happily to pleasant experiences, sadly to what is unpleasant.[3] If there were no such thing as free will, there could be no actions by any creatures, for free will is the highest created form; and, if this remained potential and unrealized, everything else, as coming after free will, would remain so.[4]

The case for the existence of free will can be seen in all the rational pursuits of man; did it not exist, sheer blindness would rule and man himself could not exist.[5] Thus free will is as much a part of man as any other of his essential qualities: a substance is the cause of its accidents; to deny one is to deny both.

[1] 'Corollarium, quod non ideo dicitur liberum Arbitrium, quia libere potest velle et nolle quodcunque, sed quia libere potest velle quodcunque obiectum suum volubile, et nolle quodcunque obiectum suum nolubile' (cor. to cap. 2, bk. II, p. 448).

[2] 'Et credo quod posset saltem per accidens, si videlicet nolendo et re-spuendo aliquod paruum bonum posset consequi aliquod maius bonum, vel vitare aliquod maius malum, sicut et potest velle malum . . .' (p. 447).

[3] 'Item omnis apprehensio actualis convenientis obiecti causat delec-tationem, et maior et convenientioris maiorem sicut quilibet experitur' (p. 533).

[4] 'Luce siquidem clarius patet cunctis, quod si actus liberi arbitrii nihil sit, nec actus alicuius alterius potentiae siue formae est aliquid: Nam liberum arbitrium est perfectissima potentia seu forma creata . . .' (p. 529).

[5] 'Item si hominem intelligere, non est aliquid, nec hominem esse intel-ligentem est aliquid; ergo nec hominem esse calceatum, aut armatum est aliquid, quare et praedicamentum habitus deperibit' (p. 534).

THE SCOPE OF THE WILL

What then is the scope of free will and where does it lie in relation
to God and to natural forces? Bradwardine replies that it holds a
position between the divine spirit on the one hand, and appetite
on the other.[1] With regard to natural forces, man's will is free
from all necessity; and it is here that his free will lies.[2]

Bradwardine rejects out of hand all necessity, either astral
coercion, natural compulsion, or the psychological enticement
from other creatures, as moving man. His freedom of will comes
from his primacy over all other creatures and blind forces. In all
natural affairs he can act or not act: nothing created can force
him to do good or to sin.[3] He has to fear only the weakness of his
own will.

It is alone in man's relations with God that he is in any way
directed. The principle of divine participation makes God the
senior partner in all that man does. No rational creature, in consequence, can be confirmed or resolved by his own nature; nor
can he move by his own free will: he is completely dependent
upon God's grace.[4]

It is not therefore possible to talk about human free will in
absolute terms. Bradwardine expresses this in three different
ways: naturally, theologically and logically. In natural terms, it
means that, in anything common to God and a second cause, God
is first; in theological terms, that God wills everything unconditionally; in logical terms that no proposition which treats of
any secondary cause, or anything inferior to God, can really be
considered as a first cause.[5] Bradwardine once more uses this

---

[1] 'Inter diuinum spiritum et carnis appetitum, tenet medium quendam
locum liberum arbitrium . . .' (p. 476).

[2] 'Quod nulla causa inferior potest necessitare voluntatem creatam ad
rationalem et liberum actum suum ad meritum proprie, vel peccatum'
(cap. 3, bk. II, p. 449).

[3] 'Homo autem nulli necessitati subiicitur naturali. Patet ergo quod nullum delectabile tristabileue creatum potest necessitare hominem ad volendum vel ad nolendum, praesertim quamdiu liberum arbitrium manet sanum'
(p. 454).

[4] Quod nulla creatura rationalis potest confirmari vel obstinari immutabiliter per naturam' (cap. 17, p. 527).

[5] 'Corollarium habet triplex porisma: Unum naturale, quod est in omni
causatione communi Deo et causae secundae, Deum causare prius naturaliter
quam causam secundam: Aliud Theologicum, Deum videlicet conditiona-

supremacy of the first cause over secondary causes to press his conclusions to their farthest possible extremes. Because no secondary cause can be absolute in its own right, by virtue of deriving from a first cause, he takes this to mean that God's will has direct guidance in everything that concerns His creatures. Thus, he says, His will is the coefficient of human will; it cannot be otherwise.[1] Moreover, because it is impossible to regard an act of free will as separate from God's will,[2] the two cannot be distinguished in their joint action. Their union is so complete that, far from each playing a certain part, they are totally involved together.[3]

Bradwardine takes this Thomist axiom not, like St Thomas, to give man complete freedom as a secondary cause, but to deny him any power at all. As a result, he makes grace the source of all goodness, refusing that a man could have even a good intention without it.[4] This, in effect, was to imply that free will could do no good in its purely natural state and that there could be no non-evil act without grace.[5] All that can be said is that God's will must come first;[6] that He directs the created will;[7] and that without His immediate willing, there would be no question

liter nihil velle: Tertium Logicum, nullam scilicet propositionem tribuentem quamcunque causationem cuicunque causae inferiori et posteriori voluntate diuina, seu aliud quicquam positiuum inferius cuicunque sub Deo esse de primo simpliciter, ratione primitatis subiecti, non causae: Plurimae tamen tales secundum quid et in arto genere sunt de primo' (cor. to cap. 30, bk. II, p. 596.)

[1] 'Quod cuiuslibet actus voluntatis creatae Deus est necessarius coeffector' (cap. 20, bk. II, p. 540).

[2] 'Corollarium, quod quicquid effecerit voluntas creata, necesse est ut et illud coefficiat increata; et quicquid operata fecerit voluntas Angelica vel humana, necesse est ut et illud cooperetur diuina; quod omnem actum voluntatis creatae totum efficit voluntas creata, et totum similiter increata' (cor. to cap. 20, bk. II, p. 554).

[3] '... ita tamen quod a sola gratia captum est, pariter ab utroque perficietur, ut mixtum, non sigillatum, simul, non vicissim per singulos effectus operetur, non partim gratia, partim liberum arbitrium, sed totum singula opere indiuiduo peragunt: totum quidem hoc, et totum illa, sed ut totum in illa, sic totum ex illa' (p. 554).

[4] *Ibid.* p. 335.   [5] We shall discuss this in ch. II below, pp. 155–6.

[6] 'Quod voluntas increata et creata in coefficiendo actum voluntatis creatae, non sunt coaequales, nec coaequaeuae in ordine naturali' (cap. 29, bk. II, p. 577).

[7] 'Quod in omni actione communi voluntatum increatae, et creatae, increata creatam naturaliter antecedit' (cap. 30, bk. II, p. 578).

of free will at all, to say nothing of its wanting or doing good.[1]

The centre, then, of Bradwardine's view of free will lies in regarding God as its first and most immediate mover. This, on the one hand, frees it from dependence upon natural and impersonal forces, and, on the other, makes God its source of freedom, so that in subjecting itself to His will it is only realizing its own nature. These are the reasons which Bradwardine employs to show that the will is free.

Furthermore, with Bradwardine, God's will is not to be regarded in the way the Arab philosophers saw it, as a universal and impersonal first cause acting implacably through a hierarchy of secondary causes, such as planets and celestial spheres. Bradwardine's God is essentially personal and immediate; the whole of his view of divine participation flows from His direct presence. In support of this, Etienne Tempier's condemnations of those making God an indirect mover are constantly to hand.[2] In the second place, Bradwardine holds it to be absurd to regard divine participation as divine identity: there is all the difference here between monotheism and pantheism. He characterizes as false the assertion that God alone creates all acts of the created will.[3] Were this so, what Bradwardine now writes at Oxford, his father, too, would be writing at Chichester.[4] Identity between the divine and created wills cannot exist for the very reason that to have free will means that its holder can incline either to faith or to disobedience.[5] Free will, by its very incapacity to do good, cannot be identified with God's will; it must have, as we have seen,[6] a special gift from God to act with Him to good. This necessity for God's special grace derives from the inadequacy of free will, even with created grace, to do God's will alone; disparity between divine and created will, not identity, is therefore the cause of divine participation. This is confirmed when we remember the

---

[1] 'Certum est nos velle cum volumus, sed ille facit ut velimus bonum . . .' (p. 569).

[2] For example, see *ibid.* p. 543.

[3] 'Recitat sex falsas responsiones; quarum Prima dicit, quod ideo solum Deum dicitur facere omnem actum voluntatis creatae, quia facit omnem voluntatem creatam, quae sola vere et proprie efficit suum actum . . .' (cap. 21, bk. II, p. 555).

[4] 'Per similem etiam rationem, quicquid nunc scribo Oxoniae, scriberet pater meus Cicestriae' (p. 559).

[5] *Ibid.* p. 556.   [6] See pp. 71 *et seq.* above.

state of the human will: it can often mistake the good for the bad and the bad for the good. God is not the cause of the will's mistakes either in what it sees, or the way in which it sees. The onus is here on free will.[1]

We have arrived at a negative interpretation of free will; it exists in so far as it can act of its own wrongly; but, even so, this is still caused by God's non-acting, and, in this sense, must be regarded as the result of His will.[2] God, then, as the positive cause of everything, existent or non-existent, is also the cause of free will's omissions and commissions. There is no way of escaping His ordinances.[3]

The paradox with which Bradwardine confronts us is very different from that of St Augustine and St Thomas. While for them the excellence of God's power was the source of free will even were it to go against Him, Bradwardine makes God's rigid control of free will, and its subjection to His immediate decrees, the source. Clearly, there is here far less ground for conviction that free will exists at all. On the one hand, Bradwardine makes God the cause, positive or negative, of all that man does or does not; on the other, man is free to accept or refuse any course open to him. Is there any means of reconciling these contradictory assertions? Bradwardine, in effect, has recognized that he cannot. For him, free will only remains free when dealing with nature and the created world; in this, man and his wisdom are supreme, immune from all compulsion. So soon, however, as God's will is involved, free will loses its independence: it is as though Bradwardine had carefully nursed and nourished free will the better to offer it to God's will as a worthy sacrifice. He has left it with no real resources of its own: he regards it, at best, as but a feeble

---

[1] 'Recitat sex falsas responsiones quarum. . . . Quarta, quod Deus facit obiectum et omnia mouentia voluntatem' (cap. 21, p. 555).

[2] 'Quod in omni non actione Deo et creaturae communi, prius naturaliter est Deum ibi non agere quam ipsam, et est, quia Deus certam actionem per creaturam non agit, ideo creatura illam non agit, et non e contra' (cap. 32, bk. II, p. 610).

[3] 'Ex his autem non improbabiliter videtur inferri, quod Deum non dare scientiam, gratiam, aut perseuerantiam, seu quodlibet munus suum creaturae capaci, est causa quare ipsa non accipit, et non habet, et quia Deus non dat, ideo creatura non accipit, et non e contra' (cor. to cap. 32, bk. II, p. 612).

attempt by reason to control impulse, and, even in this, without God's aid, it cannot prevail.

Bradwardine, indeed, by his principle of divine participation, has made man free to fall by his own weakness. Unlike, say, St Thomas he never gives him the choice to want to do good and thus to progress from sufficient grace to efficacious. Nevertheless, he realizes that to have free will is better than to be without it: it brings man nearer to God than any other creature on earth; it tempers his appetite with understanding; it is the divine spark which gives him knowledge and science and mastery over nature and the irrational brutes. Clearly, then, Bradwardine is at odds with the demands of his argument and the demands of Christian humanism. That the two cannot really meet and both live can be seen in the next chapter, where he attempts to relate the deeds of free will to God's will.

CHAPTER VI

NECESSITY, LIBERTY AND CONTINGENCY

THEIR RELATIONSHIP

BRADWARDINE, having asserted the existence of free will, has now the task of reconciling it with the overwhelming power of God's will. This is indeed the heart of the problem of *De causa Dei*, and its solution must clearly stamp it as determinist or otherwise. It is clear at once what the verdict will be, for Bradwardine is concerned to make God the source both of necessity and contingency, thereby justifying His eternal decrees in the name of freedom. God, he says, is the source of an act of free will.[1] This very act of will by God is both necessary and free: for He freely wills that an act be freely done and His ordinance makes this free act necessary. Liberty is *ipso facto* necessary; the one involves the other. In this way, therefore, contingency and necessity do not contradict, for they have a common source.[2]

This is the general principle upon which Bradwardine discusses freedom and necessity; it flows from each aspect of the principle of divine participation: first, that no second cause can itself be entirely the first cause of an effect, since it is not absolute; second, that God's will is the direct cause of all that His creatures do: He must, therefore, be involved in their own contingent

---

[1] 'In primis igitur ostendendum, Deum posse necessitare quodammodo omnem voluntatem creatam ad liberum, imo ad liberum actum suum, et ad liberam cessationem et vacationem ab actu. Deus enim potest velle voluntatem creatam producere liberum arbitrium suum, et hoc antecedenter, et prius naturaliter voluntate creata; quare, et per 10 primi, illa de necessitate obediret, et hoc, quamdiu Deus sic voluerit ipsam velle. Quoniam enim quod Deus vult, non potest non esse, cum vult hominis voluntatem nulla cogi vel prohiberi necessitate ad volendum vel non volendum; et vult effectum sequi voluntatem, tunc necesse est voluntatem esse liberam, et esse quod vult' (p. 637).

[2] 'Corollarium, quod aliqualis necessitas et libertas, ac meritum casusque et fortuna inuicem non repugnant: de fati quoque praescientiae, praedestinationis et gratiae cum libero arbitrio ac merito concordia generali' (cor. to cap. I, bk. III, p. 640).

actions. In this way contingency is as much a part of God's necessity as of free will; this relationship can be expressed in the paradox that God necessitates free will.[1] From this, Bradwardine goes on to examine each aspect in turn.

Necessity. There are, he says, two different kinds of necessity: preceding necessity which causes anything to be, and the necessity concomitant with anything caused, that is, its own effect. Every creature is subject to the first necessity, for it is the means by which it exists.[2] Only God, who constitutes preceding necessity, can remain outside it, for He alone is uncaused.[3] This means that free will can only deal with concomitant necessity, since preceding necessity is beyond the control of any creature; a secondary cause therefore, has only a relative liberty subject to God's decree. Bradwardine rejects natural compulsion as having anything in common with necessity. True necessity cannot be described in natural terms, but comes from God. Similarly, liberty does not consist in the absence of violence, either fatal or natural; but, with true necessity, belongs in God.[4]

Contingency and liberty. This is the framework in which contingency must be discussed; it cannot exist absolutely except in God. Bradwardine, first, seeks to define it. He divides the main different opinions on it into those which hold it to be what is future in things and those which say that it inheres in everything as potentiality, or as propositions about things, or as that which differs in them from God's will. He rejects both groups as inadequate or unsatisfactory. Contingency, he says, is anything that is

[1] 'Quod Deus quodammodo necessitat quamlibet voluntatem creatam ad quemlibet liberum actum suum et ad quamlibet liberam cessationem ac vacationem ab actu, et hoc necessitate naturaliter praecedente' (cap. 2, bk. III, p. 646).

[2] 'Ex quo videtur perspicue colligi quaedam regula generalis, quod videlicet universaliter omnis effectus a quocunque agente rationali vel irrationali, et libero producatur hoc modo, quod posito suo agenti cum omnibus suis dispositionibus sufficientibus naturaliter praeuiis quibus illum producit, necessario et indefectibiliter sequitur ipsum produci et producitur ex necessitate praecedente' (p. 646).

[3] 'Necessitas siquidem per se primo accipitur pro vehementia essendi illius quod per se et primo est necesse est, quod est Deus, et sic proprie definiri non potest. . .' (p. 678).

[4] See *ibid*.

possible: which can be or not be.[1] Thus something is contingent which is the act of a free agent, which, having considered the consequences which will naturally follow a certain action, does not necessarily adopt it, but considers equally the alternative.[2]

Contingency, like liberty, cannot stand alone; it must be both cause and effect, for it derives from a previous cause: if it did not, it would be necessary and not contingent. Thus only God as the first cause is not, of His nature, contingent.[3]

Bradwardine sums up his views on contingency under thirteen headings.[4] These deal (i) with the nature of contingency,[5] (ii) with its scope and limits,[6] and (iii) with its cause.[7]

(i) It is in the nature of contingency that the opposite of a particular action could equally have taken place: in the case of going for a walk, for example, it could have been equally possible not to have walked. Nothing contingent is therefore absolute, but as, say, in a king's decrees, the contingent is conditional upon circumstances. A contingent action must therefore result from freedom of choice and not be determined.

(ii) The scope of contingency is in no way contradicted by necessity; for everything that is contingent is necessary as coming from the first cause; conversely, everything necessary must be contingent by virtue of the infinite freedom which resides in the first cause. In this sense contingency is absolute. There is, however, a second aspect of contingency as the transient expression of the contingent choice in the secondary cause which derives from the first cause; for example, to move one's hand or to walk. This represents the free choice of an individual, for he may equally have decided not to have moved his hand or to have walked. Yet it is not absolutely contingent for only through the first cause is

[1] '. . . dicendo videlicet illud et ideo esse contingens aequaliter seu ad utrumlibet, quod et quia Deus vult posse sic esse et non esse, videtur definire idem per seipsum' (p. 652).

[2] 'Quare videtur mihi, quod contingens aequaliter per se et primo acceptum potest sic congrue definiri, quod est actus agentis liberi per se et primus, quo posito cum omnibus dispositionibus naturaliter praeuiis cum quibus illum producit, non necessario sequitur illum ipsum produci, sed utralibet partium potest stare aequaliter' (ibid.).

[3] 'Quis enim dixerit, quod Deus est sic contingens, et sic contingere Deum esse? Causa autem per se et primo non est sic contingens. Nam causa quae est ab alio non est ab alio in quantum causa, sed in quantum causatum' (ibid.).

[4] Cap. 5, bk. III, p. 653.   [5] Points 1, 2, 3, 4, 5.
[6] Points 6, 7, 8, 9, 10.   [7] Points 11, 12, 13.

this choice given; it is a combination both of cause and effect, for it is by a cause which is itself an effect.[1]

In the order of secondary causes, therefore, neither contingency nor its necessity is absolute in its own right[2] and they do not conflict, since only by the movement of a first cause do they arise. Similarly contingency, as part of the nature of a secondary cause, cannot be regarded as only belonging to the future: if it exists, it will belong to the present;[3] for, as Scotus said,[4] contingency, as the cause of what is possible, must be present if the possible is to take effect; as inherent in the nature of a thing it is constant and independent of time.[5] This, moreover, applies equally to liberty, since liberty and contingency are part of one another.[6] If a thing is not necessary it must be free and contingent; and, as contingent, it has arisen from liberty of choice.

(iii) From this it follows necessarily that God, as the unmoved mover, the first cause, and the principle of freedom, can alone do all that He does *absolutely*. His will is completely free and contingent in all that He does: He acts without any compulsion; but, having once done so, His decrees are absolute and necessary in all that they concern. Thus the source of all necessity and contingency is in Him; everything else is contingent upon His will.[7]

---

[1] 'Sciendum igitur . . . quod contingens dupliciter potest sumi: uno modo, per se proprie et in primo gradu contingentiae, cuiusmodi est actus primus et immanens agentis rationalis et liberi contradictorie puta velle: et talis contingentia et sequens necessitas non repugnant, sicut iam erat ostensum. Alio modo autem potest sumi contingens per accidens quodammodo, siue per aliud secundario denominatiue, et in secundo gradu, qualis est actus transiens et extrinsecus praedicti agentis descendens a primo, puta mouere manum, baculum et percutere: ubi et secundum propinquitatem et remotionem possent assignari ulterius plures modi; qui ideo dicitur contingens aequaliter, quia a contingentia huiusmodi deriuatur. Talis autem effectus est necessarius respectu suae causae totalis, sicut proximum huius docet, et contingens similiter modo dicto: unde et evidenter apparet, quod contingentia sic accepta, et antecedens necessitas non repugnant' (p. 655).

[2] Points 9 and 10.   [3] Point 7.

[4] 'Contingens aequaliter, per se primo proprieque acceptum est actus causae actualiter praesentialiterque agentis' (p. 655).

[5] 'Non modo est contingens causa, quae praeexistebat ante illud instans in quo causat, et tunc ut praeexistens potuit causare vel non causare; quia sicut hoc ens, quando est, est necessarium vel contingens, ita causa quando causat tunc causat necessario vel contingenter: ex quo igitur in isto instanti voluntas causat hoc velle, et non necessario, ideo contingenter' (*ibid.*).

[6] See points 1–5, p. 653.   [7] Points 11, 12 and 13, p. 654.

Having discussed the relation between necessity, liberty and contingency, it remains to discover the particular part that free will has in producing them. Is there, in fact, any freedom that does not come from God? In answering this question, Bradwardine distinguishes between two different kinds of power: active and passive. All the power that men, as God's creatures, possess is that of choosing between alternatives; there is no active power in their hands: that is to say, men have not the ability to create the alternatives, in the first instance; they can only accept or reject what is put before them. It is essentially this passive, conditioned power which belongs to men, as God's creatures.[1]

This power of limited choice is too often mistaken for God acting on men indirectly through secondary causes. In reality, He governs the whole universe and our only power lies in serving Him and obeying His decrees.[2] This is men's role; and by this means they can attain the highest freedom, for they turn to its source. They are, however, neither coerced nor compelled to follow God. On the contrary, this is an honour which, far from degrading men, through their dependence upon Him, exalts them.[3] Man is in the highly honoured position of being next to God among His creatures on earth. The worth and purpose of his own resources lie in changing his will for the better; but to do this he must be helped by God.[4] By his association with God, man is made doubly free: free by aspiring to the one source of liberty, and free from all three secondary forms of necessity: natural, fatal and violent. Man cannot, therefore, be his own master for his true end lies beyond himself in God.[5]

This is Bradwardine's conclusion on the relation of liberty and contingency to necessity. In itself, it does not violate the existence of free will; nor does it go against tradition in conceiving

---

[1] 'Quare omne illud et solum illud dicitur esse in potestate nostra, quod est in nostra libera potestate, libera inquam consimili libertate, scilicet contradictionis . . . nullus actus noster est simpliciter in nostra potestate libera . . . sed secundum quid tantum, scilicet respectu causarum omnium secundarum' (p. 675).

[2] *Ibid.*   [3] *Ibid.*   [4] *Ibid.*

[5] 'Nullus ergo homo est dominus sui actus omnino simpliciter et penitus absolute, summe, antecedenter, et sufficienter sine indigentia scilicet alicuius, quod suae potestati siue dominio non sit subiectum, sed tantum secundum quid, scilicet respectu causarum omnium secundarum subseruiens necessario causae primae, et hoc necessitate naturaliter praecedente' (p. 676).

everything created in secondary terms, as the effect of a first cause. With God as the source of all that His creatures do, it must follow that their actions are subject to His will and cannot be absolute in themselves. Here Bradwardine has once more combined the Aristotelian principle of causes with the Scotist view of God's will. He has united them to free God's creatures from all necessity other than God's will, thereby driving out any element of an impersonal, remote control. In this way, God possesses within Himself the contingency and liberty which go with necessity; they are inseparable and so cannot contradict one another. It is from here, once more from thoroughly prepared positions, that Bradwardine advances to extremes in dealing with the question of future contingents. Having completely armed God, he is not prepared to modify His power for the sake of men.

FUTURE CONTINGENTS

This problem is an essential part of Bradwardine's defence against the *Pelagiani moderni*: although he rarely uses the term 'Pelagian' in this dispute,[1] through obvious limits to its application, he devotes nearly two hundred pages to asserting God's primacy in all things future.[2]

No less than grace, the relation of God's knowledge of the future to freedom of action for His creatures involves the full range of the divine and created wills. In essence, the difficulty to be solved is how God's eternal knowledge of everything, possible and impossible, past, present and future, can be reconciled with free will in man: that is, if God is to know in advance everything that, say, Socrates, will do, how can it be said that Socrates acts from freedom of choice? It would appear either that God's foreknowledge violates Socrates's freedom, which is to be able equally to do or not to do, by knowing beforehand what he will do; or that, for the decision to rest with Socrates alone, God cannot be a party to its knowledge in advance. The problem raised is, in effect, no less than that of free will and determinism: it involves defining man's degree of freedom from God. Is God to control all that man does? Is man able to flout God? Is there a mean so that man, though not going against God, can act without His assent?

[1] See, for example, *ibid.* p. 715.   [2] *Ibid.* pp. 688–872.

In fine, is free will compatible with God's omnipotence, and, if so, how?

Now it is upon the future that the problem revolves, for both the present and past as already in being must be taken for granted; with the future, however, Socrates is still to act and the effects of God's will have yet to be felt. Accordingly, the implications of Bradwardine's discussion on contingency can only be seen when he turns to the future.

As we have already seen, Bradwardine regards liberty and contingency for God's creatures as relative; as the product of secondary causes they are equally dependent upon God's will as their first cause. Moreover, God's will is the means by which He knows His creatures, and so His knowledge of their contingent actions is active. This makes God's willing their cause. As a consequence, His forewilling must equally be the cause of their future, contingent actions. God, therefore, must know all that is future through His forewilling it. Such are the steps by which Bradwardine moves from the present and past to the future. They are along the line drawn by his principle of divine participation in which everything created is inseparable from God's will.

In Bradwardine's eyes there can be no contradiction between freedom and necessity. God's will, far from preventing freedom of choice, is the means for its existence. His forewilling is the prerequisite for future contingents.[1] Bradwardine sums up his position in the corollary to chapter 50.[2] Firstly, every act of divine

---

[1] 'Ponamus igitur simul esse et praescientiam Dei, quam sequi necessitas futurarum rerum videtur, et libertatem arbitrii, per quam multa sine ulla necessitate fieri creduntur. . . . Sed si aliquid est futurum sine necessitate, hoc ipsum possit praescire Deus qui praescit omnia futura; quod autem praescit Deus futurum est sicut praescitur necesse esse igitur aliquid esse futurum sine necessitate, vel praesciri sine veritate. Nequaquam ergo recte intelligenti nomen, repugnare videntur praescientia, quam sequitur haec necessitas, et libertas arbitrii, a qua remouetur necessitas, quoniam et necesse est, quae Deus praescit futura esse, et Deus praescit aliquid esse futurum sine omne necessitate' (p. 685).

[2] '. . . quod omnem actum volutionis et cognitionis diuinae praesentem necesse est, necessitate sequente praedicta, semper fuisse, et similiter semper fore; quare et quod omnia quae praesentialiter sunt, fiunt aut eueniunt simili necessitate sunt, fiunt et eueniunt in praesenti; et quod omnia quae euenient, simili necessitate euenient in futuro; imo et quod omnia quae nunc fiunt, de aliqua necessitate praecedente nunc fiunt; et quod omnia, quae eueniunt de aliqua necessitate precedente, euenient in futuro' (cor. to cap. 50, bk. III, p. 823).

will, past, present and future, must have existed eternally. Secondly, in the same way, all that is about to be, and all that will be, must, of necessity, come to be. Thirdly, that everything, therefore, whether past, present or future, is subject to the same act of creation, and its temporal order bears no relation to the certainty and eternity of its existence in God. The use to which Bradwardine puts these conclusions shows clearly where he departs from tradition: he transforms the eternal instant in God to deny the future any independent existence. Where St Thomas was content to allow that God saw everything through His own essence which in no way necessitated what He foresaw, Bradwardine changes this neutral intelligence into active approbation: with him, what God foresees, He forewills.[1] As a result, the future is as determined as the past and the present: it cannot not come about.[2]

Bradwardine, in having staked everything with the immutability of God's will, has made the future as immutable. He has demolished all intermediate positions between the future as undetermined or as the working out of an eternal ordinance. In choosing the latter, he combats three main groups of opinion. The first is that everything is determined by an inexorable necessity, in the manner of the Stoics and the Arabs. These make up the early chapters of over forty which he devotes to future contingents.[3] His concern with these is to vindicate both God and men from an impersonal determinism, even though it, too, denies the future. He frequently draws his support from Etienne Tempier's condemnations of such views; and this offers good evidence of Bradwardine's preoccupation with the Greco-Arabian determinism as one of the main dangers to his personal concept of God. Accordingly, Bradwardine, in answering them, is prepared to assert the existence both of freedom and of the future.

---

[1] 'Item apud Deum est determinata scientia omnium futurorum, quia per causam determinatam, per suam scilicet voluntatem, per quam scit ea. . . . Item omnia sunt semper praesentia in aeternitate et intrinsice apud Deum. . .' (p. 864).

[2] 'Omne quod est quando est, necesse est esse, et quod fit et factum esse fieri et factum esse, et Deum velle sic esse' (p. 853).

[3] All the chapters cited below belong to book III of *De causa Dei*: caps. 12 (p. 688); 15 (p. 690); 16 (p. 691); 17 (p. 692); 19 (p. 695).

In the second group[1] Bradwardine argues against diverse views: all these views would, firstly, deny God knowledge of the future, either as existing outside Him or taking place without His willing it; secondly, they would make His knowledge of the future incomplete so that, for example, He would foresee only good, not evil,[2] or that a man could act without Him, or oppose Him, and make Him dependent for His knowledge upon things known;[3] thirdly, as a result, they would remove any order between merit, free actions, and reward, denying God's will to be their cause and making the past, present and future all completely contingent and free from necessity.[4] In arguing against this group, he is vindicating the omnipotence of God's will as the active and eternal cause of everything created.

Bradwardine, having now freed God both from an impersonal necessity (group I) and from contingency (group II), reaches the main argument in the third group.[5] This holds that while the past and present, as actually in being, are necessary, the future, as yet to come, is not: it is accordingly free either to be or not to be and so may never take place at all. This either makes God's knowledge of the future liable to change, or it makes the future of anything contingent free from His knowledge. As we shall see in Part II below,[6] this was the way in which Bradwardine's opponents argued in asserting freedom for the future; they regarded these as the alternatives to an eternal determinism and, by implication, denied that God's knowledge of a contingent was not itself liable to change. The consequences of this opinion, which Bradwardine calls the most famous of them all, are at once apparent: God is denied absolute control over men; free will is given priority over God's foreknowledge; and His attributes of eternal omniscience and immutability of will are sacrificed in the interests of human liberty of action. It need hardly be said that Bradwardine's entire position depends upon their rebuttal; it could not stand for an instant without God's eternal forewilling as its stay and motive.

This dispute shows how far the balance of the thirteenth cen-

---

[1] Caps. 13 (p. 689); 14 (*ibid.*); 18 (p. 693); 20 (p. 696); 21 (*ibid.*) and 22 (*ibid.*).   [2] Cap. 22 (*ibid.*).   [3] Caps. 23 (p. 697); 24 (p. 698); 25 (p. 699).
[4] Cap. 25 (*ibid.*).   [5] Cap. 26, opinion 33 (p. 702).
[6] See Durandus, Aureole, Holcot, Buckingham and Woodham on future contingents.

tury between God's will and free will had, by this time, been upset; the ordered relationship of, say, St Thomas, with God as the
ultimate cause of all that His creatures did, had been broken
through the rejection by fourteenth-century thinkers of any
meeting ground between them. Because neither Bradwardine
nor his opponents could see this point of contact between the uncreated and the created as beyond the range of metaphysics and
logic, each must inevitably favour one in preference to the other.
This is shown in the conclusions that were being drawn from the
opinion under discussion. By making the future mutable, God's
essence, revelation, and Christ's knowledge and belief were all
subjected to doubt. Bradwardine in support of his view had first
to combat six opinions all of which questioned the truth of God's
essence as revealed in the Word, and the certainty of revelation
in general,[1] and Christ's knowledge in particular, holding that
Christ could have been deceived or could have believed falsely.[2]
Thus Bradwardine, in defending his own view of the future as
forewilled eternally by God, was also asserting authority. It need
hardly be said that all that he held was at stake in this struggle
over the future, for it involved both revelation, as the foundation
of truth, and divine participation as its means. Were God not
eternally to preordain everything by His will, all established
order between Him, as first and immediate cause, and His
creatures would be overturned.

It is along these lines of defending God's cause that Bradwardine argues against opinion 33. All that God does, he says,
though freely willed, is necessary once He wills it;[3] all that He
knows is constant and immutable. He, as first cause of all that is,
could be in no way dependent for His knowledge on what He
has created.[4] Far from revelation being uncertain and Christ
liable to be deceived and to deceive, as the Pelagians assert,[5]

---

[1] Caps. 33–41 (pp. 758–83).   [2] Caps. 42–50 (pp. 785–808).

[3] 'Si igitur Diuina voluntas est immutabilis, posito quod aliquid velit,
necesse est ex suppositione eum hoc velle. Item omne aeternum est necessarium, Deum autem velle aliquid causatum esse, est aeternum; sicut enim
esse suum, ita et velle aeternitate mensuratur; Est ergo necessarium, sed non
absolute consideratum, quia voluntas Dei non habet necessarium habitudi-
nem ad hoc volutum; est ergo necessarium ex suppositione' (p. 814).

[4] '. . . omnia autem futura sunt aeternaliter praeordinata, et prescripta
atque praedicta in voluntate et mente diuina. . . . Omnia ergo futura euenient
de necessitate huiusmodi ordinata' (p. 805).   [5] Ibid. p. 715.

these are evidence of God's eternal foreknowledge. Bradwardine accordingly takes the same arguments of revelation[1] to disprove what his opponents proved. Where they see revelation as evidence of God's lack of eternal knowledge of future contingents, Bradwardine regards it as evidence of God's foreknowledge. Bradwardine also demonstrates the truth of his arguments by the evidence of the apostles and saints[2] and by the nature of eternity[3] where he shows that everything in God is part of the eternal instant.

Bradwardine concludes his argument by showing that, as contingency comes from God's will, He could logically have willed a course different from that which He has willed. But once He has decided, His decision remains eternal, for He is willing it eternally; it becomes, through His infinite freedom of choice, *ipso facto* necessary. In the same way, whatever He has not willed, He rejects eternally. God, therefore, having made His choice, wants equally to maintain it, that His will may be done; it is in this sense that He cannot not will what He has already willed. To do so would involve Him in contradiction, rendering Him mutable and impairing His omnipotence.[4]

The mistake, then, of his opponents lies in confusing this eternity in God with temporal measurements, thereby trying to judge the infinite by finite standards.[5] This can only lead to dividing what is indivisible in Him. Bradwardine's solution is to refuse to recognize any difference in this world which is not also in God. As a result, rather than acknowledge the problem of the future, he denies it. This is the outcome of his discussion on future contingents; it is remarkable for its rigour and extremity.

[1] Caps. 33–46 (pp. 758–93).   [2] Caps. 47–9 (pp. 794–808).
[3] Caps. 51–2 (pp. 826–72.)
[4] 'Quod Deus vult non potest non velle, quia aliter sua voluntas esset mutabilis' (p. 843).
[5] 'Sic forte in Deo, ubi non est aliqua temporalis praecessio, sed causalis, si respiciatur ipsa Dei natura non in ratione agendi, et comparetur liberae voluntati hominis nudae ab actu antequam velit, verum erit dicere, Deum potest non velle quod vult: Si vero respiciatur ipsa diuina natura in ratione agendi, et comparetur liberae voluntati hominis cum iam actu vult, verum erit dicere Deum necesse est velle quod vult, et non velle quod non vult: Impossibile est enim eum non velle quod vult, vel velle quod non vult. Quam distinctionem facit in nostro posse et actu prioritas temporalis hanc ibidem facit prioritas causalis et subiecti super quod redit praedicatio diuersa . . .' (p. 841).

Bradwardine, in his defence of God's cause, has not hesitated to jettison the last elements of human autonomy. Not only has he vindicated God's future knowledge, but, in doing so, he has virtually excluded contingency from any real place in human affairs. It comes through God's will alone. By the principle of divine participation, then, all freedom becomes part of a supernatural association; it is not possible to regard it in its own terms but only with reference to God. In this way, Bradwardine reconciles necessity with liberty and contingency: since they are one in God they cannot be separable in His creatures. No plainer evidence is required to show that Bradwardine's God has no real room for a separate created order: He is too absolute and free in His own nature to allow similar qualities to exist outside Himself.

Bradwardine's view of creation may be likened to a precise machine devoid in itself of any direction or movement. Its workings are beyond its own knowledge and power. It needs the constant current of God's will to infuse it with life and purpose. It cannot, therefore, be judged in itself, for without God's impulsion it is like a propeller without an engine. Nothing can be left to its own resources.

CHAPTER VII

ASSESSMENT

So much of Bradwardine's system can be recognized as deriving from one or other of the main streams of medieval thought that, at first sight, he may seem simply to be an eclectic. His originality would then come not so much from anything new of his own, but through his combination of diverse and previously established elements. Yet, true as this is up to a point, to go no further would be to fail to do justice to Bradwardine or to his thought. It would mean that the pieces did not fit once he had brought them together. But in fact the most striking thing about *De causa Dei* is its coherence of argument and its rigour of application; in achieving this, Bradwardine has reached a position different from other systems previously. However, before attempting to assess the originality of his outlook, its main components must first be examined.

SOURCES OF 'DE CAUSA DEI'

It is always dangerous to equate the number of times a writer is quoted with his importance. This is especially true in Bradwardine's case: the numerical strength of a particular source bears no relation to its significance. This can be clearly seen with Averroes, above all, and also with Aristotle, the Lombard and Damascenus, to mention only a few names. Each of these is, at least once, the target for Bradwardine's wrath or disagreement. Moreover, the way in which a source is used is also important; there is all the difference between quoting a name in connexion with an anecdote, or on a matter of historical fact, and treating him as an authority on a matter of high doctrinal importance. Thus St Thomas Aquinas and Duns Scotus do not have more space given to them in Bradwardine's sources than Isidore of Seville or Boethius; but they are both far more important than the latter in his system. This is also the case with Robert Grosseteste, who is only quoted a bare dozen times, but each time his opinion lends an almost decisive weight to the argument in hand.

It is proposed, therefore, briefly to classify Bradwardine's sources under the following heads: (i) those who may be called policy-makers, the thinkers who provide the components, as it were, of *De causa Dei*; (ii) those whom he considers important for reinforcing a particular aspect of his thought, though they do not add to it; (iii) those whom he opposes for one reason or another; (iv) those whose interest lies in showing the width of Bradwardine's references and interests, without having any effect upon the main lines of his doctrines as, for example, writers of poetry and history. It goes without saying that none of these divisions is complete or absolute, and very often a particular source could answer to more than one. But they do give an indication of those thinkers who have influenced Bradwardine most.

I. There is a further division here between those who set the tone and those from whom Bradwardine operates his system. In the first group there are St Augustine, the Scriptures in general, with St Paul in particular, and St Anselm. The most popular works of St Augustine are his *Retractationes, Confessiones, De civitate Dei, Contra Julianum, Contra Pelagianos, De libero arbitrio, De correptione et gratia, De praedestinatione, De Trinitate, Super Genesim, Super Psalmos* and *Enchiridion*; that is to say, those works, and parts of works, which deal with grace and the relation between God and man, and which oppose Pelagianism. Two sayings, one from St Paul[1] and the other from St John,[2] qualify as the most repeated expressions in *De causa Dei*. In the case of St Paul, Bradwardine takes most of his quotations from his Epistle to the Romans and Epistles to the Corinthians, especially in his references to the supremacy of faith above all else. Of the Bible in general, and the prophets in particular, Bradwardine cannot emphasize too often that this is the source of all knowledge as directly inspired by God.

Bradwardine is indebted to St Anselm for the ontological proof of God's existence and of the love which is His motive. Throughout *De causa Dei* this view of God as the highest good colours all

---

[1] Therefore it is not in him that willeth, nor in him that runneth, but in God that sheweth mercy (Rom. ix. 16).

[2] Without me ye can do nothing (John, xv. 5).

that Bradwardine discusses: indeed at its broadest St Anselm's view of God may be said to be the justification for St Augustine's view of man, though this is not to imply that either had a monopoly of one view as opposed to the other.

In addition to their being the main sources of Bradwardine's outlook, these authorities are also distinguished for their regular appearance. Unlike Bradwardine's other references, these are constantly to hand, because their views apply to whatever he is discussing. This is in marked contrast to the second group of policy-makers, in particular, who are invoked far more for a specific purpose.

The second group, the practitioners, consists of Aristotle, St Thomas, Duns Scotus, and Robert Grosseteste. As suggested, their importance lies in their being the means by which Bradwardine can apply his guiding principles, and they are therefore the prerequisites of his system. Aristotle, it has already been pointed out,[1] is the main authority by which Bradwardine's system is built. He provides the second thesis of *De causa Dei*, namely, the need for a first cause in everything; and it is through this that Bradwardine is able to make everything created flow from God. Similarly, Bradwardine's view of matter and his laws of science are from Aristotle. His main works cited include the *Metaphysics*, *Ethics*, *Physics*, *Prior Analytics*, and *Posterior Analytics*, *Topics*, *De coelo*, *De anima*, *De (animalium) generatione*, *Politics*, *Rhetoric*; also the pseudo-Aristotelian works, *De bona fortuna* and *De mundo*.

St Thomas gives Bradwardine not a little of the necessity which he attributes to creation: although never exactly using the words 'existence' and 'essence' to describe God, Bradwardine's means of distinguishing and defining God from his creatures, by their modes of existence, is similar to his. From St Thomas, too, Bradwardine draws the conclusion that every effect of a secondary cause must be known to God since everything is ultimately subject to Him as first cause. Thus one may say that the physical basis of God's existence comes from St Thomas. Duns Scotus's theory of God's will, as the means of His knowledge of His creatures, transforms God into the active first cause from which Bradwardine derives his principle of divine participation.

[1] See p. 18 above.

There remains only to consider Grosseteste in this section; and his position is not so evident as those of the other authorities here. He seems to stand in the wings, rarely openly displaying his ideas, but giving final judgement when required. Bradwardine[1] makes one of the few personal references in *De causa Dei* to Grosseteste: 'the most subtle of thinkers and a very profound theologian'. This, of itself, suggests the high respect in which he held Grosseteste. He is cited most in the discussion on God's knowledge of future contingents and on free will. But it is rather to his method than to the frequency of his entries that we should look for his influence upon Bradwardine: his combination of Augustinianism with the works of Aristotle, his union of theology and science, and his adherence to the traditional outlook. These, as expressing the Oxford tradition of the time, can be seen clearly in Bradwardine; and it is in this light that Grosseteste must be given a high place among Bradwardine's antecedents.

II. In this second group there is again a division between those who lend a general confirmation to Bradwardine's positions and those who add specific embellishments. In each case their importance is secondary and they do not give fire of their own.

In the general authorities there are most of the standard texts, such as Peter Lombard's *Book of Sentences*, Gregory's *Moralia*, Ambrose, and sometimes the Greek Fathers such as Chrysostom and Damascenus. Bradwardine gives great importance to Gregory, in particular, but it is hard to discern any special influence from him. Other accepted authorities include St Jerome, St Bernard, Hugh of St Victor, St Cyprian and St Isidore of Seville.

Among the special authorities are the Arabs and the Neoplatonists. The first include Avicenna, Algazel, Alacens, Albamazar, and Averroes. They are usually quoted in support of one or other of Aristotle's principles; but the position of Averroes must be qualified, in view of the severe attacks that Bradwardine makes upon him personally, and on his determinism in general.

The use of the Neoplatonists is to give tongue to Bradwardine's own glorification of God. Dionysius, in particular, is frequently

[1] *De causa Dei*, p. 810.

I

invoked in this connexion, and from him Bradwardine borrows expressions like 'super-essentiality' and 'monad'. They add to Bradwardine's picture as elaborations add to lines that have already been firmly drawn; and they cannot be said to play a formative part in his system.

The interest of both these groups lies rather in illustrating the range of Bradwardine's sources and the thoroughness with which he includes all that is germane to the argument. This power of selecting and combining positions, at first sight irreconcilable, is one of his most marked faculties.

III. Those whom Bradwardine opposes are, broadly speaking, Pelagians and Averroists and all those who, by chance, take up positions approximating to either. Unfortunately, among the first, his real opponents are never named, for Bradwardine follows custom in not specifying contemporaries. On occasions, however, he attacks those whom he otherwise accepts and draws upon. Notable among these are the Lombard and Damascenus, and by reason of each holding a position which would give man's free will some independent power, either before or after the fall.[1] In the case of such authors, however, Bradwardine criticizes them for their specific mistakes and not, of course, as heretics.

In his opposition to the determinism of the Arabs, by which the whole universe runs on impersonal, eternal and inexorable lines, thus making the first cause equally subject to necessity, it is Averroes whom Bradwardine opposes chiefly by name. This is especially so in connexion with Averroes's Universal Soul and his theory of the eternity of the world;[2] Aristotle is also attacked for his denial of creation.[3] In addition, there are the general references that Bradwardine makes to the 1277 condemnations of those theses which regarded God as an impersonal and indirect mover.[4] Mainly, however, it is against positions whose supporters he does not name that attack is made;[5] indeed, the whole of De causa Dei is a battle against these two groups, with the Pelagians as the foremost enemy.

IV. Finally, there is that vast array of quotations which shows

[1] See pp. 73–4 above.   [2] See De causa Dei, pp. 65 et seq.   [3] Ibid.
[4] For example, see ibid. pp. 653, 678.   [5] Ibid. pp. 688 et seq.

the wide range of Bradwardine's interests and knowledge. Ovid
and Virgil are the two poets, especially Ovid, from whom on two
occasions poems are transcribed,[1] dealing mainly with the fates.
Pliny's *Natural History* is mentioned in support of natural facts;
and, for history, Josephus. Nor does Bradwardine let English
writers pass unnoticed: he makes mention of Bede, John of Salis-
bury, and William of Malmesbury.

Other names in general include Solinus, Ammonius, Marco
the Venetian, Ptolemy, Seneca, Boethius, Cassiodorus, Al-
cuin, and also the Jewish philosophers, Avicebrol and Mai-
monides.

Plato's *Timaeus* is his one work to which Bradwardine refers,
and then not over frequently. Cicero is also known to Bradwardine; and chapter 13 of book III is devoted to rebutting his assertion that God has no knowledge of the future.

The most noticeable features about Bradwardine's sources are,
first, their range, second, his selective use of them, and, third, the
complete absence of reference by name to his contemporaries. It
is this last point which leaves our knowledge about the circumstances of *De causa Dei* so incomplete. The *Pelagiani moderni*
are in almost every page of the treatise, but never once by name.
Until this space is completely filled, there can be nothing definitive about the novelty and the importance of *De causa Dei*
in Bradwardine's day. Nevertheless, on the available evidence,
certain conclusions can, provisionally, be drawn.

HIS SYSTEM AND ITS ORIGINALITY

The question to be answered is how far it is possible to designate
Bradwardine in traditional terms and how far he can be said to
represent a new outlook.

From the point of view of the traditional systems, Bradwardine's thought can be recognized as deriving from those sources
named in section I above. That is to say, Aristotle, St Augustine,
St Paul, St Anselm, St Thomas, Duns Scotus, with the Bible
and Grosseteste in general support. Now if we try to break these
down further, we get a certain order between them.

First, in general: St Augustine and St Paul colour Bradwar-

---

[1] *Ibid.* pp. 40 and 73.

dine's outlook on the relations between God and man as a whole. They provide him with his extremely high view of God's grace and the complete unknowability of His ways; and correspondingly, he follows their severe view of man's natural powers, of their inability to do good of their own resources, and of the overriding necessity of grace. In this sense, we may say that St Augustine and St Paul provide the framework within which Bradwardine works.

Second, in particular: Bradwardine adds to the company; and here we see clearly that his system is arrayed in the order of the fourteenth century and not of the fourth. It would only be true to call Bradwardine an Augustinian if so little were added to his general outlook and conclusions that, with the additions stripped away, the system would still stand. But this is not the case, as the preceding commentary has shown. In the first place, Bradwardine's view of God[1] has three inter-related parts: his view of God's spirit is that of Anselm in which His goodness is to be felt by all who believe. This infinite goodness is the quality which moves God to such rigorous activity; for, when Bradwardine says that He acts from love, he means this as the cause of His every action. God's love and goodness are the justification, were any needed, for divine participation. Added to St Anselm's definition of God is St Thomas's and Aristotle's view of His mode of being and His relation to His creations. They are established by the laws of physics; and they provide the mechanics by which God is both completely distinguished from His creatures and is their first cause. While St Anselm presents God's nature completely and intuitively, St Thomas and Aristotle describe the laws of His existence. Finally, the Scotist view of God's will shows God in His activity and movement. His will, as the principle of everything created, gives effect to God's love for His creatures as their first cause. Clearly, then, Bradwardine's view of God would be incomplete without any of these aspects: to His love there must be added secondary causes to receive it; and to both there must be His will to direct it; only in this way can God's participation take the form that Bradwardine assigns to it.

In the second place, in relation to man, it is St Augustine's view, above all, that Bradwardine follows; but even here, the means by

[1] See Ch. 1 above.

which God's predominance over man is asserted is not Augustinian: it is by the principle of divine participation, and he pays far less attention to the fall than St Augustine did. Indeed, God's will has been used to such effect over His creatures that man's dependence is far more in the eternal order of things than the result of any action entirely his own. Although, with Bradwardine, the necessity of grace depresses man even more than with St Augustine, yet, as coming from divine will, its source is different. In Bradwardine's sense, man is not to be condemned for his weakness, for that is inherent in his nature: he sins when he tries to assert his own powers.

Bradwardine, then, has so interwoven his sources that they have become merged and none remains the same. If his system is Augustinian in direction, the route and the vehicle are from others; and the completed journey must be seen as Bradwardine's. Each of his main authors plays too important a part to leave any of them out of the final reckoning; and together, at Bradwardine's hands, they combine in such a way that, for all their individual diversities, the final effect belongs to him. It is in this light that we must regard *De causa Dei*: to call its thought after one school, rather than another, involves so many qualifications that the effort becomes pointless and without meaning, besides destroying what is his alone. It is not enough, either, to dismiss Bradwardine's system as a capable arrangement of other people's ideas, for this, too, destroys and misleads: whatever else can be said about Bradwardine, his outlook has an iron unity; there are certainly no awkward joints or glimpses of light between the parts: indeed, as in his treatment of sin, to pull one part is to pull it all.

Bradwardine's originality lies in two main directions. In the first place, there is his principle of divine participation. This is the motor of his system; it is something new, and liable to great dangers; for it brings God into such ever-present contact with the created world that His creatures lose all autonomy. It constitutes a departure more radical than anything ever expressed in the traditional schools of thought; and would alone suffice to distinguish Bradwardine from them. A new dimension, as it were, is introduced into divine and human relations; or, rather, these relations become one-dimensional—the merging of the natural in the supernatural. For the first time, moreover, there is a threat to man's existence, and therein lies the danger of divine participation: for even Christ, whose merits are the beacon for all to see, is denied any special treatment as a man.

In the second place, Bradwardine's method, in its unity of exposition, is distinct from that of previous thinkers. Despite the diversity of his sources, everything is subjected so ruthlessly to his argument that *De causa Dei* takes on the nature of a sustained polemic over nearly 900 folio pages. Both in method and in spirit it is distinguished by a lack of humanity; its traits are vigour and ruthlessness; its nature is proselytizing; its effects are to daze rather than to guide. The clarity of his intentions and the extremity of his conclusions unfold his system stage by stage in a way that makes everything he writes of compelling relevance, if the argument is to be followed.

As a result, a new spirit emerges from his work which regards divine and human relations by almost startlingly unwonted standards: it is as if one were to judge a finely vaulted roof not by the beauty of its design but by the necessity of its keystones. With Bradwardine the created has nothing of value to offer except in so far as it is the extension of God's will. Such an outlook must ultimately lead to a rejection of all outward forms of life and worship for inner faith alone. It is here, above all, that Bradwardine's importance and novelty lie.

THEOLOGY VERSUS PHILOSOPHY

Bradwardine can in no way be regarded as having wished to heal the breach between faith and reason, in the sense of giving each its own sphere. His whole aim was to eliminate free will and human merit as endangering the sovereignty of God's will; far from acting as a mediator, he entered the arena as the deliberate protagonist of the claims of faith. It might be replied that this is to do Bradwardine an injustice; that his whole method and combination of sources show that he was, in fact, creating a new synthesis in which there was a place both for Aristotle and for St Augustine; and that, far from following Duns Scotus and Ockham in their rejection of physical proofs for God's existence, Bradwardine made a return to the *modus vivendi* of St Thomas's system. This, however, is to withdraw attention from Bradwardine's teaching, and to look solely at his rare combination of personal gifts. The central feature of *De causa Dei* is that God, through His will, is the first mover in every created, and human, action. God participates immediately, therefore, in all that goes on in the created world; not only has Bradwardine not returned to St Thomas, but by his principle of divine participation he has merged the created world with God. The natural, in fact, has been swallowed into the supernatural, and only in this sense can the two be said to be reunited. It is as if a tidal wave had engulfed a once independent area, leaving little to be done but to ensure whether anything remained with the devastated, created world. This must now be our task.

Bradwardine is so explicit about the complete limitations of the power of speculation and metaphysics to know anything of God that it only remained for him to write its epitaph. How, he asks, can a poor, finite soul reach to God's infinite nature? It shames philosophy to make such a claim.[1]

Only through God Himself giving us the power to do so can we know Him, thus making revelation alone the means by which this is possible. Now this, broadly, is the viewpoint accepted by all orthodox medieval thinkers. While St Thomas had solved the problem by his use of analogy, through which we might obtain the dimmest approximation to God's image, Duns Scotus and Ockham rejected any way but that of revelation: philosophy and metaphysics could not discuss truths that belonged to faith alone. Bradwardine accepts this view only to take it to its full extreme. He demonstrates the difficulty of knowing even the minute particulars of our own lives, and from this asks how infinitely more must this apply to our inability to know God. With Him as with geometry, he says, we can only reach the

[1] 'Imo erubesce Philosophe, et scientia superbiens, dedignare tam paruum Deum habere, ut tu paruus, per paruam mentem tuam totum ipsum scruteris, omnia secreta rimeris, capias et cognoscas plenarie ipsum totum. Deus namque sicut infinitae entitatis, ita et infinitae veritatis et cognoscibilitatis; quare a nullo finito per virtutem suam finitam plene cognoscitur: sed tantummodo a seipso per seipsum per virtutem suam propriam infinitam, nisi fortassis accomodet homini oculum suum, et virtutem suam cognoscitiuam infinitam, totum videlicet semetipsum, ut sic per ipsum totum Deum, possit quoquo modo cognoscere totum Deum' (p. 27).

conclusions through first knowing the premises; and these cannot be reached through our own powers of understanding.[1] It is presumption to think that philosophy can deal with the infinite: it is barely adequate to cope with the finite and the petty.[2]

The highest truth in philosophy, therefore, is that we cannot by ourselves know God.[3]

Bradwardine emphasizes very strongly the essentially unreliable nature of human knowledge in being able to recognize and understand the truth: this can be seen in the way in which our opinions constantly vary, so that we are influenced to change them by sheer weight of numbers instead of having the certitude which comes from faith alone.[4] In this Bradwardine says that he agrees with the philosophers of the Academy for not having placed much value upon material knowledge. So far as God is concerned, moreover, we are, in trying to understand Him, confronted with His will. But His will is the cause of our reason; and so there can be no approach from our reason to His will; for these are two different qualities at infinitely different levels. God reveals Himself to us by His Word as found in the Scriptures. It is only through the evidence of the prophets and the other writings that we may hope to understand Him.[5]

It is clear, then, that Bradwardine does not recognize speculation as a means of reaching the truth. Not only his remarks upon the limitations of philosophy, but the method of *De causa Dei* illustrate this. Throughout he made faith the touchstone, basing his entire cause upon the tenets of authority. Truths come from God alone; we can only find them if God reveals them to us. We are placed, as it were, between the object, on the one hand, and its truth, on the other. One is from experience; the other is from God: there is no room for philosophy. This is really the applica-

[1] 'Quare etiam correspondenter conclusiones Geometricae infinitae, etiam sese ordinabiliter consequentes, ita quod posterior sciri non potest, nisi per priorem' (p. 27).

[2] 'Vos ergo omnes pariter Philosophi infiniti, quot scitis de istis conclusionibus infinitis? finitas procul dubio, finitas et paucas . . . nullus vestrum per se aliquam scire potest, nec omnes pariter scire possunt' (*ibid.*).

[3] 'Sapiat ergo sobrie quicunque philosophus et istam veritatem pro maxima Philosophia agnoscat, nihil citra Deum posse cognoscere plene Deum nisi forte per eum' (*ibid.*).

[4] 'Cui ergo sententiae certitudinaliter adhaerebo? . . . Quid ergo in talibus nisi fides, nec ulla sincera scientiae certitudo? (p. 28).   [5] *Ibid.* pp. 29–46.

tion of Bradwardine's principle of divine participation to his theory of knowledge, for everything that we see in this world is an aspect of its complete truth, to which God must direct us. Nothing, therefore, can be explained in natural terms. Such is Bradwardine's mode of argument; the appeal is always from theological truth to a scientific fact, or a logical conclusion. By this means, as we have already noticed,[1] Bradwardine has no difficulty in discussing any subject, for it is always with reference to absolute theological truth.

The place of theology is accordingly supreme; it is on a pedestal of its own with no rival. Only the Scriptures have the right to be called truth; they are the source for all that may be said about God and indeed the world. Bradwardine does not reach the point of Luther's appeal to the Scriptures as the sole authority, but his emphasis upon their importance is more striking than his occasional references to the Church. It makes all truth, in effect, theological: dogma and certainty are his means of arguments; he allows no place to speculation. Accordingly Bradwardine never pauses to consider what may or may not be discussed; he displays none of the wariness of, say, St Thomas Aquinas to be ready to take note when the argument should change from philosophical to theological ground; that is to say, when demonstration by reason ends and assertion by faith begins. There is never, for Bradwardine, a 'no man's land', where questions remain open because faith and reason could give different replies—as in the creation of the world. As with St Augustine, all truth must be theological. From the central truth of God's existence, and His infinitely good and powerful nature, everything else must follow: nothing else is needed. Thus the task of ascertaining truth, as Bradwardine viewed it, resolved itself into clarifying the precise way in which God works, and His relation to His creatures. This Bradwardine does by the simple extension of God's powers to imply, on the one hand, His ever-present activity, and, on the other, the impotence of His creatures, men included. Everything created becomes an aspect of divine activity, with God as sole reference. In this way, all that is comes from Him, and all that is not, equally, has its non-being in His will.

[1] See pp. 33–4 above.

Bradwardine never speculates about a truth or probes for the reason of a particular thing; he simply demonstrates its relation to God. Logic and physics, therefore, far from being part of an autonomous discipline in disengaging the truth, act as confirmation to theology; they are used to support an essentially theological system. This outlook may be likened to what E. Gilson has called 'theologism',[1] in which the explanation for everything is in supernatural terms. There is no clear-cut demarcation between the supernatural and the natural, the uncreated and the created; there is no place of halt between two different spheres, and a change from one gauge to another. God sweeps into all that is created; and the method by which God is asserted is equally the method to be used in dealing with His creatures. Bradwardine, in his desire to set God so completely above His creatures, has made them share the same law. The impetus of his system has been almost too strong: and, at times, the divine and the created are almost perilously hard to disengage.

Consequently, since the same terms of reference apply universally, every time Bradwardine discusses man or the created world, he is also, in greater or lesser degree, dealing with God. It may be granted that this, to an extent, is inherent in any description which tries to combine the two spheres. But the significance here lies in the denial of any autonomy to the created world. There is no independent value given to the natural and the philosophical, as helping to reach the theological and the supernatural. By making God the active principle of all his creatures, there is no room for any division between their respective activities; nor, in consequence, any power among His creatures to do or to know without God's participation. Determinism and theologism in Bradwardine's system are different aspects of divine participation: as the one removes independent action the other removes independent speculation.

Does Bradwardine's system rob man of the need to make moral judgements? This question can only be answered by examining whether Bradwardine has left any power to human free will; if the answer is No, then there is neither need nor place for independent human decisions. Firstly, it is necessary to recall Brad-

[1] E. Gilson, *The Unity of Philosophical Experience*, ch. II.

wardine's answer: he would reply in favour both of human free will and man's need to choose the good. God's will as the first principle of justice and freedom is the source whence they flow to man. Without a free first cause, the universe would be governed by necessity. Because God is free man has free will together with the choice of wanting and doing good. Therefore, if man loves God, he will be just and want to do good; and, conversely, to want to do good is to love God. Since, moreover, God wants all men to be saved, it is not He who causes them to sin, but their lack of His grace. In short, love of God and the desire and power to do good run together. Man needs God's will for everything worth while.

In terms of Bradwardine's own system, this reply is adequate; for, granted that God does participate in every human action, only by His will can men do good. But, so soon as the practical conditions of the created world are considered, there are insuperable difficulties. In the first place, because of the arbitrary nature of God's will, and with it the necessary and entirely uncaused nature of grace, how can a man do good unless He has first so ordained it? God's will is eternal; He therefore decides to move us to carry out the action that He forewills. In that case, though God's will is both free and just, we are not able to be in either state apart from it. Thus, it may be argued, if we move and want to do good, this power comes from His will; and if we do not, this too, comes through His will in not moving us. There is no need to try to move of our own accord, for only He can enable us to do so; far better to wait for God's impulsion than seek that which we do not feel arise in us. Moreover, Bradwardine himself has stressed that, not only do our wish and power for good come from God alone, but that if we try to act alone, of our own free will, we can only do so for evil.

In the second place, throughout Bradwardine's system, there is no place for natural law, just as there is no place for the natural in any form. Hence it is impossible to appeal to any absolute and constant standard in this world; no bridge is provided to traverse the gulf between God's will and man's reason, no intermediate plane joining the infinite to the finite. Justice, goodness and love can only reach God's creatures through His will; they are supernatural virtues; and if they are not infused by Him they cannot appear in the world. Another possible means of natural guidance is thereby denied to men. Such a position would seem to suggest that, in practice, outside the immediate terms of *De causa Dei*, there is no incitement to free will. Indeed, the warning against independent human action has been trumpeted long and loud, and all merit has been virtually annihilated. In the circumstances, the earnest soul would lose confidence and prefer to do nothing, and the indifferent one would be prepared to follow his impulses as the surest way of avoiding effort and trouble. Bradwardine's determinism thus gets enmeshed in its own rigour. It must either end in theocracy or in an individual belief, essentially personal and emotional. The weakness of his system lies in its failure to recognize the practical effects of its tenets. While to accept one method rather than another in explaining God's ways and existence is a matter, above all, for conviction and belief, this is not the case with its effects on the created world. To discount man, for example, though perhaps justifiable within the theological terms of Bradwardine's system, involves accepting or denying these conclusions in practice. It is in human and created terms that Bradwardine is open to criticism on two counts: first, because his view of man barely gives him the right to be considered according to Christian ethics; and second, because, in fact, it frees man from any effort to do good. In both of these, therefore, Bradwardine goes against the ideals he is defending. Man's infirmity can become the basis for his amorality; and lack of individual worth can mean lack of an individual ethic.

In this sense it is not unjust to talk of Bradwardine's determinism. He has annexed the direct control of the world and of its deeds to God. The effect of depressing the status of men has made itself felt. Either direct inspiration and personal contact with the Almighty, as with Luther, or the directly ordained application of God's decrees through a theocratic government in the manner of Calvin, are the consequences. In either case, man has no natural autonomy. Bradwardine has prepared the ground for each: for, in whichever of these directions the truth may lie, it has no place in reason or science or secular practice. The faith that lies in the heart has no need of the hand or the head. Bradwardine, by failing to render unto Caesar any value of his own, has impoverished him too much to allow him to render unto God.

PART II
THE PELAGIANS

CHAPTER VIII

THE PELAGIANS

A s we have suggested in the Introduction, Pelagianism for Bradwardine meant more than its strict technical definition. It was in his view primarily to express an attitude of human vainglory and lack of faith in God; and it was directed against all those who denied God and the supernatural, no matter how little or for what pretext. Wide though his definition was, it had a singular relevance to the times. In the scepticism of Ockham and his followers what started as an attitude of neutrality towards God and the supernatural seemed inevitably to lead to partisanship for men and the natural. By limiting knowledge to tangible experience they could find no place for God or for His ways; and in excluding theology and metaphysics they were forced back upon a logical and rational explanation which applied only to the natural order. This, as we have already suggested, meant a break between faith and reason. It was this stark division between the two realms which formed the starting-point for what Bradwardine regarded as Pelagianism.

Bradwardine, throughout *De causa Dei*, was primarily at strife with this attitude which refused to make God the centre of our knowledge and experience. His view of Pelagianism accordingly must be seen in this light; it is not the sharply defined heresy of the fourth century, but the product of fourteenth-century scepticism casting doubt upon all that it encountered, God included. Since we are concerned with Bradwardine's view of Pelagianism, this must be the definition we accept here: his are the only terms of reference.

THE SOURCE OF SCEPTICISM

This attitude of scepticism originated in Ockham's theory of knowledge, which he distinguished as intuitive and abstract. Intuitive knowledge dealt only with the existence of an object; it was not concerned with discussing it.[1] Abstract knowledge, on the other hand, involved a mental process in which the mind reflected upon what had been brought to its attention, even though the original object were no longer present.[2] By this distinction Ockham was able to show that the process of knowing (abstract knowledge) did not guarantee the existence of the object known (intuitive knowledge). Accordingly, all our concepts, abstractions and values derived from the mind and not from the object itself; they were not synonymous with the immediate experience of reality, which only intuitive knowledge could provide. In consequence, Ockham regarded all discussion and thought as the ordering of terms (*suppositiones*) and not involving the objects themselves. Man, for example, according to Ockham could have three different terms: as the word itself as a material sound (*suppositio materialis*), as the individual Socrates (*suppositio personalis*) and as the species, human being (*suppositio simplex*).[3] These three *suppositiones* applied to every word.

Now the supreme importance of this outlook lies in its denial of an independent reality to anything not perceived by the senses; in taking as alone real the objects encountered in intuitive knowledge Ockham could find no place for the universal. Nothing but the individual counted and everything else became a purely mental concept whose existence was beyond the bounds of experience. Thus the *suppositio simplex* could not be subject to proof for it did not correspond to any fact known to experience. The effect of this was to erect a barrier between practical experience and super-sensory knowledge; it meant the dismissal of metaphysics, concepts of value and, above all, theology, as beyond the ken of reason: to discuss them was not to discuss facts but to speculate upon possibilities; since they were not subject to verification they could not be regarded as certain.

It is in this sense that the scepticism of Ockham and his followers must be viewed; unlike that associated with Hume it did not doubt the existence of all extra-mental reality. On the contrary,

---

[1] '. . . notitia intuitiva rei est talis notitia: virtute cuius potest sciri utrum res sit vel non' (Commentary on Sentences, Prologue, qu. 1 z).

[2] 'Abstractiva autem est ista virtute cuius de re contingenti non potest sciri evidenter utrum sit vel non sit' (*ibid.*).

[3] Sentences, bk. I, dist. 2, qu. 4 M.

for Ockham the individual stone and chair and man were so complete in themselves that there was no call to look away from them; he did not question the reality of this world, but of all that was beyond it; he stopped at the real, not the mental. Only when one moved beyond the tangible did uncertainty arise and an attitude of doubt and speculation replace practical knowledge. Accordingly it was towards metaphysics and theology that there was scepticism, for these shared the very uncertainty common to everything super-sensory. It is in this sense that we shall regard it here.

It was K. Michalski[1] who first made an extensive examination of the scepticism of the fourteenth century. He saw it primarily as the substitution of the probable for the certain in the way discussed above. Thus, in Michalski's view, the refusal to accept, say, God's existence as certain, but only as logically probable, was the hallmark of the fourteenth-century scepticism.

While it is true that probability was frequently invoked, its identification by Michalski with scepticism seems inadequate: firstly, because probability of itself does not necessarily imply an attitude of scepticism, and, secondly, because Michalski failed to take note of the different treatment accorded by Ockham to questions of knowledge in general and to matters of faith in particular. So far as the first is concerned, any thinker, St Thomas Aquinas included, can at certain junctures refuse to go beyond asserting that something is probable, rather than certain, and yet not be a sceptic. Indeed, the expression is frequently to be met in most scholastic writings, not least by Bradwardine, the archenemy of Pelagianism. In one sense, such an attitude of reserve is inherent in reason's very attempt to attain to the supernatural.

In the second case, instead of using any single term to describe fourteenth-century scepticism, we may see three operating at the two different levels of reason and faith: they are neutrality, possibility and indeterminacy. The first provided the general framework within which the sceptics decided all questions beyond the scope of practical experience; the latter two were the effects of such an attitude when applied to God.

Once the scope of knowledge has been limited to fact, everything else becomes, as we have suggested, the province of specula-

[1] See Bibliography below, p. 272.

K

tion; there is no means of correlating it with practical experience. Hence, in the absence of evidence to the contrary, God's existence can either be or not be; there is no rational means of establishing one of these alternatives to the exclusion of the other. To the definitive terms, 'yes' and 'no', a third, 'perhaps', can be added. Such an attitude is essentially one of neutrality; it implies that what is under discussion could be equally true or false. It was implicit in the sceptics' denial of the proofs for the existence of God or in their refusal to apply reason to what lay beyond it: it was, in effect, a confession of ignorance. While no claim is made here that this is equivalent to a three-value logic, in which there is a middle term to those of true and false, the effect is not dissimilar, as we shall see in its applications to questions of faith.[1]

Possibility is the corollary of neutrality: once it is conceded that an object need not be A to the exclusion of B it follows that either is possible. It is by this means that the sceptics discussed God and His ways, allowing that it was possible for Him to follow any course of action. This in turn led to indeterminacy: the lack of any certain order to which possibility gives rise. Thus when one course is as likely for God as another (neutrality), any is possible (possibility) and there is no means of determining the outcome (indeterminacy).

It is only when neutrality becomes expressed in these two ways that scepticism is transformed from a mere theory of knowledge into an active challenge to faith; and the instrument in achieving this was the sceptics' use of God's absolute power (*potentia absoluta*). It made up, together with God's ordained power (*potentia ordinata*), the generally accepted division of God's omnipotence. God's *potentia ordinata* referred only to the world which He had created; it was the law by which it was governed, providing the regulations for everything. It was to be found in His Word and authority which, as the expression of His eternal

---

[1] Ph. Boehner, in his edition of Ockham's *Tractatus de praedestinatione et de praescientia dei et futuris contingentibus*, pp. 43 *et seq.*, attacks the view that Ockham favoured a three-value logic. While this may be true in the strict meaning of the term, this view fails to take into account the attitude of doubt which he and his followers displayed to all but fact. Thus Aureole's view of future contingents was, as we shall see, founded upon the neutrality which governs all that is not certain.

decrees, were immutable. In this sense, God's ordained power applied less to His own nature than to His creatures, for it was inseparable from their existence. It ordained fixed and requisite standards for everything, as in the case of grace, which it had decreed to precede an act of merit.

God's *potentia absoluta*, on the other hand, denoted God's omnipotence purely and simply; as one of His attributes it was outside all space and time and not directed to any specific universe, or to sustaining any fixed order. Infinite freedom was its only law; to will, its *raison d'être*. It could override the decrees of God's ordained power as a sovereign his ambassador; for like the latter, God's *potentia ordinata* constituted only the specific application of a wider authority. Thus, to take the case of grace and merit again: by God's *potentia absoluta* merit was not dependent upon grace, as it was under God's *potentia ordinata*. It enabled God to do anything.

Now it was in the use of God's *potentia absoluta* that the real effects of Ockham's scepticism are to be found; it combined those three features of neutrality, possibility and indeterminacy, and applied them to God and to revelation. Its central theme was that nothing was impossible for God in His absolute power; and in removing the bar of impossibility it opened the way to neutrality and indeterminacy. Neutrality was expressed in the refusal to limit God so that any course was as likely as another in His infinite freedom; accordingly the sceptics refused to limit themselves in what could be said about Him; it enabled them to join the blasphemous to the devotional, to make black part of white, to consider the impossible as possible, all in the name of His freedom. Nothing could be excluded which could not be disproved, for it offered no inherent reason for being less eligible. As a result God was as He willed; His attributes dissolved before the blaze of His omnipotence, making Him unknowable not only in the wider and accepted sense, but in those traits which were virtually a precondition for belief. His goodness, perfection, mercy, justice and wisdom all faded from man's vision as beyond his ken. He could only be known by His ability ever to do differently than He had done. God, therefore, lost His certainty; He became identified with infinite possibility rather than with any fixed and ascertainable order. Hence anything could be posited of

Him, for His *potentia absoluta* substituted speculation for understanding.

This in turn led to indeterminacy: with God so free that anything was possible there was no means of ascribing to His actions any constant order. Since He was unknowable, and our propositions about Him as likely to be true as false, there was no ascertainable relation between His will on high and man's deeds on earth. With anything and everything possible to Him in His infinite freedom, nothing could give man empirical knowledge of Him on earth. Thus it was utterly impossible to establish any causal chain between Him and His creatures. The infinite freedom of the divine will could transcend any course of action; it was fruitless to attempt to establish an order by which it operated. God could by-pass all the ways of His ordained power and none could gainsay Him.

Clearly God's *potentia absoluta* threatened the entire foundation of His ordained law, and the latter, at its hands, became the most fleeting of contingencies, ever liable to be dispensed with. This was the way in which it was employed by the Pelagians; it constituted the application of their neutrality to matters of faith, serving the double purpose of freeing God from reason and reason from theology. Thus the rigid limits of Ockham's logic, by which everything extra-sensory was rejected as unreal, found their true counterpart in God's *potentia absoluta* towards matters of faith. Where reason ended God's *potentia absoluta* began, taking charge of all that was not subject to verification and showing how uncertain it was. It carried to its conclusion scepticism's denial of reason to a place in faith, by applying an attitude of neutrality towards dogma and authority. The implication of God's *potentia absoluta* was that, if reason were to be committed to faith, the latter became meaningless and void; only by keeping them separate could each remain unimpaired. Thus upon whatsoever God's *potentia absoluta* turned, it succeeded in casting doubt. There was no means of saying that God was good; for by His *potentia absoluta* He could equally be bad: He could mislead Christ or desire a man to sin, and His will was justification enough; there could be no judgement apart from it. Hence God's *potentia absoluta* refused to exclude contingency in the name of the contingency in God's will.

God's *potentia absoluta* in effect showed that the uncertainty to which all that was unproven was subject involved God and revelation equally. It enabled the sceptics to avoid accepting the authority of God's ordained law by speculating upon what He in His absolute power could do. It showed that to discuss the divine was to reach absurdity in that possibility became the only criterion. Rather than that, it implied, keep each to its own sphere. So long as theology remained a matter of faith it need not be doubted; but when reason was invoked in its support it then had to submit to the same speculation which governed all that was unverifiable. The penalty for such misuse was God's *potentia absoluta*. God's *potentia absoluta* was thus the main instrument of the sceptics in their denial of the validity of reason in faith.

That this was its primary purpose, and not, as P. Vignaux has suggested,[1] merely to emphasize the radical contingency of everything created, can be seen in the manner in which it was employed. Apart from other occasional mentions to show, for example, that God could work a miracle, or that He could have ordained affairs differently, it was confined almost entirely to those questions where faith and reason clashed; that is to say, where each offered a different answer to the same question and where practical experience was controverted by authority. Thus it was mainly employed over the relation of grace, free will and merit, and, with Adam of Woodham, over future contingents. These matters could be approached either from dogma or from an empirical examination: it was from the latter that scepticism started, with the result, as we shall see, that free will and its actions, as coming within practical experience, were asserted at the expense of grace and habits, which were outside it. At no time was God's *potentia absoluta* used indiscriminately: far from subjecting all knowledge to its scrutiny it was used to delimit the intangible from the tangible. This was its paradox: the sceptics employed a standard immune from reason in order to assert the place of reason.

It is, I submit, in God's *potentia absoluta* that the main force of scepticism lay. It was, in the first place, the theological justification for surgically separating faith from reason, keeping each to its own sphere. In the second place, it transferred the neutrality

[1] *Nominalisme au XIVe siècle*, pp. 22–4.

towards all but fact to the divine. In the third place, in the name of God's freedom it was able to override all the traditional concepts and obliterate all the known landmarks of God's ordained power: to say that God could mislead, that Christ could be misled, that revelation could falsify, that the mortal sinner could be loved more than the man in grace, that there was no inherent evil in the one, nor goodness in the other, that God could want a man to hate Him, that grace and mortal sin could coexist, that God loved the act of free will more than the habit of grace, all testify to the change wrought by God's *potentia absoluta*. It displayed more than a mere exercise in God's omnipotence and His creatures' contingency; it was primarily the *reductio ad absurdum* of reason in faith, showing how impossible it was to discuss what was beyond discussion; it allowed speculation and uncertainty to reign where knowledge and proof were lacking.

God's *potentia absoluta* marked the real division in Bradwardine's time: it illustrates, where the more traditional doctrines cannot, what put him on one side and the sceptics on the other; why, although both he and Holcot could be called Augustinians, their differences are greater than their similarities. While Bradwardine stands by the authority of tradition and the supremacy of faith over reason, his opponents denied their compatibility with reason. They refused to allow knowledge to pass beyond fact, where Bradwardine made knowledge subject to faith. Although scepticism was possible without God's *potentia absoluta*, as the case of Pierre Aureole shows, it lacked its power and audacity. Rather it resembled a blue-print, waiting to be given actuality: and this God's *potentia absoluta* did.

The importance of God's *potentia absoluta* has not yet been appreciated in modern times. Michalski himself barely refers to it and, even when discussed, it is generally seen as simply the means for asserting God's freedom, without due regard to its application.[1] Contemporary references are still scanty, but two may be mentioned: first its rejection by the Masters who condemned Ockham at Avignon, in 1326, as extenuating the opinions put forward in its name;[2] second, Wyclif's description of the 'modern

---

[1] 'Les courants critiques et sceptiques', *Bulletin de l'Académie polonaise de science et de lettres* (1927), pp. 65–6.

[2] See pp. 189–93 below.

Pelagians' as those who, by the use of God's *potentia absoluta*, give human actions priority over God's co-operation and who allow that men may gain merit without grace.[1] These are exactly the kind of arguments put forward by Bradwardine's opponents and discussed below. Although neither proves conclusively that the modern Pelagians were identified with God's *potentia absoluta*, together they lend support to such a view. What is certain is that it was by such means that the sceptics argued their cause, which was, in turn, condemned by Bradwardine.

THE QUESTIONS AT ISSUE

The most important effect of the sceptics' use of God's *potentia absoluta* is the breach it caused between faith and reason: on the one hand it made God so unknowable that nothing could be said about Him; on the other it prevented any analogy between Him and His creatures. In the circumstances the hierarchy between God and man, the foundation of the thirteenth-century syntheses, was destroyed and each, in effect, became virtually self-sufficient. Thus, in the name of God's absolute power man was made virtually independent of God. Because God was so infinitely free, men might find themselves exalted above their mortal stations. The infinity in God's power meant a corresponding absence of limits to human powers; far from man rising at the expense of God, in the manner of the original Pelagians, because God's stature was infinite that of man was correspondingly unrestricted.

This is the other extreme to which the power of God's will can be taken: where for Bradwardine it meant the utter debasement of man as worthless and impotent when not moved by God's will, Ockham and the sceptics let him soar unaided to the divine heights, if God so willed it. Each view started from the same circumstances.

Bradwardine treated the separation of the natural from the supernatural in a manner which obliterated the natural as an autonomous sphere; he invoked the supremacy of God's will over His creatures to subject them to its minute and immediate

---

[1] *De ente librorum duorum excerpta*, Wyclif Society (London, 1909), p. 195. I owe this information to Mr J. A. Robson.

control. Ockham and his followers used this same division between the natural and the supernatural to treat them as separate,
each complete in its own right. They, therefore, tended to discuss man and the world in very much more full and self-sufficient
terms, refusing to move beyond ascertainable fact. They used
God's will, in its absolute power, as the means for justifying man's
independence; this was the furthest extent to which they relied
upon God in support of reason: He never emerged as the chief
actor holding the centre of the stage, but remained for ever in the
wings, His own absolute power being the justification for His
absence.

When we come to examine the questions at issue we must regard them in the light of these conflicting views of God's will.
It has already been mentioned that the matters of dispute between Bradwardine and the Pelagians were much wider than the
direct question of man after the fall.[1] They were concerned, above
all, with God's relation to men, and, more specifically, with the
effect of God's will upon free will. Broadly speaking, while the
Pelagians in their emphasis upon God's infinite freedom were
prepared to assert its lack of restriction on free will, Bradwardine's whole aim was to make man subject to God. Their opposition centred on two main groups of questions: the place of the
supernatural virtues; and future contingents. The first was
mainly concerned with the resources of free will; the second with
its scope. Both involved two quite contrary views of God and
His attributes, man and his resources, and the principles by
which they operated.

The quarrel on the supernatural virtues was primarily over the
place of created grace and charity. Was it necessary for God in
His omnipotence to have recourse to a supernaturally infused
habit in order that a man might be acceptable to Him and rewarded with His glory? It is at once clear that this raised questions of the first importance: first, did God work to an eternal
order, or was His omnipotence to be seen in His freedom to
change? Second, were there absolutes which governed God's
actions and His dealings with His creatures? If grace did not inherently make dear, it could have no intrinsic goodness and sin
could live with it. Third, from this, was grace necessarily the

[1] See Introduction, p. 13 above.

means to glory and sin the means to reprobation? If God could by-pass them and deal direct with men, without regard to their state, were they superfluous? Fourth, in that case, was the strength of free will sufficient of itself to be free from supernatural habits? If it was, then it could reach God alone. Fifth, what, then, was the place of merit? Did it depend upon a supernatural habit or could it come from free will alone? These were some of the issues which occupied Bradwardine and his opponents. At every turn, they were pervaded by an order of priorities which ultimately must go in favour of either God or men.

In the same way, the dispute over future contingents brought out their differing attitudes. If God knew the future eternally and His knowledge was all-embracing, could free will then be undetermined? The Pelagians said No. For free will to be preserved, they held, either God's knowledge must leave man freedom to carry out his own detailed actions without His foreseeing them, or He must allow His knowledge of them to be contingent, as subject to change as free will was free to change its course of action. To follow the first course was to allow God's omniscience to be limited; to follow the second was to put revelation in doubt: for if all that concerned the freedom of the future could not be preordained, then the Word itself must be contingent. Anything God or Christ said about the future could turn out differently and so they could mislead. To accept either of these alternatives was to be on the side of free will; and Bradwardine in opposition to the Pelagians, as we saw, rejected both of them.[1]

Between them, therefore, these two groups of question covered the whole canvas of theology and belief. God's nature, knowledge, will and ways were all in question. Ultimately it had to be asked whether He was the justification for flux and disorder or the source of an eternal and immutable order which it was blasphemous to question. Similarly, man's nature and resources were disputed. Was he capable, alone, of good and was his will so free as to make him master of his own fate? Finally, the standards common both to God and man were subjected to doubt. Ethics and values, good and evil, wavered between the uncertainty of God's will and the absolute values eternally in Him. For the

[1] See pp. 103–9 above.

Pelagians they were as God willed them; for Bradwardine they were immutable.

The issue is clear in every case: either theology must mean belief in an accepted God whose nature and decrees are the source of His creatures' actions and standards; or there must be scepticism towards Him. While Bradwardine followed the first to the exclusion of God's creatures, the Pelagians made the omnipotence of God's will their justification for disregarding Him.

With such a broad field of questions, it would be idle to pretend that Bradwardine's Pelagians can be easily defined and identified. There may well be reason enough for a score or more of his contemporaries to come within the term; and it will take many years before they can be assembled with any certainty. Moreover, lack of firm historical facts in tracing anonymous literary opponents makes the evidence at best circumstantial. Only in the case of Pierre Aureole is there any personal allusion by Bradwardine himself. Above all, the looseness of the term Pelagian, as used by Bradwardine, makes a general survey of conflicting ideas, as discussed above, the only fruitful approach, even though this itself increases the difficulty of identification. With these considerations in mind, six thinkers, contemporaries or near contemporaries of Bradwardine, have been chosen as forming an important influence upon his views and as most probably constituting some, at least, of his Pelagians. That this cannot be proved conclusively, even by an examination of the relevant texts, is far less important than that they form part of the climate of thought which produced *De causa Dei*.

All these thinkers were prominent and influential among their contemporaries.[1] When they held to views attacked by Bradwardine, it seems more than probable that they, rather than the lesser fry, were his target. If Ockham were to voice an opinion, it is far more likely that he would attract attention than if an obscure bachelor said the same thing. Furthermore, Bradwardine was writing expressly to stem a flood tide of unorthodox views which had become current in the schools. It was no idle exercise on his part, but a burning mission to repel Pelagianism, that urged on his *De causa Dei*. He would hardly have felt this threat to be so

---

[1] For details of their lives, except for Buckingham, see *Dictionnaire de théologie catholique*. Buckingham was Chancellor of Exeter.

acute had thinkers such as Ockham and Durandus been neutral, if not on his side.

Thus, although lacking the final stamp of established fact, there is a strong case for regarding those thinkers included here as Bradwardine's adversaries. Beyond saying that they were important advocates of views opposed by Bradwardine, I make no other claim at present. This does not *ipso facto* make them the *Pelagiani moderni*; but their importance for Bradwardine's thought must be recognized. They were the more prominent representatives of a host of his opponents reaching down throughout the schools of Oxford and Paris. Whether or not Bradwardine actually included them in this number, men of the stature of Durandus, Ockham, Aureole, Holcot, Buckingham and Woodham cannot be neglected in assessing Bradwardine's position.

CHAPTER IX

THE TRADITIONAL BACKGROUND TO THE DISPUTES BETWEEN BRADWARDINE AND THE PELAGIANS[1]

ALTHOUGH the controversy between Bradwardine and his opponents was, above all, over the relation of faith to reason and of the divine to the created, it also raised doctrinal and theological issues of the first importance. Questions of orthodoxy are therefore involved; and while it is no part of the present study to pass final judgement upon the contentions of either side, their respective positions must be considered.

Difficult though it is to separate the dogmatic and the philosophical, the historical and the orthodox, in such questions as grace, free will and merit, an attempt must be made to distinguish what was common in the fourteenth century and what has since become accepted. While, ultimately, each side must be judged by what is now the orthodox teaching, it is important to remember that much that is now clear-cut was not so in the fourteenth century. Accordingly, we shall attempt here, first, to state the traditional doctrines, over each question mentioned, in the fourteenth century; next to take the views of the contestants themselves; and finally to relate them both to what went before them and to what has since been decreed.[2] In this way it is hoped to do justice both to the thinkers themselves and also to post-Tridentine dogma.

GRACE[3]

As we suggested in the preceding chapter, the controversies over grace involved more than the mere question of its presence or

[1] The whole of this section is based primarily on the relevant articles in *Dictionnaire de théologie catholique* [*Dict. théol. cath.*] referred to in the footnotes. The views of Bradwardine and the Pelagians are all to be found in other parts of the present work as specified.

[2] Readers are referred to Appendix II below for a summary of the modern divisions and terms of grace in order that the differences between fourteenth century and modern usage may be noted.

[3] *Dict. théol. cath.* VI, cols. 1156 *et seq.*

absence in a certain form; it called into question the accepted tenets of belief in God, man, and their relationship to one another.
This can be seen the better when the concept of grace itself is
considered.

Grace is generally defined as a supernatural gift, or the sum of
supernatural gifts, given to a rational creature for its final salvation. Its award distinguishes man from the brutes and from the
inanimate. The Fathers regarded grace as the infusion of the
Holy Spirit and this view was developed by the scholastics, until,
as at present regarded, it has manifold aspects.

The great division in grace is between uncreated and created.
While there are many further divisions in the latter, as we shall
mention, they all in some way express a supernatural gift which
is from God, but which remains distinct from Him. Uncreated
grace, on the other hand, is God Himself acting directly through
His will: in this sense it is less a distinct quality than an attribute
of His nature. It is the source of all created grace, and divine im-
pulsions, and the ultimate cause for dividing the saved from the
damned. Traditionally, therefore, uncreated grace was not the
main object of attention, for it did not lend itself to the minute
examination and division which could be applied to created
grace. It is only mentioned here in some detail because it plays an
important, though different, part with both Bradwardine and the
Pelagians. Created grace, as a supernatural gift from God, though
deriving from His will, was distinct from it. It had two main
functions: to cure man's moral infirmity (*sanans*) which had
come from the fall; and to elevate him to God (*elevans*) by enabling Him to do good. Its twofold purpose was to keep man from
mortal sin and to move him to fulfil God's mandates, endowing
his actions with a supernatural value.

Now, although no hard and fast division can be made, there
are two main kinds of created grace corresponding to these
divisions: habitual, sanctifying grace and actual grace. The first
denotes a permanent state of grace for the just man not in mortal
sin; the second a transitory act, or series of acts, for the accom-
plishment of specific salutary acts.

Before we inquire further into these two different types, it is
important to stress that during the Middle Ages they lacked the
distinctness of the present day, being rather implicit than clearly

expressed. St Thomas Aquinas,[1] for instance, did not use the term actual grace, and the terms for the different kinds of supernatural aid differed with individual thinkers. Thus the Lombard called habitual grace *gratia gratis dans*[2] and actual grace *gratia gratis data*; Alexander of Hales[3] called graces distinct from the Holy Spirit *gratiae gratis datae*, whether actual or habitual; St Bonaventure followed Alexander of Hales.[4] St Thomas,[5] on the other hand, while also making *gratia gratum faciens* sanctifying grace, regarded *gratia gratis data* as the gift whereby he who received it co-operated in leading others to salvation. This is the modern meaning of the two terms,[6] but their diversity in the twelfth and thirteenth centuries can be appreciated. When we come to the thinkers under consideration here, we find the same terms but again used in a contrary way. Bradwardine[7] distinguishes *gratia gratificans* as uncreated grace, and *gratia gratis data* as created. Frequently, he uses the term *gratia creata*, rarely specifying a division which would correspond to actual and habitual grace. The same lack of a clear distinction between the two is to be found in Ockham and his followers,[8] and in Bradwardine as well as among them the dispute is far more over the need for a supernatural gift at all than over its specific form.

Both these different kinds of grace had been recognized by the Fathers (especially St Augustine) and by the early Church councils (e.g. the Second Council of Orange). Sanctifying grace was generally a supernatural form infused into the soul, where it resided as a habit; it was not an integral part of the soul, since it was additional to its natural make-up; nor was it a separate substance, since a substance cannot share itself with another substance. It was rather an accidental form which could be dissipated by mortal sin and, conversely, could be infused into one in whom it had not previously existed. Sanctifying, habitual grace had two aspects: one was its sacramental nature by which it was infused through the sacraments (e.g. baptism and penance). The other was as the formal cause of justification by which a sinner, through a series of good acts, could be infused with sanctifying grace. Its

---

[1] *Dict. théol. cath.* VI, col. 1558.   [2] *Ibid.* XII, col. 1271.
[3] *Ibid.*   [4] *Ibid.*   [5] *Ibid.*
[6] See Appendix II, p. 267 below.
[7] *De causa Dei*, pp. 247 and 325.   [8] See below *passim*.

effect was to render him into whom it was infused just and to make his soul capable of receiving an intuitive vision of God. Although a gift distinct from God, it was physically a participation in the divine nature, making the man in whom it resided love Him and want to follow His ways. Its presence excluded mortal sin, but it could not of itself suffice for perseverance in good or for the accomplishing of every good act: it was a state of justice from which good was desired.

It was left to actual grace to achieve those salutary actions which either derived from a state of grace or which led to it. Actual grace, as concerned only with the deed itself, consisted of a variety of aids ranging from external gifts such as revealed truth to internal graces such as the illumination of the Holy Spirit. It had two main functions: the first to move men to salutary actions, as a preliminary to receiving habitual grace; and the second to move the justified man to good and to preserve him from mortal sin. Actual grace consisted essentially of an involuntary impulsion, in which God's immediate influence was superadded to natural energy. St Thomas upheld this view in seeing God's co-operation in every physical act.[1] This divine influence was to be found in both habitual and actual grace; it was operating when it excited the soul to want good, and co-operating when the will was moved towards it by a salutary action.

Could either habitual or actual grace alone suffice for salutary actions and preservation from mortal sin? The answer was No. From the point of view of actual grace it was essentially the means to the end of making a man just: the deeds it activated were either towards a state of justification or towards preserving that state. So far as habitual grace was concerned, it could not of its own remain the safeguard from sin and the instrument of good. 'No man, even after having been re-born by the grace of baptism, is capable of conquering the snares of the devil or resisting the desires of the flesh except by daily succour from God to persevere in goodness.'[2] Thus to avoid sin habitual grace was not enough. It is in this light that the special grace of final perseverance must be seen; it constituted that special aid from God by which one in

---

[1] *Dict. théol. cath.* VI, col. 1643.
[2] *Ibid.* col. 1591 quoted from *De gratia Dei indiculus* (Denzinger Bannwart, 182, 806, 832.)

grace might persevere until the end. It is usually regarded as the ensemble of efficacious graces,[1] a special gift reserved for the elect. St Augustine[2] had first enunciated such a special gift for the predestined in *De correptione et gratia, De praedestinatione sanctorum* and finally *De dono perseverentiae*. Its existence had been implicitly accepted by succeeding Church councils, such as the Second Council of Orange,[3] and it was left to St Thomas to take it up in the same definitive way. His own views[4] on the subject bear signs of evolution from the 'Commentary on the Sentences', where he spoke of actual grace sufficing to avoid mortal sin, to *De veritate*[5] where he stressed the need not only for habitual grace but for a special additional gift. This was later canonized by the Council of Trent.

Thus there were three main aspects to created grace: the transitory aids and illuminations of actual grace, the state of grace and justice which came from habitual grace, as the cause of justification, and the special divine gift of final perseverance by which this state could be maintained to the end. We have now to ask why some received such gifts and not others.

The history of these concepts is too multifarious to be recounted here. It is enough to take as a foundation the main questions at issue between St Augustine and the Pelagians; for these formed a turning point not only in St Augustine's outlook, but subsequently in that of the Church and dogma. The dispute between St Augustine and Pelagius may be said to have centred around three themes:[6] firstly, the Pelagians' lack of any distinction between natural law and the law that came from revelation, which prevented them from considering powers beyond man's reach; secondly, their denial of the effects of original sin with their view of Adam's sin as personal to himself and not transmitted after his death to those unrelated to him—as a consequence, death and mortality were regarded by the Pelagians as natural to humanity and they did not acknowledge that man's natural powers had been impaired—; thirdly, the claim that grace was not held necessary for accomplishing God's commands or for avoiding mortal sin,

---

[1] *Dict. théol. cath.* col. 1594.   [2] *Ibid.* XII, cols. 1265 *et seq.*
[3] *Ibid.* col. 1270.   [4] *Ibid.* cols. 1275 *et seq.*
[5] *Ibid.* cols. 1278 *et seq.* (Denzinger, 884).
[6] *Ibid.* arts. 'St Augustine', 'Pélagianisme' and 'Grace'.

and that man was considered able to fulfil all divine mandates of his own resources, in return for which he had the right to grace.

These views show clearly how little the Pelagians considered God when considering man; there was no concept of an elect or of predestination; and everything was regarded in natural terms. It was in combating these views that St Augustine gave coherence to the hitherto scattered views on grace. Briefly, St Augustine[1] identified grace with the saving will of God, which, as his doctrine was finally developed, was prevenient to every good action on the part of man. In man's present state it had the double function, already mentioned, of *sanans* and *elevans*, but even before the fall man had needed grace to remain whole. St Augustine stressed particularly the need for baptism, to heal his fallen state, and for the special gift of final perseverance to maintain a man in God's grace. Without these he was damned.

Augustine's outlook on grace as the beginning of all salutary activity became part of established dogma. The Second Council of Orange took it up, regarding prevenient grace as the means by which an adult reached justification.[2] God, it held, touched man by an illumination or inspiration of the Holy Spirit, and he could freely accept or reject it.

This raises the problem of why grace works in some and not in others; or, put more technically, the difference between sufficient and efficacious grace. All men, it was held, received sufficient grace to observe the commandments and consequently to persevere in justice and be saved. As the Council of Orange, following St Augustine, said, there was sufficient grace to all men wanting to avoid sin and sanctifying grace to those not in mortal sin.[3] Sufficient grace comprehended all actual graces given to men, such as supernatural illuminations; but these of themselves did not mean the achievement of salutary actions: the power they bestowed had first to become efficacious, transformed from the power to act to the act itself. This could only come about through the co-operation of him to whom such grace had been given. St Augustine taught that efficacious grace lay in obtaining the consent of men, but that the reason why some responded and others did not remained a mystery.[4] The same doctrine was expressed

---

[1] *Ibid.* vi, col. 1577.   [2] *Ibid.* col. 1639 (Denzinger, 180).
[3] *Ibid.* col. 1596.   [4] *Ibid.* cols. 1657 *et seq.*

L

by the Second Council of Orange:[1] grace was inefficacious, not in itself, but if a man refused to consent. God foresaw the response a man would make, but in His mercy awarded the power to act even though it should not be used. To realize this power another predetermining grace was needed, though neither St Augustine nor, later, St Thomas specified a further act on God's part for this co-operation. However, in contradistinction to the Molinists, St Thomas never held that grace was efficacious solely because of free will:[2] for the very act of free will was the result of God's will. Thus it was in keeping with St Thomas's views on the relation of causes that grace was efficacious both entirely from God as first cause and entirely from man as second cause, and their respective actions could not be delimited.[3] Accordingly the difference between sufficient and efficacious grace was not one of substance but of accident: the former remained potential, while the latter became actual.

Although the cause of a good action came from the co-operation of free will, the distribution of grace was a mystery. It belonged to God alone to predetermine some to damnation and others to glory and no one could gain grace unless eternally ordained by God.

The traditional doctrines of grace, then, up to the age of Ockham, were founded upon the dual supports of predestination and the fall. Whether expressed in the more direct theological terms of the Augustinians or viewed in the Aristotelian sense of a first mover, it was universally held that God decreed those who were in grace and those in mortal sin. Whatever the specific mode, the prevenient grace which came from His will was the source of all salutary actions and justification. Similarly, the effects of the fall had rendered man dependent upon God's grace for being cleansed from sin and remaining free from it. Alone, no man could long remain whole and he certainly could not do God's will on earth.

It is against this background that we must try to assess the orthodoxy and deviations of the modern Pelagians and Bradwardine. So far as the modern Pelagians were concerned it is not

---

[1] *Dict. théol. cath.* VI, col. 1659.   [2] See Appendix II below.

[3] *Dict. théol. cath.* VI, cols. 1663 *et seq.*; and R. Garrigou-Lagrange, *Dieu*, p. 474.

hard to see how flagrantly they departed from tradition; and in recounting their main lapses we shall be brought in mind again of those of the original Pelagians. They differ from each other in their source and aim,[1] but in their effects they show marked similarities.

In the first place, the modern Pelagians, like their predecessors, took no account of the difference between a natural and a supernatural action. There was no inherent distinction, for them, in regarding God as first cause and as God. Similarly, they recognized no intrinsic goodness in grace and therefore they did not distinguish a natural from a supernatural deed:[2] Ockham and his followers viewed an act only as an act and in doing so denied the need for grace to give an act a supernatural value. This meant, in the second place, that the modern Pelagians paid as little attention to the effects of original sin as their forerunners. Their starting-point was not the present fallen state of man, but man as God in His absolute power could accept him. Finally, in the third place, this led to a rejection of the intrinsic need and place of grace. It was not so much—as in the case of the first Pelagians—that man could win grace as that man had no need of it at all.

The result of these positions went flagrantly in the face of both tradition and subsequent dogmatic teaching. Firstly, the existence of created grace was questioned and its need denied. Accordingly, there was no acceptance of the orthodox view that both habitual and actual grace were needed to remain free of mortal sin and to fulfil God's mandates. Secondly, this led to the complete neglect of final perseverance as a special and indispensable gift from God to the elect: instead Ockham adopted Cassian's view by which the elect were eternally predestined to glory,[3] but that those not elected could win salvation by the right use of their natural powers. None of the modern Pelagians made any mention of final perseverance at all and it had no place with them in either name or in fact. Similarly, the traditional teaching on predestination was rejected and with it the view of prevenient grace as the beginning of all salutary deeds. No causal connexion was made between grace and glory, and in the words of Ockham the end did not necessarily require the means.[4]

[1] See preceding chapter.   [2] See below, *passim*.
[3] See pp. 206–10 below, and also O. Chadwick, *John Cassian: a Study in Primitive Monasticism*.   [4] See p. 195 below.

Thirdly, the essence of grace as a supernatural aid bestowing good was denied. Each of the modern Pelagians averred the possibility of grace and sin coexisting, and Adam of Woodham went so far as to include mortal sin.[1] In the same way none of them regarded grace as the source of goodness or the means by which a soul was brought to God. Although their main attack was upon the supernatural habit of grace and charity they at no time substituted the need of a series of actual graces instead, thereby providing for the existence of some supernatural aid.

Fourthly, because the modern Pelagians had no inherent place for grace, because they saw no causal link between its presence and glory, and because they denied it to be the source of goodness, they allowed no room for the traditional view of justification. This was not, for them, the state of grace to which an adult was led by a series of transitory actual graces, and in which he was maintained by God's aid. On the contrary, God could accept any sinner who repented without any supernatural impulsion moving him.[2] Moreover, in the paradoxical world of the modern Pelagians, God could reward him who hated Him and disobeyed Him, whilst to be in His grace were no sign at all of His love.[3] In consequence, there was no order between grace and glory, sin and reprobation, for nothing was inherently good or evil.

It is clear, then, that the modern Pelagians by their use of God's *potentia absoluta* dispensed with the need for created grace altogether. Although this was usually done in the name of God's absolute power, it was sometimes supported by the term uncreated grace. This was taken by Ockham to mean God's will acting directly through the Holy Spirit,[4] and while the use of Peter Lombard's name in its support tended to lend the idea a certain respectability, it did not alter their fundamental position. To say that uncreated grace was God's will and that, in the face of its efficacy, created supernatural gifts were not necessary was only to say that there was no room for created grace: it still meant dispensing with the whole framework of the traditional views, and, with them, man's dependence upon supernatural aid.

[1] See p. 245 below.
[2] See, for example, Ockham's view, p. 204 below.
[3] As, for example, Holcot's assertion that God could love the sinner more than him into whom He had infused His grace; p. 217 below.
[4] See p. 199 below.

Accordingly the term 'uncreated grace' is of interest here in showing how nothing but God's will counted with the modern Pelagians.

Bradwardine's reply to these doctrines differed from the orthodox views only in the extent to which he took them. He was at one with tradition, and especially St Augustine and St Thomas, in invoking man's dependence upon a supernatural aid for preservation from mortal sin and for the fulfilment of God's mandates: his two main charges against the modern Pelagians were that they denied the need of grace for either. Yet by his manner of staking the claim for a prevenient grace in all goodness, and of accepting the need for the special gift of final perseverance to maintain a state of grace, Bradwardine left no room for man or for the actions of free will. This can be seen in two directions.

The first was in his making the distinction between created and uncreated grace the equivalent to that between sufficient and efficacious grace. Bradwardine refused to allow that, however much created grace a man might have, he could overcome any temptation, fulfil any of God's mandates, resist mortal sin or persevere.[1] This, as can be seen, differs from the traditional view by which an actual grace was needed, as well as habitual sanctifying grace, to remain free of mortal sin, and where an actual grace was needed for a salutary action. Bradwardine, however, was not content to entrust such a deed to the impact of actual grace: he specifically said that it must be aided by uncreated grace, which was God's will: 'That free will, however well endowed with created grace, cannot overcome any temptation without God's special aid.'[2] Such a view makes what were but two aspects of the same thing different qualities and, indeed, so radically different that there could be no real comparison between them. Moreover, this in turn made God's will the only factor in a good deed by a man: it was the opposite of the position which Molina and his followers were later to take up, when they held that grace became efficacious only when free will consented to co-operate with it; with Bradwardine there was no place for free will at all.[3]

This is lent support by Bradwardine's view of operating and

---

[1] *De causa Dei*, II, chapters 4–9 (inclusive).   [2] *Ibid.* p. 477.
[3] See Appendix II below.

co-operating grace. The distinction was based upon the Scriptures,[1] as exciting man to good and aiding him to realize it. The Second Council of Orange defined them similarly:[2] the good which came from God alone was operating; where man co-operated in this good it was co-operating. St Thomas, too, followed this division, explaining them as two different aspects of grace, not separate entities.[3] Operating and co-operating grace[4] were found in both sanctifying and actual grace. Sanctifying grace was operating (*non effective, sed formaliter*) in rendering a soul agreeable to God, and co-operating as the beginning of a meritorious act by a justified man working freely for good. Actual grace was operating in so far as its effect was a salutary action moved by God, and co-operating when the soul was moved at the same time. Thus, although the movement was from God, and without Him there would be no co-operation, man had a definite part to play. For Bradwardine, however, this was not apparent: God moved the will to want good (operating) and then co-operated with the will in achieving good. 'He operates that we should wish; when we so wish.... He co-operates that we should perfect [our wish].'[5] There was, with Bradwardine, clearly not the same element of free will. It was God who both operated and co-operated; and indeed Bradwardine used this very expression when he said: 'By co-operating God perfects in us what He started by operating....'[6] The same dependence upon God's will in the entire process is evident here as it was in the case of making an action efficacious. Bradwardine had gone to the other extreme in his reply to the modern Pelagians: where they allowed no room for grace, he had excluded free will from any part at all. Although of quite a different kind, Bradwardine's unorthodoxy is apparent.

The second way in which Bradwardine deviated from tradition was in his denial of the effect of human dispositions upon the degree of grace awarded. This was the position taken up by Luther who, in refusing to recognize grace as an infused virtue, but simply as faith, denied that good or bad acts could have the slightest effect in augmenting justice.[7] In contrast, St Thomas

---

[1] *Dict. théol. cath.* VI, cols. 1653 *et seq.*   [2] *Ibid.* (Denzinger, 182, 192).
[3] *Ibid.*   [4] See Appendix II below.   [5] *De causa Dei*, p. 366.
[6] *Ibid.*   [7] *Dict. théol. cath.* VI, cols. 1626 *et seq.*

had held that the degree of grace differed according to the different disposition at the time of infusion, although these differences were primarily due to God's will. Moreover, it was commonly held that grace could be augmented by virtuous actions and the observance of God's precepts.[1] The Council of Trent, in reply to Luther, had reaffirmed these doctrines.[2] Similarly, the value of negative dispositions, in destroying obstacles to grace, had been recognized; and, in the case of positive dispositions towards receiving grace, the Second Council of Orange had held these to be necessary for sanctifying grace, through actual grace.[3]

Bradwardine, however, disregarded the human element in these operations; and he never tired of dismissing all claims for the movements of free will as Pelagian: 'It is therefore a damnable Pelagian error to participate in faith or grace, namely, in initiating it or augmenting it ... for the whole is totally from God.'[4] In the light of tradition and doctrine it is clear that Bradwardine had overstepped the limits in assigning no part at all to human dispositions; under Bradwardine's ordinance man virtually ceased to be the material cause of grace, and its award approached more to an arbitrary exercise on God's part. The words of the Council of Trent form a fitting commentary on his views: 'If anyone saith that man's free will, moved and excited by God, nowise co-operates ... let him be anathema.'[5]

FREE WILL

Over free will there was the same extremity of views between Bradwardine and the modern Pelagians as over grace. As a result each went beyond the bounds of tradition. This held that, while God had endowed man with freedom to choose between different courses of action, as the result of the fall his own free will did not suffice to overcome temptation and avoid sin. Grace, as we have seen, was needed for fulfilling God's mandates, healing man's fallen nature, and leading him to God.

The history of the doctrines of free will is so inextricably part of that of original sin that the two cannot be separated. Up to the

---

[1] *Ibid.*   [2] *Ibid.* col. 1627 (Denzinger, 800, 803, 834, 842).
[3] *Ibid.* col. 1630 (Denzinger, 180).   [4] *De causa Dei*, p. 433.
[5] Session VI, taken from Garrigou-Lagrange, *op. cit.* II, p. 437.

time of Bradwardine and his contemporaries, its main development had come from St Augustine and later from the scholastic thinkers of the twelfth and thirteenth centuries. We have already mentioned the formative effect of the Pelagian controversy on St Augustine's views on grace, and this applies equally to free will. For him the fall had meant the weakening of free will and the transmission of this weakness, through propagation, to all mankind. St Augustine was so concerned for the lot of those damned (*massa damnata*) as its result that he made no real distinction between natural and supernatural goodness:[1] free will for him meant the power to do evil, when unattended by grace, and accordingly the whole of his attention was directed to the supernatural aids for leading man to salvation and for keeping him from sin. Grace was the essential antidote to the first man's loss of sanctity and, with it, his power to remain free from sin.

The Second Council of Orange[2] reaffirmed St Augustine's doctrine in every respect, regarding all goodness in supernatural terms and making no reference to moral natural actions.

With the twelfth and thirteenth centuries, and the growing attention to natural phenomena, the distinction between moral and supernatural became clearer. St Thomas held that, while there could be no distinction between what belonged to predestination and what to free will, as there was no distinction between what resulted from a first cause and what resulted from a second, man could do certain morally good deeds without grace.[3] Grace, he said, was needed for man to accomplish all his obligations and avoid all sin, a moral necessity which did not exist before the fall: *gratia elevans* had become *gratia sanans*.[4] Secondly, it was needed in addition to supernaturalize a natural action (*elevans*), as in the case of loving God above all, which came from a natural action, but required grace to observe His law. Those actions, on the other hand, in which grace was not required, included being able to obey the first precept, although a man could not completely carry it out. It was in this connexion that the distinction between the substance of an act (*substantia operum*) and the mode of acting (*quoad modum agendi*) was made.[5] The substance constituted

---

[1] *Dict. théol. cath.* xiv, 'Péché originale', cols. 385 *et seq.*
[2] *Ibid.* cols. 409 *et seq.*   [3] *Ibid.* vi, cols. 1578 *et seq.*
[4] *Ibid.* col. 1585.   [5] *Ibid.* cols. 1580–1.

what was morally required for a good action; the mode involved performing it, including its supernatural nature, and in this sense was accidental to it. Such a distinction made allowance for man's desire to do good as distinct from his limitations in achieving his aim: it took into account the fall in weakening man's moral fibre without, as in Luther's case, denying him any good at all.

The result of this distinction between substance and mode meant, firstly, that infidels could carry out good works, and, secondly, that every man in mortal sin did not necessarily sin every time he acted.[1] It allowed man a moral sphere in which he could act for good. This distinction between the moral and the supernatural was extended to the different aids which God could bring to a man. The *concursus naturalis* referred to natural moral actions and did not involve grace since no supernatural end was in question.[2]

We may conclude, then, that though grace was required to heal original sin, to prevent mortal sin and to fulfil God's mandates, there was a natural sphere in which good, moral actions might be carried out without it and where even one in sin could accomplish non-evil actions.

When we turn to the differing views of Bradwardine and the modern Pelagians we see how completely this balance between the moral and the supernatural was shattered. The modern Pelagians, as we have already noted above, reverted to many of the fundamental positions of their namesakes. In this case, however, they did not openly deny the *reatus* of original sin, nor the need or efficacy of baptism; they rather, in starting from God's *potentia absoluta*, did not regard man in his actual fallen state but as God could make him. This had the effect of making man's natural actions the preparation for glory and enabled them to be endowed with the same supernatural value which was traditionally reserved for grace.

One of the main sources of the modern Pelagians' breach with tradition was their neutrality to all but the actual fact.[3] This was extended not only to matters which were beyond experience, but also to the metaphysical properties in what was known: for Ockham and his followers there was all the difference between acknowledging the existence of individuals, such as Plato and

---

[1] *Ibid.*   [2] *Ibid.* col. 1588.   [3] See preceding chapter.

Socrates, and drawing conclusions about the human species. This was equally the case with the value of an act and its relation to a habit. Where tradition had taught that being was the foundation of any action—*agere sequitur esse*—the modern Pelagians saw nothing but the act itself as alone tangible: its value, or the habit from which it derived, was denied any real meaning. The result was that there could be no distinction between a moral and a supernatural action for the modern Pelagians, because an act was only an act. God alone, by His absolute power, endowed it with whatever value He thought fitting.

Once all actions were regarded as complete in themselves, two important consequences followed. The first was that, as we have seen, grace lost any intrinsic place. The second was that free will became the sole agent in a supernatural deed and all reward referred to its act, not to a supernatural habit, as held by tradition. Durandus and Ockham, for instance, regarded free will as capable of doing all that God willed to be necessary for salvation. Durandus, by making the moral order virtually self-sufficient and independent of God's aid, tended to ignore the traditional limitations of fallen man as though there were no call for grace in remaining free from sin. Moreover, he virtually made man's preparation for grace a *sine qua non* for its award, a position which closely approximated to Cassian's nine hundred years earlier. Ockham, too, showed the same neglect of the distinction between natural and supernatural acts, and the need for God's grace in the latter: with the rejection of supernatural habits God was able to deal directly with man, and free will's actions sufficed for His reward. 'All love of God', he said, 'can be natural . . . because God can accept an act of natural love in the same way as any other act derived from charity.'[1] This need only be compared with the views of St Augustine canonized by the Second Council of Orange mentioned above, to see how flagrantly they flouted the whole of tradition. Free will became the starting-point of all reward, a position of stark Pelagianism, though Ockham defended himself from the charge by denying that either God or man need make use of grace as a means to a meritorious action.[2]

The later sceptics tended to allot free will more definite powers,

---

[1] Sentences, bk. 1, dist. 17, qu. 2; see pp. 189 *et seq.* below.
[2] See p. 197 below.

such as loving God of its own accord and fulfilling His mandates.[1] Such views were against the whole doctrine of grace and original sin, and, in essence, though shielded by God's *potentia absoluta*, heretical. They were condemned by the Council of Trent in the following terms. 'If human nature remained in that state of integrity in which it had been established (by God in Adam) it would not be able to maintain itself there of its own resources without the aid of its creator. Consequently, since it cannot, without the grace of God, preserve its integrity, how could it, without the grace of God, recover what it has lost?'[2] Bradwardine in rebutting his opponents went to the opposite extreme: not only did he, in keeping with dogma and tradition, make prevenient grace the beginning of all salutary action, but, in doing so, he denied any power to free will at all.[3] The same signs of this attitude, seen in his views on grace, are also present here. At no time did he talk in terms of man's natural goodness or consider his moral powers. Goodness for him was synonymous with grace, and had no existence apart from it.[4] This can be seen in his constant assertions that, because no moral virtue can be absolutely right or virtuous without charity, any work which is not from grace is in some way sinful;[5] that there can be no wisdom or justice[6] without the habits of wisdom or justice; and that there can be no righteousness except through grace.[7]

From these assertions Bradwardine draws three conclusions which are not in keeping with either tradition or dogma. The first is that, since there is no true virtue in an infidel, he cannot carry out a good action and that all the works of infidels are sinful.[8] The second is that, without grace, there can be no non-evil act or intention: 'ubi fides non erat bonum opus non erat.'[9] Moreover, Bradwardine refused to allow that a man could persevere in good for even one hour without grace, which was another way of saying that lack of grace meant instantaneous sin.[10] Conversely, he held that one endowed with the gift of final perseverance could not sin, because he could not fail finally to persevere.[11] The third way in which Bradwardine displayed his unorthodoxy was in his refusal

[1] See under Holcot, Buckingham, Woodham below.
[2] Council of Trent, 19th canon quoted in *Dict. théol. cath.*, VI, col. 1577.
[3] See pp. 71–2 above.　　[4] *De causa Dei*, p. 497; and pp. 71–2 above.
[5] *De causa Dei*, p. 327.　[6] *Ibid.* p. 329.　[7] *Ibid.* p. 330.　[8] *Ibid.* p. 327.
[9] *Ibid.* p. 393.　　[10] *Ibid.* p. 497.　　[11] *Ibid.* p. 465.

to accept the division (mentioned above)[1] between the substance of an act and its mode. This is eloquent testimony to his refusal to allow free will any moral qualities which could exist in man without a supernatural aid. It is particularly striking that Bradwardine went so far as to imply that those doing so were involved in the Pelagian heresy.[2]

Each of these main points finds its reply either in the traditional doctrines of Bradwardine's time or in subsequent condemnations. The case of infidels and sinners being able to carry out a good action was generally accepted; so, too, was the division between the mode and the substance of an act attacked by Bradwardine. On the question of one persevering in the avoidance of all sin, the Council of Trent held that this applied only to the Virgin.[3] Finally, Bradwardine's virtual denial of free will's ability to do any good was rejected as matter of faith, in opposition to Luther's view;[4] and the similar position taken up by Jansen and his followers was condemned by Innocent X.[5]

MERIT

The place accorded to merit depends ultimately upon that given to grace and free will. If grace is not considered the beginning of all salutary activity (the position of the modern Pelagians), then a meritorious act will be regarded as the work of free will and a natural phenomenon. On the other hand, when grace is made the source of all supernatural reward, merit will be the effect of grace and not its cause. These were the conflicting views of the modern Pelagians and Bradwardine.

From a theological point of view, merit was regarded as the reward due to a salutary action which derived from grace. Although from free will, it was only possible through the direct influence of a supernatural aid. Accordingly, the traditional view of merit must be seen as an integral part of the doctrines of grace and free will. Only if a man were free from sin and moved by God

[1] *De causa Dei*, p. 335.
[2] 'Alii adhuc fingunt, quod homo sine gratia ex seipso potest perficere divina mandata secundum substantiam operis, non tamen intentionem mandantis, quae est quod fiant in gratia' (*ibid.*).
[3] *Dict. théol. cath.* XII, cols. 1278 and 1291 (Denzinger, 804, 833).
[4] *Ibid.* col. 1290 (Denzinger, 817).
[5] *Ibid.* (Denzinger, 1092, 1093).

could He carry out a salutary operation; his own free will, alone, did not suffice to reach Him.

With the thirteenth century, however, this general acceptance of a divine co-operation in a meritorious act became more precise; and a distinction, in keeping with the growing recognition of the natural, was made between what was from a directly supernatural impulsion and what could come from free will. By this means, merit was divided in two kinds: strict, absolute merit (*de condigno*) and a relative, conditional award (*de congruo*).[1] Merit *de condigno*, as mentioned above,[2] was distinguished from merit *de congruo* as being the product of sanctifying grace; it was supernatural in origin and not subject to human actions. It was the effect of grace, not its cause, and therefore beyond the reach of man. As such, the traditional teachings on grace and free will were expressed in merit *de condigno*: it was the reward which could come only from grace. To aver otherwise would be to fall into the error of Pelagius that man could win his own salvation by gaining God's reward for deeds carried out by his own powers. Merit *de condigno* followed justification and justification could only come from sanctifying grace, its principle.

Merit *de congruo*, on the other hand, did not depend upon a state of habitual grace; but only upon an actual, external grace. Thus a man not in a state of grace could, say, hear a sermon (an external grace) which would help him to regret his sins; if he did so, and repented, he merited *de congruo*; and this could then lead to his receiving a supernatural habit. This made merit *de congruo* not absolute in itself, but dependent upon God's liberality in accepting a disposition to good from one not in grace. While merit *de condigno* corresponded to the mode of an action, merit *de congruo* corresponded to its substance.[3]

The modern Pelagians made great play with merit *de congruo* as the direct path to salvation: it enabled them to avoid the need for grace and it recognized the value of human dispositions. This meant firstly that God could deal directly with the acts of free will, making human dispositions the initial agent in gaining God's acceptance. It mattered not the quality of such an action; God could take it up and endow it with whatever reward He willed. In

---

[1] *Ibid.* x, cols. 684 *et seq.*   [2] See pp. 74–9 above.
[3] See *Dict. théol. cath.* VI, col. 1581.

the second place, this put the onus of reward upon God's will alone, enabling Him, in His absolute power, to by-pass all the requirements of His ordained power.

Clearly, then, to accept merit *de congruo* was to offer full scope for God's *potentia absoluta*; or, put another way, merit *de congruo* was the medium for God's *potentia absoluta*: it enabled Him to dispense with habits; it offered sin as good a chance of reward as grace; it put the onus upon God and gave the glory to man.

We are not here concerned with the details of the modern Pelagians' use of merit *de congruo*; these can be seen below. Its importance lies in providing an escape for the need for grace in winning God's absolute merit and acceptance (*de condigno*). By its use, grace was of no intrinsic account in the *processus* of salvation: a man could do all that God wanted of him by his own powers without grace. It dispensed with a constant order between grace and glory, sin and reprobation. Above all, free will alone became the constant factor. In the case of contrition, for example, Ockham went beyond tradition when he held that a sinner's contrition, in being worthy of merit *de congruo*, was the means for the remission of his sins.[1] To say that hating sin sufficed for its expulsion and the infusion of grace, erred in two ways: first it gave the will a power to detest sin which by tradition only came from grace; secondly, instead of making this grace the result of either a supernatural gift or the sacraments, Ockham gave free will the power to obtain this grace unaided. This came perilously near to Pelagianism in making a natural movement the *sine qua non* for grace.

The same rejection of the traditional order between grace, merit and glory was expressed by the other modern Pelagians when they held that the right use of free will could bring merit;[2] that even one in mortal sin could act in such a way that it were meet for God to reward him;[3] and that an act of free will was far more pleasing to God than any habit.[4] These opinions clearly controverted the orthodox doctrines on both grace and free will: they denied the necessity of grace and exalted the powers of free will. In thus putting the natural before the divine the modern Pelagians participated in the same offence as their namesakes;

[1] See p. 204 below.   [2] See p. 218 below.   [3] See p. 245 below.
[4] See pp. 246–9 below.

and the condemnation of the Second Council of Orange, addressed to the latter, applies equally to them: 'God loves us so that we shall be [in His grace] by His gift, not so that we are by our own merit: since no merit precedes grace, a reward is due to good works if they are produced; but grace which is not a due, precedes [the good works] that they may be produced.'[1]

Bradwardine's reply was quite simple: there could be no such thing as merit *de congruo* because God never acted conditionally and man could not influence His actions. This was one more sign of his rejection of every deed on the part of free will. Although the Council of Trent avoided the term merit *de congruo*, as it aroused controversy, it held to the ideas it expressed. The Council spoke specifically of 'the necessity of a preparation' for justification,[2] a position quite contrary to Bradwardine's, which we have already seen condemned.

ATTRIBUTES OF GOD

Until the rise of Ockhamism God's attributes had always been given full expression in His nature. These included all those virtues which related to His own being, such as infinity, omnipresence and eternity, and to His operations, such as wisdom, providence, love, mercy and justice. They were in no way separate from God's essence but constituted an indivisible self-subsisting being. All were agreed upon this, though there were different ways of explaining this unity. St Thomas saw the divine essence as formally self-subsisting being; its attributes were not formally distinct, but only virtually; that is, the distinction between, say, God's omnipotence and wisdom was only in the human mind; omnipotence and wisdom were inherent in His essence without being formally distinct. This was in contradistinction to Duns Scotus, who made these attributes formally distinct in themselves before any human act of intellection. Similarly, where St Thomas saw infinity as the mode of God's attributes, Duns regarded the principle of God's essence as infinite being. Nevertheless, for both, God's attributes existed as qualities which could be distinguished and discussed.

[1] *Dict. théol. cath.* x, 'Mérite', col. 656 (Denzinger, 182 and 191).
[2] *Ibid.* col. 754 (Denzinger, 797, 798).

Ockham and his followers rejected this outlook. As only individuals counted, God's essence was merely the grouping of all the
perfections with no need to seek a logical priority among them.
Terms such as goodness and wisdom were merely verbal
distinctions. This was given fullest expression in the concept of
God's *potentia absoluta*, which, at the sceptics' hands, became a
means of denying all God's attributes except His will; or, put
another way, subsuming God's whole nature under His will. The
effect of this was, as we shall see, to ignore any constant principles
according to which God operated. Not only did grace become
superfluous and without intrinsic value, but so did every other
value. This outlook involved two very important breaks with
tradition. The first was that God became involved in the neutrality which the sceptics extended to all but fact. Wisdom and
mercy lost an intrinsic place in His nature, and, as a result, did not
necessarily guide and inform His actions. God could act irra-
tionally as, for example, in making a man hate Him,[1] revealing
to one in grace his future damnation;[2] or rewarding one for hating
Him, while punishing another for loving Him above all.[3] Moreover, He could mislead Christ and cause Christ to mislead the
elect;[4] and, most heinous of all, God could, according to Adam
of Woodham, sin.[5] It needs no great effort to see how contrary to
tradition such notions of Him were: He lost all resemblance to
the creator of revelation and tradition and His ordinances became
meaningless.

In the second place, the refusal to accept the traditional view of
God's nature, and of created standards, led to the rejection of
metaphysics. Being as a concept could find no place in an outlook
which denied all reality to anything but an individual act. Thus
the sceptics' rejection of habits, as of no account in judging an
act, led to more than the denial of a place to grace; it denied the
view that every action was itself the result of being: the Thomist
maxim *agere sequitur esse* became one more for the scrap-heap of
superfluities. Without being, there could be no ordered relationship between God and His creatures, the whole foundation
of scholasticism. Hence the breach they made with the past.

[1] See p. 244 below.   [2] See p. 245 below.   [3] See p. 219 below.
[4] See p. 253 below.   [5] See p. 254 below.

FUTURE CONTINGENTS

The question of future contingents is, as we have seen above,[1] another way of viewing the relation between predestination and free will. It raises the time-honoured question of how to reconcile God's eternal ordinances with the contingency which belongs to free will: if God has already foreseen how Socrates will act, how can Socrates be free not to act? Until the fourteenth century the problem had been resolved primarily as a matter of faith, not proof. Omniscience and eternal foreknowledge were accepted attributes of God;[2] predestination the accepted source of all that was created. Accordingly, the reason why God predestined man and yet man could act of his own free will was part of the mystery of the supernatural and could never be subjected to a full-fledged rational explanation. St Thomas had come closest to describing the relation between God's will and man's will in his view that every action by a creature was both entirely from its own movement as a secondary cause and entirely from God as first. Hence the very power of a secondary cause to act freely was the result of the first cause moving it to act freely. It was a proof of the excellence of God's will that He could create man to act freely.

So long as this framework was upheld and the eternity of God's ways acknowledged, there was no real danger, either to God's omniscience or to man's free will. Ultimately, the latter had to derive from the former. As St Thomas said: 'the knowledge of God is the cause of things in so far as His will is joined to them'.[3] Moreover, the future was present from all eternity, since an eternal cause had to produce it.[4] With Duns Scotus, however, came the great change in outlook to be found among the sceptics. In his emphasis upon God's will as the source of all His actions, Duns helped to break the causal chain between God's will and

---

[1] See pp. 103–9.

[2] *Dict. théol. cath.* XIV, 'Science', cols. 1598 *et seq.* We are not concerned here with the aspects of God's knowledge: speculative and practical. For all that is outside Himself, it is both, since He not only knows a thing as possible but as it will be realized. St Thomas divided God's knowledge into vision and simple intelligence: the former applied to actual things, past, present and future; the latter to the merely possible. Thus His knowledge of vision, as dealing with real things, involved His approbation and, in this sense, was their cause.

[3] From Garrigou-Lagrange, *Dieu*, II, p. 475.   [4] *Ibid.*

free will, a breach which had such marked effect upon the modern Pelagians. While Duns did not turn God's will loose in their manner, or invoke His absolute power with such persistence, he refused to see any means of correlating the divine with the created. For him, God's will was so contingent that there could be no clearly enunciated mode of His actions.

Duns's view of the future rested on two supports:[1] the first was to make God's knowledge practical only through His will; that is, all that God knows as real was the result of His willing it. In thus identifying God's external knowledge with His will, Duns made it active, approbative and undetermined by anything save His own willing. This led to the second innovation: the separation of God's knowledge into past, present and future instead of eternally the same. Duns rejected this eternity of time in God on the grounds that it would be false for God still to know as present what had become past. Accordingly God distinguished temporally, not eternally.

That both of these views were fraught with the most vital consequences can be seen in the disputes between Bradwardine and his opponents. If God's will were made the source of His external knowledge the effect could be twofold: either all order could be destroyed, breaking any connexion between God's will and free will on the grounds that God's will was too free to allow of any certain foreknowledge; or everything could be harnessed to a preordained and immutable will, which, by subjecting everything to its minute control, destroyed all contingency, the future becoming merely the temporal expression of an eternally determined course. Whichever way was chosen, it destroyed the balance between God's omniscience and free will. Either God became too free to have eternally certain knowledge, as with the modern Pelagians, or the immutability of His will allowed no autonomy to free will, as with Bradwardine.

It was not without reason that both Bradwardine and the sceptics should take over Duns's voluntarism, in fashioning their outlook on future contingents: it provided Bradwardine with his most effective instrument for asserting God's control over His creatures, permitting nothing to come about but by God's immediate direction; it enabled the sceptics to give His creatures

---

[1] Sentences, bk. I, dist. 39, 8 and 9 (Wadding edition, 1639).

full autonomy in its name, thereby discussing the future in natural and temporal terms, as it affected free will.

The consequences of Duns's rejection of the identity of time in God were even more far-reaching, for they involved nothing less than the refusal to exempt God's knowledge from temporal change. Thus for the first time the future came to constitute a real problem. Far more than his making God's will the source of His knowledge—a position, after all, which only gave God's will a more direct role—this threatened God's omniscience. God no longer knew the future *sub specie aeternitatis*, as knowledge ever present in Him, but was made subject to temporal considerations. In consequence, if God were now to know the future, as future, before it came about, He would have antedated it and robbed it of contingency; if He did not know it, His omniscience was impaired. This was the problem to which Duns's second breach with tradition led. For the first time the problem of the future involved the whole foundations of belief and these disputes of the fourteenth century were, for that reason, of a very different order from those of the sixteenth over Molina's middle knowledge.

St Thomas had recognized the consequences that would arise from distinguishing time in God when he said: 'The future is present in God and so it is definite ... but while it is future it is indifferent.'[1] In other words, to regard the future as future would be to introduce the very neutrality and indeterminacy which were the stock-in-trade of scepticism. The sceptics eagerly took up this separation of past, present and future, as we shall see below. They defended the future as independent, both in God and outside Him; while, in reply, Bradwardine reached a position which virtually denied the future at all.[2]

The sceptics, in their defence of the future, followed two different alternatives. From their common standpoint of making God recognize the future, they either denied that God knew future contingent events until they came to pass (Aureole, Durandus of St Pourçain and Holcot) or they affirmed that God's knowledge of contingents must be as contingent as the contingents He knew; for, otherwise, if it were certain, it would destroy their contingency (Buckingham and Adam of Woodham). In each case they sinned against tradition, for they impaired God's knowledge

[1] *De veritate*, qu. 2, art. 12.   [2] See pp. 106–9 above.

either in its extent or its certainty, and He no longer remained omniscient. Moreover, both sides invoked revelation in their support: Holcot maintained that the very certainty of revelation prevented God from knowing what was contingent and therefore uncertain.[1] Buckingham[2] and Woodham[3] held that, because revelation applied to the future, and what was future might never be, the truths revealed in His Word were contingent and might never come to pass. Accordingly, God could mislead Christ and Christ in turn could mislead the elect. Though Holcot defended God's revelation as eternal truth he did so at the expense of His omniscience; on the other hand, Buckingham and Woodham maintained His omniscience at the expense of His revelation. While the consequences of the latter outlook were more flagrantly contrary to tradition, Holcot, even so, cannot be absolved. Bradwardine, in his reply, went to the extent of denying the independent existence of the future. As we saw above, the future was as determined as the past and present in that it could not fail to take place.[4] Although Bradwardine, as ever, started from the side of tradition, with the sole intent of defending it, he reached a position which once more denied all autonomy to man and any real freedom to his will.

Thus in all these questions examined above, the same contrast between the claims of free will and those of God's will distinguishes them throughout. In every case it was the sceptics who violated the need for a *concursus supernaturalis*, whether over grace, free will, merit or the future. Similarly, Bradwardine, in reply, was so concerned to vindicate God's place that he could find none for man; for Bradwardine there was no *concursus naturalis*. This is the distinction between the two sides: the modern Pelagians were culpable because they wished to exclude God from any real part in the natural at all. Bradwardine, in contrast, allotted Him all. While the former dispensed with Him, the latter mistook the manner of His actions. Their respective positions must be assessed accordingly.

---

[1] See pp. 224–7 below.   [2] See pp. 234–41 below.
[3] See pp. 249–54 below.   [4] See pp. 106–9 above.

CHAPTER X

DURANDUS OF ST POURÇAIN: ONE OF THE PRECURSORS

THERE is more than one reason for Durandus of St Pourçain to be considered among Bradwardine's opponents. The central one is that he provides an essential part of what may be called the pre-history of scepticism.[1] Although there is no direct evidence of an influence upon Ockham, his system shows such signs of a breakdown in the balance between the natural and the supernatural that he cannot be ignored. Originally a Thomist, Durandus tended ultimately towards the indeterminism preached by Ockham and his followers, but he reached it in a different way. As a Dominican, he did not reject Aristotle's hierarchy of causes as the other Pelagians did; he used it to give men and secondary causes greater freedom of movement. This, combined with his use of God's *potentia absoluta*, led to views on grace and future contingents which were shared by all Bradwardine's opponents mentioned here.

The second reason is that Durandus's system is quite opposed to Bradwardine's. While Bradwardine has no place for anything but God's will, Durandus has hardly a place for God's will at all. More specifically, Durandus makes the created order so autonomous that it is self-sufficient in all things natural; it is only with supernatural matters that God need be involved. Otherwise, His will is only an indirect cause in all that man, and His creatures, do. There are clear traces here of the original Thomist division between nature and grace being pushed to the point of rupture. Although this is at the opposite pole from Ockham's voluntarism, where God's will as the cause of everything cannot be described, the same indeterminacy results; for in each case the actions of God's will cannot be ascertained. Thus there is no choice but to

---

[1] He died 1332. See J. Koch's *Durandus de S. Porciano* (Münster, 1927); he puts the date of the first of Durandus's three 'Commentaries on the Sentences' as 1308 and the third as 1327 (p. 399).

look to His creatures as the only sure evidence. In Durandus's case this results from the almost self-sufficient character of natural forces; in that of Ockham, it comes through God's will being outside human terms of reference; but, in both cases, the ultimate effect is the same: to discount God, for all practical purposes, in human actions. There is here ample cause for a clash between Bradwardine and Durandus.

The third point of discord between Durandus and Bradwardine springs from the second. Durandus, in denying anything approaching divine determinism, is not committed to denying the power of natural forces, such as the stars, the planets, and the spheres. He is prepared to allow them an over-all effect upon all things created and an indirect effect upon man. This, too, flies directly in the face of Bradwardine's repeated denials of the power of astral, or any other non-divine, necessity. For these reasons, Durandus offers an important challenge to Bradwardine's belief, and one of which it is hard to believe Bradwardine was unaware.

THE SUPERNATURAL VIRTUES

Two features stand out in Durandus's views here. The first is the virtual self-sufficiency of the moral and the natural; the second, his use of the distinction between God's two kinds of power so that God, by His *potentia absoluta*, is able to evade the decrees of His ordained power. In both cases Durandus marks the transition to Ockham and the succeeding Pelagians: he does not reach Ockham's conclusion that free will and God's will are the only two essentials for an act of merit, nor those of the others that God's will alone counts, free will having no integral part to play. Rather he sees the role of free will as initiating the grace and glory that God awards: it is neither the direct mover of Ockham, nor the undefined element of the later sceptics; it is more limited than the first and more constant than the second.

Durandus, while sometimes giving them the different designation of *necessitas absoluta* and *necessitas conditionata*, employs God's two kinds of power to render created grace and charity unnecessary. There does not, by God's absolute necessity, have to be any relation between the receipt of charity and the ability to do good.[1] God can wish for man the highest good of which he is capable (beatitude) without his possessing habitual grace.[2] While Durandus does not go on to draw the conclusions of Ockham and his followers that, therefore, grace lacks intrinsic value or that one can be in grace and yet be hated by God, he has opened the way for such an attitude. For himself, however, he appears content merely to show that grace is not the *sine qua non* of glory.

From this Durandus discusses the cause of charity; it depends, he says, upon the influence of God and the response of the subject into which it is infused. The disposition of the created will to receive charity influences God in bestowing it; the greater this disposition of free will towards good, and its revulsion against evil, the greater the charity infused.[3] In this way Durandus makes the human element inseparable from the infusion of grace and charity: although these supernatural gifts are from God, the man most disposed towards them will receive them in the greatest

[1] 'Responsio . . . et sic ad quaestionem istam dicenda sunt tria. Primum est quod homo potest esse, et est Deo gratus et charus antequam habeat gratiam et charitatem sibi formaliter inhaerentem. Secundum est quod ad esse deo gratum vel charum non sequitur necessario necessitate absoluta quod homo sit habiturus quandoque gratiam vel charitatem sibi formaliter inhaerentem. Tertium est quod ad esse deo gratum vel charum sequitur de necessitate conditionata (scilicet ex suppositione ordinationis divinae) quod homo sit habiturus quandoque gratiam et charitatem habitualem formaliter inhaerentem.' (Commentary on the Sentences, bk. I, dist. 17, qu. 1, p. 46 c.)

[2] '. . . sed deus potest velle homini bonum, et summum bonum cuius ipse est capax (scilicet beatitudinem) absque hoc quod velit ei dare gratiam habitualem vel charitatem quantum est de potentia absoluta secundum quam deus potest dare et homo recipere gloriam vel beatitudinem sine gratia habituali praevia, ergo ad esse Deo dilectum vel ad esse Deo gratum vel charum non sequitur ex necessitate absoluta quod homo sit quandoque habiturus gratiam vel charitatem habitualem' (*ibid.* p. 46 d).

[3] '. . . Charitas autem dependet ex duobus scilicet ex Deo influente, et subiecto recipiente . . .' (*ibid.* qu. 3, p. 47 d).

'Alio modo attenditur inaequalitas ex parte subiecti quo ad dispositionem subiecti per quam homo reddit se aliqualiter dignum charitate saltem de congruo, et haec dispositio est conatus ad bonum qui requiritur in omnibus adultis . . . Sic dico quod infallibiliter secundum proportionem conatus datur charitas; Cuius ratio est, quia immediata dispositio voluntatis ad recipiendum charitatem est amor boni, et detestatio mali, voluntas ergo illa plus disponitur in qua actus illi magis intenduntur. Sed voluntas magis disposita recipit perfectiorem charitatem quantum est ex parte sui, sicut omne subiectum magis dispositum recipit perfectius impressionem agentis, ergo secundum intentionem conatus est intentio charitatis' (*ibid.* qu. 3, pp. 47 d and 48 a).

measure. Moreover, those who, already in a state of grace, put it to the best use will augment it,[1] just as those who misuse it diminish it.[2]

Bradwardine opposes each of these different assertions: as we have seen, grace for him is the source of all goodness and the sole means to glory. It is, moreover, entirely gratuitous, in no way dependent upon any human dispositions.[3] These are, on the contrary, the result of grace freely given by God. There is, he says, no virtue, philosophical or moral, without charity and grace, and he attacks those as Pelagian who say that man can prepare himself for God's grace, which will then be forthcoming.[4] Bradwardine calls it a damnable Pelagian error to make man participate in faith or grace either as initiating, or augmenting, them. Far from one coming from man and the other from God, the whole is given by Him.[5]

Durandus's position over grace, then, allows a definite scope for free will after the manner of Cassian; but, what is equally important, he undermines the need for supernatural habits by his

[1] 'De tertio sciendum quod non omnis actus ex charitate procedens meretur augmentum charitatis, *sed solum illi qui sunt secundum proportionem charitatis informantis voluntatem, vel excellentiores*, puta ex toto conatu voluntatis. Cuius ratio est, *quia ille solus dignus est accipiendis qui bene* utitur iam acceptis, sed habens habitum iam intensum et remisse operans non utitur debito modo suo habitu, quia actus non proportionatur intensioni habitus, ergo per tales actus non meremur augmentum charitatis sed solum per illos qui excellunt vel adaequant ipsum habitum (bk. 1, dist. 17, qu. 8, p. 51 d).
(In this and further extracts in this chapter, italic type has been used by me for emphasis; it is not in the original.)

[2] '... ergo sicut charitas educitur de imperfecto gradu ad perfectiorem per augmentum sic potest reduci de perfecto ad imperfectiorem per diminutionem ... charitas numquam minuitur nisi per demeritum nostrum de condigno, licet detur a principio propter solum meritum de congruo ...' *(ibid. qu. 10, pp. 52 c and 53 b).

[3] 'Contra quosdam Pelagianos dicentes hominem posse ex se tantum debite praeparare; quod si faciat deus dabit gratiam suam gratis' (*De causa Dei*, chapter 37, p. 316).

[4] 'Ex his igitur plane constat, quod nulla virtus Philosophica aut moralis, sine gratia charitatis, est simpliciter vera virtus recta, aut iusta, nec valet erigere voluntatem creatam ad Deum super omnia propter Deum gratuito diligendum, quin potius ipsam deflectit, deflexamue detinet, ad cuiuslibet commodium proprium ad seipsum. De necessitate ergo requiritur aliqua virtus superior supernaturalis, heroica, et divina, puta gratia gratis data a Deo ad erigendum voluntatem creatam ex seipsa' (*ibid.* p. 329).

[5] 'Est ergo error Pelagianorum damnabilis participare fidem aut gratiam, scilicet eius initium et augmentum, unum scilicet dando Deo, alterum vero nobis, totum enim est totaliter dandum Deo' (*ibid.* p. 433).

use of God's *potentia absoluta*. We shall see how both of these aspects are taken up by his successors.

FREE WILL

It is in his views on free will that Durandus illustrates his departure from the Thomist tradition; he extends the distinction between nature and grace to mean their almost complete separation so that it is hard to find any real point of contact between them. It leads to Durandus's viewing man in purely natural and moral terms which offer no apparent dependence upon the supernatural. Only where the latter is concerned is grace involved. The result is to exalt man's natural powers to an unwonted degree. In the first place, man, even in his actual state of sin, can avoid transgressions against natural law, though not against supernatural decrees,[1] where he needs divine aid.[2] He can fulfil affirmative precepts, such as honouring his parents, without his being in grace. Such deeds, however, do not go beyond natural law and they cannot gain eternal life or supernatural recognition.[3]

[1] 'Opus aliquod potest esse bonum dupliciter. Uno modo bonitate morali, quae est ex conformitate ad rectam rationem. . . . Alio modo bonitate meritoria. Primo modo potest homo sine gratia bonum opus, quia ubi sunt principia sufficientia alicuius operationis potest esse et illa operatio, sed in homine absque gratia sunt sufficientia principia bonae operationis moralis, quare, etc. Minor probatur, quia recta ratio agibilium, et voluntas per eam recta sufficiunt ad bonam operationem moralem, haec autem sunt in homine sine gratia ergo etc.' (Comm. Sent. bk. II, dist. 28, qu. 2, p. 154 a).

[2] '. . . distinguendum est de peccatis mortalibus, quia quaedam sunt contra praecepta iuris naturalis, quaedam vero sunt contra praecepta iuris divini et supernaturalis. Dicendum ergo quod peccata quae sunt contra praecepta iuris naturalis tantum possunt vitari ab homine existente in peccato praedicto modo scilicet secundum solum reatum, sed non illa quae sunt contra praecepta iuris supernaturalis. Primum patet ut prius, quia si talia peccata non possent vitari sine gratia hoc esset propter defectum gratiae vel ratione peccati praecedentis. . . . Item bonitas moralis non stat cum peccato quod est contra dictamen iuris naturalis, sed homo sine gratia potest in omne opus bonum bonitate morali quae est ex obiecto, fine, et circumstantiis . . . ergo quilibet potest sine gratia vitare quodcunque peccatum quod est contra dictamen solius iuris naturalis' (*ibid*. qu. 3, p. 154 c).

[3] 'Et eodem modo in praeceptis affirmitivis nullus est transgressus si faciat quod praecipitur, puta quod honoret parentes, licet non sit in gratia, quamvis non perveniat ad finem intentum a praecipiente, videlicet ad hoc ut facta sua sint remunerabilia vita eterna. . . .'

'Non enim est peccatum mortale, nisi sit contra aliquod praeceptum. Et ideo sicut homo sine gratia potest vitare peccata mortalia, sic potest implere praecepta' (*ibid*. qu. 4, p. 155 a).

Secondly, a man can prepare himself for grace without God's special help; for no supernatural gift is forthcoming to a man unless he prepare the way for it by the use of his free will. Were this not a condition of grace, it would be given to all men irrespective of their own efforts towards gaining it.[1] Thus, although a man cannot earn God's predestination without having previously been endowed with grace, he can prepare himself to receive grace of his own resources. This comes very close to Pelagianism and Bradwardine certainly regarded it so. Chapter 37 of *De causa Dei* is headed: 'Against certain Pelagians who say that man can, of his own powers, duly prepare himself [for grace]; that if he does so God will freely reward him with grace.'[2] This is to ignore the truth that only with God's special help can man rightly direct himself; nor does grace necessarily follow from such a disposition in a man.[3] It need hardly be reiterated that Bradwardine turns his face against any suggestion that men, either before or after the fall, could ever do good by themselves; as we have seen, it is in the very nature of men, as of all creatures, to be incapable of independent action; only with God's participation can they act for good.[4]

Thirdly, free will, for Durandus, springs from men's natural powers and is not generated by God; His part is only to conserve

---

[1] 'Quod homo possit se praeparare ad gratiam sine novo dono habituali sibi divinitus infuso, omnes concedunt, et merito, quia si homo indigeret tali dono ad praeparandum se ad gratiam per eandem rationem indigeret dono ad praeparandum se ad iam dictum donum: nullum enim donum supernaturale datur, nisi praeparatis in habentibus usum liberi arbitrii, alioquin daretur omnibus, quod non est verum . . . *ergo praeparatio ad gratiam non requirit aliquod habituale donum, et hoc omnes omnes concedunt* . . . si tamen gratia sit habituale donum tamen ad eam potest homo se disponere pure ut videtur per liberum arbitrium absque tali speciali motione. Ideo videtur aliter esse dicendum, quod si speciale adiutorium vocetur immediata motio voluntatis a deo, sine tali potest homo se praeparare ad gratiam, quia illud bonum quod habet ad gratiam immediatum ordinem videtur esse praeparatorium ad ipsam, sed bonum morale est huiusmodi. *Quum ergo in tale bonum possit homo sine immediata motione voluntatis a Deo, patet quod absque tali adiutorio potest se homo ad gratiam praeparare*' (bk. II, dist. 28, qu. 5, p. 155 a and b).

[2] *De causa Dei*, p. 313.

[3] 'Nullus tamen aliquid horum potest, hoc se quouismodo disponere sine Deo specialiter id agente. . . . Verumtamen collatio gratiae non semper sequitur praeparationem huiusmodi, sicut nec ipsam gratiam collatam perseuerantia, praedestinatiue ad vitam. . .' (*ibid*. p. 318).

[4] See above, p. 71.

the actions carried out by free will, not to direct them.[1] Sin is thus not God's responsibility but man's, and he is duly punished or rewarded for succumbing to it or resisting it.[2] The human will is capable of doing good in natural terms; it is only for the super-natural that God's help is necessary.[3] Grace in no way informs moral actions. Thus, contrary to Bradwardine, a right intention does not require faith for all its good actions, but only for those which are to be worthy of divine recompense.[4] It is this distinc-tion, he says, which allows infidels to be capable of good acts though they are unworthy of everlasting life. In the same way a supernaturally infused habit is only necessary for supernatural rewards; for moral virtue, the habits we acquire by our natural deeds suffice. Thus, so with man as with his whole system, Dur-andus makes a sharp delineation between his natural and super-natural requirements. Each has its own clear set of attributes which do not encroach upon the other. Left to themselves, there would seem to be no inherent reason why they should ever pass beyond their own boundaries; it is only when men are to be taken above their own natural limits that they need external aid, for they can then no longer rely upon themselves. At no time, how-ever, does Durandus make these limitations the centre of his attention. His system, far from making man's actual fallen state its foundation, is virtually an essay in natural self-sufficiency.

MERIT

It is over the question of merit that both the previous aspects of grace and free will receive their fullest expression. On the one hand, Durandus uses God's absolute power to dispense with the constant need for grace in a meritorious action; on the other, he

[1] '. . . Minor probatur, quia deus non est causa actionum liberi arbitrii nisi quia liberum arbitrium ab ipso et est et conservatur. . .' (Comm. Sent. bk. II, dist. 37, qu. I, p. 166 a).

[2] '. . . deus non est immediate auctor huius vel illius peccati sed mediante libero arbitrio cui imputatur bona vel mala actio ratione suae libertatis qua se determinat ad hoc vel illud et sic imputatur ei ad culpam vel meritum et sic praemiatur vel punitur' (ibid.).

[3] Ibid. dist. 39, qu. 3, p. 169.

[4] 'Restat ergo dicendum, quod directio intentionis per fidem non requiritur ad omnem bonitatem sed solum ad meritoriam vitae eternae . . .' (ibid. dist. 41, qu. I, p. 172 c).

finds scope for the natural powers of free will in initiating it. This combination does not sit uneasily upon him, for, unlike, say, Adam of Woodham, Durandus did not take God's *potentia absoluta* to such an extreme that all order was destroyed. On the contrary, Durandus does not at any time assert that good or bad lacks intrinsic meaning; that the act from free will is alone of consequence; or that God alone decides what to reward and what to punish without reference to anything but His own will. Each of these assertions is to be found among the later Pelagians, but Durandus himself stops short at having opened the way for them. He uses God's *potentia absoluta* primarily as the means of establishing the independent actions of free will.

Durandus's view of merit takes its start from the traditional concepts. There are, he says, two kinds of merit corresponding to the way in which an act is worthy of reward. The first is *de condigno*, where reward is due to the nature of the deed performed, and involves a strict proportion, based on true justice, between the deed and its worth. The second type of merit, *de congruo*, has no such inherent claim: there is nothing in the nature of such a deed to warrant recompense; this can only come from the liberality of him who grants the reward.[1]

Now, merit *de congruo*, because it lacks any complete value *per se*, cannot conform to a fixed standard. It does not, therefore, entail a state of grace; for any deed which it prompts has no worth in itself. Whether it is rewarded or not, lies not in its own achievements but in another's liberality in giving it consideration. Thus every sinner, says Durandus, though deprived of grace, can merit *de congruo* by repenting; his right intention, although alone incapable of making any demand upon God's grace, gives him a certain moral claim to be considered. If his cause is taken up,

---

[1] 'Quantum ad primum notandum est quod cum meritum dicatur actio per quam ei qui agit efficitur debitum aliquid dari, sicut est duplex debitum, ita est duplex meritum, quoddam est debitum de condigno quando ex natura et conditione operis efficitur homo dignus ut ex iustitia sibi reddatur talis merces propter aequalitatem inter opus et mercedem secundum istam aestimationem. Aliud est debitum de congruo quando non debetur talis merces ex natura operis sed redditur solum ex liberalitate dantis, aliud aliquid enim congruum est liberalem dare quod alius non meruit et condigno recipiente. Meritum ergo de condigno respicit debitum primo modo dictum, meritum autem de congruo respicit debitum secundo modo dictum' (bk. 1, dist. 17, qu. 2, p. 47 b).

however, this lies not in its justice but in God's liberality. God will then act from His bounty, not from His justice, and, for this, grace is not necessary in His creature.[1]

So far, Durandus has stated the generally accepted case for merit *de congruo*; but he now proceeds to go farther and into deeper waters. If, he says, God can by His absolute power acknowledge and reward repentance in sinners, He can, by the same token, reward such merit *de congruo* with glory and beatitude. In the same way, if Christ could thus receive the beatific vision, so could any other man. God could give glory to any man for a deed uninformed by grace, just as a king could reward a soldier with a horse for a similar act.[2]

Merit *de congruo*, in fact, has no limitations; it is as unrestricted as God's *potentia absoluta*, and as undefined. It can compass everything that God's will compasses: nothing is beyond its reach.

Merit *de condigno*, on the other hand, follows a much stricter and more absolute standard. In the first place, there are two kinds: strict merit *de condigno* (*proprie et stricte*) and a liberal, less rigid variety (*large*).[3] Strict merit *de condigno* demands full

---

[1] 'Hoc supposito dicendum est quod ad merendum solum de congruo non est necessarium ponere in nobis gratiam vel charitatem habitualem, quod patet quia secundum omnes peccator carens gratia poenitendo meretur de congruo gratiam iustificantem. . . . Congruum enim est ut bene utenti bonis naturae propter deum det deus bonae gratiae' (*ibid.*).

[2] 'Idem patet de gloriosa, posset enim Deus de potentia absoluta facere quod gloria vel beatitudo caderet sub tali merito. Si enim Christo data est beatitudo animae sine ullo merito, fortiori ratione posset deus gloriam dare cuicunque homini pro solo opere bono gratia non informato, ut sicut meremur gratiam per opus consimile. Quemadmodum enim pro consimili actu rex militi quandoque dat equum. Sic Deus pro eodem opere bono ex genere et circunstantiis posset absque gratia de potentia absoluta dare gloriam sive paradisum tanquam castrum quo nunc dat gratiam, vel charitatem tanquam equum quae nunquam excidit et utrobique esset meritum solum de congruo. Ratio autem omnium istorum est, quia meritum de congruo plus innititur liberalitati dantis quam valori operis. Dare autem gloriam pro opere bono ex genere et circunstantiis pro quo nunc datur gratia iustificans non excedit immo non adaequat liberalitatem divinam; ergo beatitudo vel gloria posset de potentia dei absoluta cadere sub merito talis operis, sicut nunc cadit gratia et sic propter tale meritum non est necesse ponere gratiam vel charitatem esse habitum creatum in anima' (*ibid.* b and c).

[3] '[De merito autem de congruo est subdistinguendum, quia quoddam est meritum de condigno dictum proprie et stricte et aliud large.] Primum meritum de condigno stricte et proprie sumptum est actio voluntaria propter quam alicui merces debetur ex iustitia sic quod si non reddatur ille ad quem pertinet

reward, such that, if this is not forthcoming, injustice will arise. This strict merit is governed on a rigid *quid pro quo* basis: each deed unconditionally merits a strict recompense; and he who carries out such a deed is a legitimate creditor.

Now, such a relationship, says Durandus, cannot exist between man and God, but only among men. The infinite difference in status between God and men precludes their acts being on a comparable footing. Grace is not, therefore, required for the operation of strict merit *de condigno*, since no divine element is involved. A simple transaction between, say, merchants must be judged according to elementary justice and does not require grace or charity.[1]

The other, more liberal, aspect of merit *de condigno* applies to actions involving both God and men. By God's *potentia ordinata* merit *de condigno* is necessary to all good deeds gaining divine recompense. Only those acts which are meritorious *de condigno* can be accepted by God as worthy of glory and eternal life. But for this to be possible men themselves must first be informed by grace and charity; for, left to their natural resources, they are incapable of approaching the divine heights. The supernatural infusion of grace and charity forms the bridge over this infinite gulf; grace and charity, therefore, are the prerequisites for merit *de condigno*.[2]

reddere iniuste facit et est simpliciter et proprie iniustus' (bk. 1, dist. 17, qu. 2, p. 47 c).

[1] 'Et tale meritum de condigno invenitur inter homines. . . . Et ideo propter meritum de condigno (cum sit homini simpliciter impossibile) non est ponendum in nobis gratiam vel charitatem habitualem' (*ibid.*).

[2] 'Aliud est meritum de condigno large sumptum pro quadam dignitate quam Deus ex sua ordinatione rationabili requirit in nobis ad hoc ut opera nostra acceptentur a Deo, et quidem ut remunerabilia vita eterna; et propter tale meritum necessarium est ponere in nobis gratiam vel charitatem habitualem' (*ibid.*).

'Est enim tale condignum ex suppositione divinae ordinationis et non absolute. . . . Inter hominem autem et deum non potest esse simpliciter iustum, sicut nec aequale, sed solum iustum secundum quid . . . quia totum quod est hominis bonum est dei et a deo et multo amplius quam actiones servi sunt domini sui in humanis, propter quod meritum hominis apud deum non potest esse simpliciter meritum de condigno, sed solum secundum praesuppositionem divinae ordinationis, ita scilicet ut homo id consequatur a deo per suam operationem quasi praemium vel mercedem, *ad quod Deus ei virtutem operandi deputavit, quae virtus operandi ad merendum beatitudinem est non solum potentia voluntatis, sed habitus gratiae vel charitatis*' (*ibid.*).

Durandus, then, allows that men of their own resources can merit glory and grace *de congruo*; but not *de condigno*. In the one case, a man can love God and win His glory without previously receiving grace; in the other, grace must have been first infused.[1]

Now, at first sight, this might appear to be stark Pelagianism, and, as we shall discuss shortly, Bradwardine considered it as such. Durandus himself is clearly aware of this danger; but he excuses himself by drawing the distinction between *de congruo* and *de condigno*. Pelagius, he says, erred by holding that it was possible to merit, without grace, *de condigno*.

Durandus, on the other hand, allows only the possibility *de congruo*. This has the effect of making any recompense the gift of God and not the prerogative of the individual who has merited.[2] Nevertheless, it has to be confessed that Durandus has carried the possibilities of merit *de congruo* to their extreme. He has not, technically, been guilty of Pelagianism in doing so. Firstly, because of his defence just cited: he has never implied that a man can of his own win merit unconditionally by fulfilling the strict requirements ordained by God, as in *de condigno*. Secondly, Durandus saves himself from Pelagianism by his use of God's absolute power. It is on this basis that he builds his argument. At no time does he say that a man can win God's grace by his own natural powers; on the contrary, it is God who decides to override human limitations by aiding those whom He thinks worthy of His aid. The onus for the reward therefore rests upon God, not man.

[1] 'Et tunc bene concluditur quod sicut sine fide infusa potest homo in deum credere, sic sine charitate infusa potest homo deum diligere: sed neuter actus est meritorius de condigno quia tale meritum ex divina ordinatione supponit gratiam vel charitatem. . .' (*ibid.*).

'Ad secundum dicendum quod nec propter meritum de solo congruo, nec propter meritum de condigno stricte ac simpliciter et proprie sumpto ponenda est gratia vel charitas habitualis: sed propter meritum quod est de condigno non simpliciter, sed secundum praesuppositionem ordinationis divinae' (*ibid.* p. 47 d).

'Ad argumentum alterius partis *dicendum est quod gratia non est necessaria propter meritum quod* est de solo congruo, sed propter meritum quod est de solo condigno non simpliciter, quia illud non est homini possibile, sed secundum praesuppositionem ordinationis divinae' (*ibid.*).

[2] 'Et ideo non sequitur quod ex puris naturalibus mereamur de condigno, ut dicit Pelagius: nec sequitur, quod apud Deum nihil possumus mereri: possumus enim mereri de solo congruo ante gratiam habitam, et post habitam de condigno modo prius frequenter exposito' (*ibid.*).

This said, however, Durandus has, in effect, breached the walls of faith. He has used God's absolute power to by-pass grace and the supernatural virtues: in the first place, he has fashioned merit *de congruo* as an instrument to lead men directly to God. A good impulse on the part of a man is worthy in its own right; although alone not strong enough to gain God's grace, it can move God to act. Good deeds, similarly, have a value in themselves: they, too, can lead to eternal rewards, if God so wills it.

Secondly, then, merit itself plays an active part in men's salvation. Although ultimately dependent upon God's grace, men can help to stir and guide it. As a consequence, human activities are worth while and cannot be ignored; even the worst crime can be palliated by genuine repentance and good deeds. Men themselves can work for their own salvation. Finally, by implication, grace loses its unconditional and irrevocable character. Although men can never take the reins of eternal life and glory into their own hands, they can twitch upon the thread in the not unfounded hope of being included on the journey. Merit and reward become far more a joint effort, in which both man and God have a part to play. Durandus never expressly makes the one a *sine qua non* for the other; but his view of merit *de congruo* in effect makes a man's act the starting-point. Here, too, as in the rest of his system, Durandus has made the natural and the moral order self-sufficient enough to move towards God unaided. It is as though men had first to qualify by their own powers before God consented to aid them by His power.

It can be seen that this active role assigned to men in gaining their own salvation moves directly against Bradwardine's view. Durandus, while technically free from Pelagianism, has in fact been able to exalt human powers in a similar way. Despite their different starting-points, Durandus has arrived at a position not far removed from that of Pelagius. Each allows men a large area of autonomy; each, Pelagius explicitly, Durandus implicitly, does not find insuperable handicaps to human action in original sin; each, again by different methods, grants to men a more than passive role in gaining their own salvation; neither of them sees grace or charity as indispensable to doing so.

While these features do not give us the right to call Durandus a Pelagian they go far towards suggesting why Bradwardine might have done so. Chapter 40 of book I of *De causa Dei* is headed: 'Against those who think that man can by himself merit the first grace *de congruo*; but not *de condigno*.'[1] This position is identical with that of Durandus, who, as we have just seen, has allowed men to reach glory alone *de congruo*, but not *de condigno*. The lengths to which this use of merit *de congruo* can be taken have also been noted, and Bradwardine seems equally to have been aware of them. This error, he says, is the greatest and most widespread of them all; for this reason it must be most conclusively repudiated. To accept this assertion would mean accepting the whole Pelagian heresy that grace comes from good works and merit; it would mean that men were able to influence God and to gain His grace by their own powers. This would, first, make merit and grace joint causes together, and so each a partial cause; secondly, merit itself would be preparatory to grace; and, thirdly, a man could then merit by his own powers and this would lead to his receiving grace; fourthly, for anyone to merit grace *de congruo* would mean that he did so before he was in grace and charity.[2]

Bradwardine and Durandus are thus in open collision over the very foundations of their different points of view. Bradwardine makes all goodness supernatural in its nature and origin; only grace can bring it about. Before the good deed must come the good intention and before both there must be grace.[3] If, he says, our natural resources sufficed for all that we could achieve, the supernatural virtues would be in vain, which they clearly are not.[4] He has no place in his system for any natural quality which could enable men to direct themselves. This is the great gulf between Bradwardine and all his opponents, Durandus included. Unlike them, he rarely mentions God's *potentia absoluta*.[5] There is no

---

[1] *De causa Dei*, p. 325. Also see p. 75 above. I am here following my commentary, pp. 74-9 above. [2] *De causa Dei*, p. 325.

[3] 'Nullus enim operando meretur, nisi habeat intentionem rectam, scilicet recti finis. . . . Talis autem extra charitatem non habet intentionem rectam' (*ibid.*).

[4] 'Frustra ergo ponuntur hi tres habitus, scilicet, fides, spes, et charitas supernaturaliter nobis infusi, cum sine his naturalia nostra nobis sufficiant ad faciendum et servandum omnia diuina mandata' (*ibid.*).

[5] And then only to show that God could have annihilated what He had created (p. 67) or that a habit could suffice without an act (p. 417). These are the only two occasions on which I have been able to trace it in *De causa Dei*.

N

question of denying its existence, but of condemning the use to which it is put. Thus, like the *magistri* in Ockham's condemnation at Avignon, Bradwardine directs his attention to the views which it shields.

God's will is so much the beginning and end of Bradwardine's outlook that it is the only touchstone. In this sense, the conflict between him and his opponents is really between God's *potentia ordinata* and God's *potentia absoluta*. Authority is his one reply to the scepticism of the Pelagians. For Bradwardine the truth is to be found in the actual ordinances which God has imposed upon this world; they allow of no speculation. It is along these lines that Bradwardine condemns merit *de congruo*: whatever is fitting for God cannot be simply good relatively (*de congruo*) but absolutely (*de condigno*).[1] Bradwardine, therefore, rejects merit *de congruo* in all its aspects as the most dangerous of falsehoods. In particular, like Durandus, he takes the same image of a king rewarding a subject. Durandus[2] had used this as an example of the way merit *de congruo* is recompensed: as the king gives his knight a horse or a castle so God gives a man grace and charity: in each case the power of reward lies in the will of the donor, though the prompting has come from the recipient.

The similarity in image is interesting and it is tempting to think that Bradwardine in taking it up was making a direct reply to Durandus. This, however, can only be conjectured; what can be said is that their differences in outlook stand clearly marked under this same light. That which Durandus defends, Bradwardine attacks; he will not hear of such a parallel as that between God and a king. This would be to make Him act conditionally in response to a previous cause; but the very essence of all that God does is that it is unconditional and uncaused and prior to everything else. Here, then, is the heart of their difference. For Durandus the created in general, and man in particular, have their own autonomous powers and they can influence divine deeds, however slightly: for Bradwardine, on the other hand, God and His will come first in such a way that everything else can only be

[1] 'Item si fit ita, congruum est Deum dare gratiam sic merenti, quia hoc volutum est a Deo: ergo hoc nedum congruum ut hi dicunt, sed etiam condignum, quicquid Deus vult fieri dignum et iustum fieri' (*De causa Dei*, p. 346).
[2] See p. 173 above.

discussed as the extension of His power: to talk of merit or human good is therefore only to describe the effects of God's will. The danger of Durandus's use of merit *de congruo* to such an outlook is not hard to see. It cuts at the root of Bradwardine's one-dimensional absolutism; it gives human beings an active and important part to play in their own salvation; and, above all, it prepares the way, taken by Ockham and his followers, for disregarding anything but God's will and free will. While Durandus still pays deference to the traditional teachings, he has also undermined them. It is hard not to feel that Bradwardine had Durandus in mind when he castigated merit *de congruo* as 'this error ... the most famous in these days'. It offered safe passage to dangerous doctrines.

FUTURE CONTINGENTS

The marked division which runs through the whole of Durandus's outlook between the divine and created is particularly apparent in his views on future contingents. It springs, above all, from the indirect role of God; neither His will nor His knowledge is the immediate cause of created things. His intellect directs; His will incites and inclines; but neither puts into immediate effect.[1] God, says Durandus, does not act more immediately than any creature; he is not, therefore, the immediate cause of His creatures' actions.[2] This arises because God does not either

---

[1] 'Et dicendum quod scientia dei est causa creaturarum per modum dirigentis. Voluntas autem est causa per modum inclinantis et inducentis. *Neutra autem est immediata causa rerum,* potentia vero est causa rerum, sicut exsequens et immediate movens, haec autem patent' (Comm. Sent. bk. I, dist. 38, qu. I, p. 88 c).

[2] 'Ideo dicendum est aliter quod ea quae, fiunt a Deo mediantibus causis secundis non fiunt ab eo immediate sicut ipsemet rationes terminorum videntur sonare. Quod apparet primo sic, si Deus ageret immediate ad productionem effectuum causae secundae (ut cum ignis generat ignem) aut ageret eadem actione qua creatura, aut alia. Non eadem propter duo. Primo quia illam potest habere creatura sine speciali influxu dei (supposita conservatione suae naturae et suae virtutis activae) quia actio quae non excedit virtutem speciei agentis sufficienter elicitur a sola virtute speciei, *frustra ergo poneretur principium aliud immediatum eliciens talem actionem.*

'*Secundo, quia impossibile est eandem actionem numero esse a duobus vel pluribus agentibus ita quod a quolibet sit immediate et perfecte, nisi in illis sit eadem virtus numero. Sed in Deo et creatura non potest esse eadem virtus numero, ergo impossibile est quod eadem actio numero sit ab utroque immediate et perfecte. Actio autem creaturae, immediate est a creatura et perfecte, cum non*

produce an immediate effect (as fire causes fire), nor does He share
the same actions with His creatures. A creature can act, without
special help from God, in anything that does not exceed its
capacities: thus it would be vain to postulate an additional
immediate cause for what it can accomplish of its own. Furthermore, God and His creatures cannot be measured together;
therefore, He cannot be the immediate and perfect participant in
their actions. God's role is to act as the universal cause, remote
and perfect in conserving all that exists. He does so indirectly,
providing the framework, as it were, but leaving the particulars
to be filled out from themselves. This is of course not to say that
God could not intervene directly, if He so desired; but, says
Durandus, if He did, His creatures would then have no part
to play. Thus God conserves the power of secondary causes to
move, without directing them, a situation quite the reverse of
that depicted by Bradwardine.

It is not surprising that, where Bradwardine saw the most
rigorous and exclusive determinism on God's part, Durandus
barely finds a meeting place between God and His creatures; so
much is left to the interplay of secondary causes that there are
many rivals to His power. This gives Durandus's system consequences strikingly at variance with Bradwardine's. In the first
place, the power of the spheres becomes important. Durandus
discusses their influence in book II.[1] To the question whether
they act as a cause upon things inferior to them, Durandus replies
that they exert power over all *generabilia et corruptibilia*. For
that which is unalterable and unmoved will always have effect
upon that which is changeable and can be moved.[2]

---

excedat virtutem suae speciei, ergo eadem actio non est immediate a Deo' (bk. II,
dist. I, qu. 5, p. III c).

   'Patet igitur quod ea quae producuntur per actionem creaturae non producuntur
a deo immediate. Posset tamen deus ea immediata producere si vellet, *sed tunc
creatura nihil ibi ageret*' (*ibid.* p. III d).

   [1] *Ibid.* dists. 14 and 15.

   [2] 'Quod autem coelum habeat causalitatem super omnia generabilia et
corruptibilia. Patet sic, Alterans inalterabile est causa omnis alterationis, sed
coelem est alterans inalterabile, ergo etc. Maior patet, sicut enim omnis
motus reducitur ad movens immobile, quod est prima causa omnis motus, sic
omnis alteratio reducitur ad alterans inalterabile, quod est causa omnis
alterationis. Minor simpliciter patet, quia alterans inalterabile non est
intelligentia, quia non movet immediate ad formam. . .' (*ibid.* dist. 15, qu. 1,
p. 134 d).

Durandus compares the spheres to a seed; while not itself a full, living being, it is the source of life. The spheres, too, though not themselves living, give life to other things. They do so not because of any created intelligence, but because God has made them the origin of all *generabilia et corruptibilia*.[1] If the celestial spheres are the origin of everything that comes into being and dies, have they, Durandus asks, any influence upon free will? His reply is a roundabout one; but ultimately he concedes that the spheres have an influence here, too. They cannot, he says, affect free will by governing its nature and its actions; or by directing its inclinations and inciting it to perform certain actions; or by directly impeding it. Yet, indirectly, the celestial spheres can upset free will by removing the objects of its attention. Since all natural things are subject to the spheres, says Durandus, the latter can both introduce and remove obstacles to free will, thus playing a part in its movements.[2]

Durandus by denying to God any but indirect control over His creatures has given entry to other indirect forces as well. While he

---

[1] 'Ideo dicendum quod sicut in semine, quod non est vivens, est virtus generativa rei viventis, pro eo quod semen decisum est a vivente. Sic in coelo licet non sit vivens, est virtus generativa rei viventis, non quia motum ab intelligentia, nec quia virtus sit ei influxa ab aliqua intelligentia creata: Sed quia productum est a Deo tanquam quoddam semen omnium generabilium et corruptibilium: et sic cum coelum agit in virtute Dei ad productionem viventium, sicut semen equi in virtute equi generantis ad producendum equum' (*ibid.*).

[2] 'Nunc restat considerare de quarto membro, in quo et tertium omissum implicabitur. Videndum ergo utrum liberum arbitrium possit impediri per actionem corporis coelestis, indirecte removendo obiectum, et patet quod sic, quia omne quod sit per solam alterationem corporis subiacet actioni corporis coelestis, quia coelum cum sit alterans inalterabile est causa omnis alterationis. . . . *Sed impedimentum electionis voluntatis per absentiam objecti sit per solam alterationem corporis.* . . .

'. . . Sic igitur patet quod coelum habet causalitatem super liberum arbitrium, impediendo actum eius indirecte per impedimentum virium sensitivarum. Et per idem patet quod habet causalitatem super ipsum causando actum eius, ut removens prohibens . . . Sed corpus coeleste habet causalitatem super omnem corporalem alterationem, ergo, etc.' (*ibid.* qu. 2, p. 135 b).

'Ad secundum dicendum quod coelum non est causa animae quantum ad esse quod habet in corpore, nisi dispositive, quia esse animae in corpore est a deo, qui eam creat infundendo, et infundit creando. Corpus autem coeleste est solum causa disponens subiectum. Et simili modo coelum non habet causalitatem discretam super actiones proprias animae inclinando in eas directe impediendo, sed solum indirecte in quantum dispositio corporis facit ad praesentationem obiecti modis quibus expositum est' (*ibid.*).

refuses the celestial spheres an immediate influence upon free will, he is prepared to grant them indirect control. It is hard to see, *prima facie*, where God's power is any greater than that of the spheres, or which is more likely to exercise greater control upon things created. Once again, there is abundant fuel to feed the flame of Bradwardine's wrath. We have noted in Part I that Bradwardine's opposition to natural determinism is only second to his hatred of Pelagianism.[1] Time and again he thrusts at those who uphold the power of the spheres and other intermediary causes between God and His creatures.[2] It must not be forgotten that the subtitle of *De causa Dei* is *Contra Pelagium et de virtute causarum*; Bradwardine saw the attack upon the Pelagians as an attack also upon those who challenged divine determinism with a natural determinism. He makes constant references to Etienne Tempier's condemnation in 1277 of such determinist theses;[3] and the whole of his treatise is directed to emphasizing God's unchallenged necessity. Thus the views of Durandus upon the spheres cut at the root of Bradwardine's system. It is a struggle between the remote and indirect power of the Greco-Arabian God and the direct and personal control of the Augustinian and Scotist God. Bradwardine here takes the side of the latter in his desire to rescue God's power from intermediaries; he differs only in the use to which he puts it.

This leads to the second great consequence of God's indirect control: its relation to His knowledge of future contingents. We have already noted that the future only became a problem of the first importance with the division of God's eternal knowledge into past, present and future: for then it involved God's foreknowing the future as future before it had come about. Consequently, for the first time, God's omniscience was contraposed to contingency: it either meant determinism or the exclusion of contingency. Durandus seems aware of this problem, for his own solution betrays those same traits of holding to tradition and yet opening the way for innovation. Central to his argument is his recognition of the need to conserve the future as future in God, as well as in the created order. As a result, he is concerned to allow that, on the one hand, God knows everything eternally; but, on

[1] See Introduction above, pp. 15–16.
[2] E.g. *De causa Dei*, p. 543; also pp. 653, 655, 681–2, 695.   [3] *Ibid.*

the other, He cannot know as actual that which has not yet come into being. In this he has in effect conceded to the new outlook, preferring to conserve the future rather than God's omniscience.

We have already noted that, for Durandus, neither God's knowledge nor His will is the immediate cause of all things; they cannot, therefore, be the cause of future contingents. The way in which God knows is through His essence.[1] He knows all things not only absolutely in themselves, but in their relationship to one another. But, and here is Durandus's first qualification, God does not know future contingents in their actual existence; if He did they would be present not future; God, rather, knows them as they will be.[2] This prevents God from making something future come into being in the present, and yet enables Him to know how it will be when the time is due for it to come into being. Any other method, Durandus shows, would make God know

[1] 'Nunc autem Deus non solum cognoscit causam contingentem in se et absolute, quia sic in ea vel per eam non cognosceretur infallibiliter aliquis effectus nisi tantum coniectura probabili (ut bene dicunt alii) sed cognoscit omnia quae eam determinare possunt et quae determinabunt, insuper cognoscit omnia quae eam impedire possunt et quae impedient vel non impedient, ergo Deus in causa contingente sic cognita potest certitudinaliter cognoscere effectum futurum contingentem. Item Deus non cognoscit alia a se nisi per cognitionem suae essentiae, futura ergo contingentia si novit, novit per notitiam suae essentiae. . .' (Comm. Sent. bk. I, dist. 38, qu. 3, p. 89 c).

[2] '. . . Quantum ad secundum, scilicet utrum Deus cognoscat futura contingentia quantum ad eorum actualem existentiam. Sciendum quod potest habere duplicem intellectum, unum utrum deus cognoscat futura contingentia quantum ad suam actualem existentiam, id est, ea actu existere, et sic constat quod non, quia intellectus dicens esse quod non est, est falsus, sed futura contingentia nondum sunt actu, alioquin non essent futura contingentia sed praesentia, ergo si Deus intelligeret ea actu existere intellectus eius esset falsus, quod est impossibile, deus ergo non cognoscit futura contingentia quantum ad eorum actualem existentiam sic quod cognoscat ea actu existere. Alius potest esse intellectus, scilicet quod Deus cognoscat futura contingentia quantum ad suam actualem existentiam non quod Deus cognoscat ea iam existere, sed quia Deus ab aeterno novit illam propriam et distinctam et actualem existentiam quam habebunt processu temporis in seipsis, et hoc modo Deus cognoscit futura contingentia quantum ad eorum actualem existentiam. Cuius ratio est, constat enim quod Deus cognoscit contingens dum est praesens, puta sortem currere, alioquin ego cognoscerem illud quod Deus ignoraret, si ergo non cognoscebat hoc prius quando fuit futurum, sequeretur quod aliquid accrevisset suae essentiae quod est impossibile. . . . Sic igitur patet qualiter Deus cognoscit futura contingentia, quia cognoscit ea determinate quantum ad suas proprias et determinatas actualitates quas habebunt . . . cognitio tamen utrorumque dependet a cognitione divinae essentiae' (ibid. p. 89 c and d).

falsely what did not yet exist; or else prevent it from being in the future at all; or force Him to be dependent upon future contingents for His knowledge.

Durandus, in keeping with his view of the indirect nature of divine control, reaches two conclusions which limit the extent and nature of God's foreknowledge, showing clearly the direction the discussion was taking. The first springs from the division which he makes between things caused by God and things deriving from secondary causes. This enables God's knowledge to remain free from determinism in each case: so far as His own knowledge is concerned, God's intellect does not impose it upon His will, which, as the cause of things, is free to act independently. In the case of those things not from His will, they are not influenced by God's foreknowledge, since they result from secondary causes.[1] The effect of this is to give secondary causes their own *raison d'être* with or without God's approval; it is to come close to the same conclusion drawn by Buckingham that free will is so free that it can act even in spite of God.[2] Like Buckingham, Durandus has left a gap between God and His creatures, so that He is not in complete command of them. The second conclusion which Durandus reaches is over the nature of God's foreknowledge itself. God's knowledge, he says, is so free that He is able not to know what He knows and know what He does not

[1] 'Quantum ad tertium scilicet an scientia Dei imponat necessitatem rebus scitis. Notandum quod scientia Dei comparatur ad res dupliciter. Uno modo, ut causa. Alio modo, ut cognitio infallibilis et certa, et neutro eorum modorum imponit necessitatem rebus. Quod non ut causa patet primo sic, aliqua futura dependent a solo deo sicut a causa, alia vero dependent ab ipso mediantibus causis secundis, sed scientia divina neutris imponit necessitatem, ergo etc. Minor probatur quantum ad utramque partem, quod enim scientia dei ut causa non imponat necessitatem futuris quae dependent a solo deo, probatur sic, scientia dei non est causa eorum quae fiunt a Deo, nisi mediante voluntate, ut patet ex supradictis, sed voluntas Dei non necessario vult quicquid Deus scit, sed libere vult et potest non velle omne aliud ab ipso, ergo scientia dei, ut causa non imponit necessitatem rebus futuris. . . . Item patet de his quae producuntur a deo mediantibus causis secundis sic, omnis effectus contingens et contingenter eveniens, cuius aliqua causa per se est impedibilis potest impediri, sed eorum quae fiunt a Deo mediantibus causis secundis multa sunt quae praeter scientiam divinam habent causas impedibiles, vel per actionem contrarii, vel per dispositionem materiae, ergo talia non obstante causalitate divinae scientiae contingenter eveniunt' (bk. 1, dist. 38, qu. 3, pp. 89 d and 90 a).

[2] See p. 184 below.

know. To say that all that God knows is necessarily true can, says Durandus, be understood in two ways: either as absolute necessity, in which sense it is not true, or in terms of the contingency to which it refers, and in this case men are equally as infallible in their knowledge as God. When, for example, Socrates runs, he who sees Socrates running knows it as necessarily and as infallibly as God.[1] Thus God's knowledge of contingents can only be necessary *ex suppositione* and not absolutely; it is as certain as the contingent.

Durandus does not go on to infer the possible effects of God's lack of certainty over contingents: he neither denies Him knowledge of them (as Aureole and Holcot) nor does he openly make His knowledge of contingents contingent (as Buckingham and Woodham). As with his views over grace, free will and merit, Durandus seems content to leave such conclusions unpressed, himself only posing the questions. There are, then, in Durandus's views on the future, four main strands. Firstly, the recognition in God of the difference between past, present and future, which, while enabling Him to know each future event as it will be, prevents Him from knowing it as actually in being. Second, the power he gives to secondary causes, enabling them to determine their own courses without God's intervention. Thirdly, the lack of any direction by God's foreknowledge so that He could know what He Himself did not will. Finally, Durandus's recognition that the future differs from the past and the present in such a way that God cannot have necessary knowledge of it.

Accordingly, when we turn to Bradwardine's views on the

---

[1] '. . . deus potest nescire quod scit, et scire quod nescit, et ideo non necessario scit talia, sed libere, sicut libere vult ea fore vel non fore, si autem determinet materiam verbi, scilicet *a* fore, sic est falsa et divisa, sub hoc sensu Deus praevidit *a* fore necessario quod non est verum, immo praevidit *a* fore contingenter, modo sic est quod consequens non infertur ex antecedente ratione compositionis verbi ad subiectum quae est necessaria, sed solum ratione materiae verbi, quae est contingens. . .' (Comm. Sent. bk. I, dist. 38, qu. 3, p. 90 b).
'Modo quum dicitur omne scitum a deo necessario est verum si intelligatur de necessario simpliciter et absolute non est verum. Necessarium enim ex suppositione quae stat cum contingentia simpliciter potest esse scitum infallibiliter, non solum a Deo, sed etiam a nobis, ut cum scio sortem actu currere . . . propter quod sequitur quod conclusio ex maiore sit necessaria necessitate suppositionis solum, et non simpliciter, quod concessum est' (*ibid*. p. 90 c).

question, there are at least four points of dispute between him and Durandus. It will be recalled that Bradwardine takes up over two hundred pages of *De causa Dei* in combating more than thirty erroneous opinions, on God's foreknowledge, before he arrives at opinion 33, the central one.[1] If we examine these in chronological order we shall see how sharply Bradwardine was reacting against an attitude such as Durandus's. Opinion 8 in chapter 19 of book III is condemned for holding that secondary causes are subject to the necessity of intermediate forces and not the result of God's free dispensation.[2] In his support Bradwardine invokes Etienne Tempier's condemnation of two articles on necessity. Opinion 10, averring that God does not will the effects of the created order, comes very close to Durandus's that a contingent exists regardless of God's knowledge.[3] In the sixteenth opinion[4] Bradwardine condemns the view, upheld by Durandus, that God does not will the act of free will before the latter, and in the seventeenth,[5] the view that, while God acts together with any creature, it could act alone. Similarly, against opinions 22, 23 and 24,[6] Bradwardine defends the divine will as the immediate and determining cause of all created acts, in contrast to Durandus's position where God does not move more immediately than any other cause and His will does not impose any necessity. Bradwardine opposes the idea that God's will is not always necessary (opinion 22); that it is not the efficient cause, only the assent of the divine intellect being required for secondary causes to act by themselves (opinion 23); and that the divine will never compels, but persuades (opinion 24). In opinion 25, Bradwardine attacks the view, implicit in the use of God's *potentia absoluta* by all the Pelagians, that God does not make stages between merit, free acts and rewards.[7]

All of these opinions here are the preliminary to opinion 33; they show clearly that, as with Durandus, secondary causes are not subject to God's constant and immediate direction, while for Bradwardine they are. Accordingly, their different responses to the problem raised by the thirty-third opinion must be considered in this light: the view of each towards the future will depend upon the manner in which they regard God's relations to His

---

[1] See pp. 103 *et seq.* above.   [2] *De causa Dei*, p. 695.   [3] *Ibid.* p. 696.
[4] *Ibid. p.* 697.   [5] *Ibid.*   [6] *Ibid.* p. 698.   [7] *Ibid.* p. 699.

creatures. Briefly, opinion 33 held that while the past and present, as already in being, were determined, the future, as yet to come, was not;[1] it was not, therefore, compelled to come about. For Bradwardine, as we have seen,[2] this was out of the question, for, if the future were mutable, then God's will would be mutable and the whole of his system would fall to the ground. Durandus, on the other hand, has already denied that the future is the same for God as the past and the present, on the grounds that if it were already in being it would not be future. Thus, by implication, though not explicitly, Durandus has recognized that the future is distinguished from the past and present by its indeterminacy. Although Durandus, as we have seen, does not openly take up the defence of the future in the way of the later Pelagians, he has prepared the ground for them.

The clash between Bradwardine and Durandus is more in the nature of an extensive reconnaissance than a sustained battle at any one sector. It covers the whole front of the divine and created wills without ever reaching the same pitch as that, say, with Ockham. Both in his views over grace, merit and free will and over future contingents Durandus marks a turning point: he is content to establish his new positions without exploiting them further. Nevertheless he has given ample evidence of the break which they constituted with tradition. There was fertile soil for conflict between his outlook and one such as Bradwardine's, and it is not hard to see Durandus as being foremost among the Pelagians.

[1] *Ibid.* p. 807; see also pp. 107–9 above. [2] Above, *ibid.*

CHAPTER XI

WILLIAM OF OCKHAM: THE CENTRAL FIGURE

B RADWARDINE'S clash with Ockham, though it has many similarities with his struggle against Durandus, differs in scope and source. While it is true to say that Ockham takes substantially the same position on the supernatural virtues and merit as Durandus, he does not range so widely beyond them, that is, in a Pelagian sense. Questions of secondary causes, of future contingents and of men's moral powers do not come in for the same treatment as Durandus gives to them. On the whole, Ockham's Pelagianism is concentrated around the questions of grace and predestination. Now this is no accident; for the source of Ockham's Pelagianism lies far less in the nature of his system, as it did with Durandus, than in his scepticism: that is to say, his view of knowledge as being limited to experience. This has two important consequences. First, by this limit Ockham's method never passes beyond what is logically tenable; thus what Bradwardine asserts as irrefutable, as for example God's existence, Ockham rejects as unproved. Secondly, this means that, to all intents and purposes, God is outside his terms of reference; beyond assertion by faith little can be said about Him. Ockham accordingly tends to confine God to the margins of the argument; although ever present, His influence is indeterminate: for the very omnipresence of God's will renders it beyond precise delineation. As the cause of everything in general, it is too vast to be applied to particulars.

By invoking God's absolute power Ockham opens the way to his seemingly Pelagian views; for God can do anything, and, in discussing what is possible for man, Ockham is only discussing what is possible for God. Man can rise beyond any restrictions because God is free from all restrictions. Thus there is no question, for Ockham, of man usurping divine power, as in the case of Pelagius. The only yardstick for Ockham is that which God wills. Hence, all the grades of charity and grace and all our actions are merely contingent, to be accepted, rejected or ignored, as God pleases. This is the root of Ockham's views and of what his contemporaries considered to be his Pelagianism.

THE 51 ARTICLES AT AVIGNON

In their condemnation at Avignon in 1326 of the fifty-one articles taken from Ockham's 'Sentences' the *magistri* called the first four Pelagian. In addition, other questions (5, 6, 7, 8, 10, 35, 46) denying intrinsic values, as, for example, that God could enable a man to hate Him, that beatitude could be inefficacious, or that grace and sin could coexist, were equally condemned as going against authority. The first four questions all invoked God's *potentia absoluta* as enabling a man to carry out a meritorious act without supernatural help. The first article holds that, from God's absolute power, a man can, of his own will, do good and that God can accept this action as worthy of His grace. Therefore, says Ockham, a good act, to be meritorious, does not require a supernatural habit such as charity.[1]

It is not more contradictory for a meritorious act to come from men's own powers, if God so wills it, than for them to commit a bad act unaided. Moreover, says Ockham, an act is only meritorious if it is voluntary and of our own accord; and for this to be possible our wills must so direct us. Our wills, therefore, rather than any habits, are the principal cause of merit because they act freely. A habit of itself is neither good nor bad, but indifferent: only God makes it good, and for this reason He can dispense with it entirely.[2]

[1] 'Reprobando communem modum, quo ponuntur quod habitus caritatis requiritur ad actum meritorium dicit sic: Istud reputo falsum simpliciter, quia bonum motum voluntatis ex puris naturalibus elicitum potest deus acceptare de gratia sua, et per consequens talis actus ex gratuita dei acceptatione erit meritorius. Ergo ad hoc quod talis actus sit meritorius, non requiritur talis habitus. Praeterea omne illud, quod potest ex se sufficienter in actum demeritorium, potest de potentia dei absoluta in actum meritorium ex se, quia, cum actus meritorius et demeritorius sunt contrarii, non est maior repugnantia actus meritorii ad naturam in puris naturalibus constitutam. Ergo non includit contradictionem voluntatem in puris naturalibus ferri in actum meritorium' (Art. 1 from A. Pelzer's article in *Revue d'histoire ecclésiastique*, XVIII (1922), p. 250).

[2] 'Praeterea nihil est meritorium, nisi quia voluntarium, et hoc, nisi quia libere elicitum vel factum, quia nihil est meritorium, nisi quod est in nobis et

Thus, for Ockham, a habit, either supernatural or acquired, is devoid of intrinsic value. The two conditions for a meritorious act are that it must be freely done by a man and freely rewarded by God; His absolute will only accepts actions which please Him and for this no intermediary habit is needed. The reply of the *magistri* to this is that it smacks of Pelagianism and worse. Ockham, they say, equates the possibility of our natural powers doing good with the good that comes from charity. This can only mean that there is no such habit as charity, or, if there is, it is to no purpose since it in no way leads to merit. Accordingly, they see it as Ockham's aim to eliminate the need for charity.[1]

Most significant in their round condemnation of Ockham's views as Pelagian is their equally round rejection of his use of God's *potentia absoluta* in extenuation. They refuse to allow that God's absolute power makes any difference; for, they say, all that Ockham states could sound equally well without it.[2]

in nostra potestate. Sed nihil est in nostra potestate, quod possimus agere et non agere, nisi quia a voluntate tanquam a principio movente et non ab habitu, quia habitus, cum sit causa naturalis, nihil est indifferens propter habitum. Ergo ratio meriti principaliter consistit penes voluntatem ex hoc quod ipsa libere elicit. Ergo ut actus sit meritorius, non requiritur habitus.

'Praeterea omnis actus, qui cum aliqua circumstantia, que non est de se laudabilis, est meritorius, potest esse meritorius de potentia dei absoluta sine ista circumstantia. Sed actus diligendi deum super omnia cum caritate, que non est est de se laudabilis, est meritorius. Ergo sine ea potest esse meritorius' (Pelzer, *loc. cit.*).

[1] 'Dicimus quod iste longe processus in predicto articulo est erroneus et sapit haeresim Pelagianam vel peius. Adequat enim quantum ad rationem meriti nobis in praesenti vita possibilis, opus factum sine caritate operi facto cum caritate. Et per totam deductionem apparet quod ipse et intendit quod nullus est habitus caritatis aut, si est, frustra est, quia nihil penitus facit ad meritum, quod est expresse contra dictum Apostoli prima ad Corinthios 13. ...

'Et quod intendat excludere caritatem a merito, patet in singulis contentis in sua deductione. Dicit enim primo quod bonus motus voluntatis ex puris naturalibus elicitus potest esse meritorius ex gratuita dei acceptatione, nec ad hoc requiritur aliquis alius habitus.

'Et hoc quod dicit: habitum caritatis non requiri ad meritum et hoc intelligat qualiter hoc intelligat, apparet per rationem, quam ad hoc probandum inducit. Arguit enim, sic: Omne illud, quod potest ex se sufficienter in actum demeritorium, potest de potentia dei absoluta in actum meritorium ex se. Et per hoc vult concludere quod sicut voluntas ex se sufficienter potest demereri, sic sufficienter ex se potest mereri, et sic sequeretur quod caritas non solum non est necessaria ad merendum, sed quod omnino superfluit, quia sola voluntas ex se sufficit' (*ibid.* pp. 251–2).

[2] 'Nec potest excusari per illam addicionem, quam ponit: de potentia dei

In this dismissal of Ockham's use of God's absolute power lie two important considerations. First, that his opponents in general are not prepared to acknowledge the validity of this new outlook as applied to God. They refuse to allow hypothesis to circumvent revelation. What has been ordained by God is the only criterion; to destroy the laws that apply to this world by laws which apply to none is equivalent to rejecting all standards. Thus the *magistri* see Ockham's method as essentially an attack upon the foundations of the established tenets, even though it is carried out in the name of God's omnipotence. Second, this rejection by the *magistri* of Ockham's use of God's *potentia absoluta* provides some clue to Bradwardine's attitude towards it. While they brush it aside explicitly, albeit without taking the trouble to confute it, Bradwardine rejects it by implication. Never once does he mention its use as a cloak for openly professed Pelagian views; though, as we have seen with Durandus, he attacks the views put forward in the name of God's absolute power. It seems probable, therefore, that, as with the *magistri*, Bradwardine did not consider it worth refuting and preferred to concentrate upon what was actually expressed.

Lastly, in this first article, the *magistri* attack Ockham's assertion that it is the will which counts in any act of merit and that neither a habit nor charity has any intrinsic value. To say that God's absolute power can make an act, neutral in itself, good, and that, equally, charity bears no value in itself is against the Scriptures.[1]

The next two articles the *magistri* also condemn as Pelagian. By the second article Ockham holds that God can accept a man as deserving of eternal glory without his possessing grace, and,

absoluta, quia argumentum suum eque procedit absque illa condicione sicut cum illa. Propositio autem, quam assumit, est heretica et conclusio heretica' (*ibid*. p. 252).

[1] 'Idem patet ex 2a ratione, quam adducit dicens quod nihil est meritorium nisi quia voluntarium et a voluntate libere elicitum vel factum et non ab aliquo habitu, et sic totum meritum, quantum est possibile homini viatori, attribuit libertati voluntatis et nihil caritati vel alii habitui. Idem patet ex 3a ratione, in qua dicit sic quod omnis actus, qui cum aliqua circumstancia, que non sit de se laudabilis, est meritorius, potest esse meritorius de potentia dei absoluta sine illa circumstancia. Et assumit quod caritas de se non est laudabilis, quod est non solum contra philosophiam moralem, que dicit quod virtuti debetur laus, sed contra sacram scripturam. . .' (*ibid*. p. 252).

correspondingly, He can damn him without his having sinned.[1]

The third article simply specifies that for divine acceptance charity is not needed. To both of these the *magistri* give the same rejoinder that this is to fall into Pelagius's error.[2]

The fourth article follows the same pattern. God, says Ockham, can, by His absolute power, remit sin without the sinner first needing grace.[3] This, too, the *magistri* condemn as Pelagianism.

Thus there are four articles among those condemned at Avignon which are cited as Pelagian. This is in itself evidence that Ockham was openly associated with heretical tendencies in a way that could not have escaped attention, least of all by Bradwardine, the arch-enemy of Pelagianism. Moreover, as has been suggested earlier, anything associated with Ockham would have more than ordinary implications.[4] With his following and reputation it is clear that views voiced by him would be likely to be taken up in a chorus by his followers. With these attributes, therefore, and as the direct contemporary of Bradwardine, it is not too fanciful to see Ockham as the centre of Bradwardine's target. Certainly it is views such as those cited above that Bradwardine engages against, as a closer examination will show.

There are two main aspects to Ockham's Pelagianism: the place of supernatural virtues with the attendant problems of grace, charity and merit; and the process and cause of predestination. The field is much narrower than in the case of Durandus; but, in a sense, it is correspondingly more deeply worked.

---

[1] 'Deus potest aliquem existentem in puris naturalibus primo acceptare tanquam dignum vita eterna et sine omni sui demerito reprobare' (Pelzer, *loc. cit.* p. 253).

[2] 'Illud quod dicitur: tanquam dignum, reputamus erroneum quod ex solis naturalibus acceptetur tanquam dignus, cum adequat hominem existentem in puris naturalibus homini existenti in caritate in esse dignum vita eterna et incidit in errorem Pelagii accipiendo dignum, prout de eo loquuntur sancti et doctores' (*ibid.*).

[3] 'Deus de sua potentia absoluta potest remittere culpam sine collatione gratie. Cuius ratio est, quia quemcumque potest acceptare tanquam dignum vita eterna sine omni gratia inherente. . . . Confirmatur, quia non videtur contradictio quia deus possit dare alicui existenti in peccato mortali visionem essentie sue in illo instanti, in quo potest sibi dare gratiam' (*ibid.*).

[4] See p. 139 above.

THE SUPERNATURAL VIRTUES

The main lines of Ockham's arguments follow the extracts contained in the four articles quoted above. As we have already seen, their basis is God's absolute power, and little other reference is made to Him. It is hard to place Ockham's views here in terms of a wider outlook, as with Durandus. The ideas he expresses seem to have no aim save that of cutting away superfluous concepts. It appears far more to be an essay in economy than part of a firmly grounded outlook. Scepticism sets its tone; the abiding effect is reason's inability to discuss God save in terms of possibility.

A supernatural habit, he says, is not necessary for a man to be accepted by God as worthy of eternal life.[1] There is no rigid order by God's absolute power. God can enable an infant to be born free from sin, actual and original. He can also ordain it to eternal life without first giving it any supernatural habit. Thus God, if He so wills, can dispense with all such means in awarding a man eternal glory.[2]

Ockham reaches three conclusions on supernatural habits. First, that we cannot prove by reason that they are necessary for following God's ways; second, that it cannot be proved that they are necessary for beatitude; third, that in the case of those habits that we can have, these can be natural, not supernatural.[3]

Habits, for Ockham, therefore, have no part to play in leading

---

[1] 'Contra istum primum . . . quod non opportet ponere talem habitum informantem animam ad quid aliquis sit acceptus a deo tanquam dignum vita eterna. . . . Et hoc dico quoniam deus de potentia absoluta posset quemcumque acceptare sine tali habitu: licet non de potentia ordinata' (Commentary on the Sentences, bk. III, qu. 5 E).

[2] 'Minor probatur, quia deus de potentia sua absoluta potest facere puerum aliquem nasci sine peccato actuali et originali . . . et per consequens . . . nihil habeat repugnans divine acceptationi potest deum talem puerum ordinare ad vitam eternam, et sibi dare vitam absque hoc quod det sibi talem habitum. . . . Si deus disponat dare vitam eternam alicui viatori: non est necesse talem esse in gratia et charum deo, et hoc potest sine omni habitu. . .' (ibid.).

[3] 'Et hic teneo tres conclusiones. Prima quod non potest probari ratione naturali quod indigemus habitu supernaturali quocumque ad consequendum finem ultimam. Secunda est quod ex hoc quod credo quod beatitudo est mihi conferenda propter merita non potest concludi consequentia formali quod habitus supernaturales sunt nobis necessarii. Tertia est quod respectu omnium habituum quos possumus habere, possumus habere habitum naturalem naturaliter inclinantem. Ideo dico . . . quod habitus supernaturales sunt nobis necessarii de potentia dei ordinata non absoluta' (ibid. qu. 8 A and C).

o

a man to God. A vast segment of divine and human relations has been broken off, leaving men in their natural powers and God in His omnipotence face to face. The importance of this step is plain to see. In the first place, the supernatural virtues have of themselves no value, so that, even where they are present, they offer no guarantee of God's acceptance.[1] It is to turn the route, for so long regarded as the only means of reaching the cherished destination, into an inconsequential by-way; both the privilege of using it and the certainty of its goal have gone. Nor has it been replaced by a broader highway, but by a magic broomstick following no accepted landmarks. In the second place, the breaking of this link between God and man bids fair to circumvent the very place of the Church. Once again, as in Bradwardine's dismissal of human achievements, Ockham has robbed of efficacy everything but God's will. Though from opposite extremes, they have reached a similar point in thrusting aside intermediary forms between God and His creatures. In the third place, however, and here, in relation to Bradwardine and his contemporaries, the crucial issue, Ockham cannot but exalt man's independence by his application of God's absolute power. Although, as we have already remarked, the onus for this rests upon God's infinite freedom, the effect is nevertheless to make man far more self-sufficient and free from the compelling need for grace. This his accusers saw as leading to Pelagianism and as going against the authority of the Scriptures. The effects of Ockham's views, whatever his intentions, could only, in the eyes of his opponents, spell a rejection of the established teachings and invite men to ignore them for their own God-given powers.

The conflict between Ockham and Bradwardine issues directly from their views on supernatural virtues: for the one, they are accidents, of no account in themselves, to be employed or discarded as God wills; for the other, they are God's means of directly participating in His creatures' actions, an inseparable constituent in any good deed. The conflict may, for the sake of clarity, be said to have three aspects: first, the place of the supernatural virtues; second, the role of the human will; and third, the

---

[1] '. . . potest talis forma existere in anima; et tamen non opportet deum acceptare eam informatam tali, ergo non necessario ad talem formam sequitur acceptatio divina' (bk. III, qu. 5 E).

relationship of each to merit and reward. Clearly, these can be no more than strands in a single pattern: though each can be fleetingly picked out, it is too closely interwoven with the others to mean anything alone.

As to the first aspect, little more need be added. Ockham treats the supernatural virtues in much the same way as casual acquaintances are to be regarded: despite the passing pleasantry, one can live as well without them. Bradwardine makes their need imperative; there would be no life without them.[1] For him they have a definite and essential place, where for Ockham they have none. Grace and glory, says Ockham, are two effects produced by God: grace comes first because it applies to this life while glory is its consummation. This means, he continues, that God could confer grace and charity upon a person without also giving him glory; similarly God, having given a man grace and charity, could annihilate him: there is no need for charity to involve divine acceptance. God, in His absolute power, is bound by no conditions.[2]

This complete jettisoning of any established relationship between good acts and supernatural virtues, grace and glory, removes all causality from the actions of God and man. Bradwardine attacks this as going against his whole view of divine participation; and the heading of chapter 46 (book 1) of *De causa Dei* is remarkable for being an almost word for word reply to the view just put forward by Ockham: 'Against all those who acknowledge predestination and reprobation to glory and punishment; yet who deny that these follow any definite stages.'[3] On the

[1] 'De necessitate ergo requiritur aliqua virtus superior supernaturalis, heroica et diuina, puta gratia gratis data a Deo, ad erigendum voluntatem creatam ex seipsa' (*De causa Dei*, p. 329).

[2] '. . . gratia et gloria sunt duo effectus producti a deo; gratia est prior, quare est in viatore, et gloria est posterior, quia est in consummatione, igitur potest deus conferre alicui gratiam et caritatem et non conferre sibi gloriam . . . non obstante quod conferat sibi gratiam . . . viatori cuicumque potest conferre gratiam et caritatem et statim post potest eum annihilare, et per consequens potest sibi conferre gratiam et dispositionem et eum annihilare. . . .

'Ideo dico . . . ad istam conclusionem quod caritas nec quicumque alius habitus necessitat deum ad dandum alicui vitam eternam; imo de potentia dei absoluta potest alicui conferre caritatem et eum potest annihilare' (Sentences, bk. III, qu. 5 E and H).

[3] 'Contra quosdam concedentes praedestinationem et reprobationem ad

contrary, he says, God has distinct and eternal knowledge of every stage of grace and merit, glory or punishment.[1] Ockham's attitude to a habit, as without intrinsic significance, leads him to regard the supernaturally infused habit as not really different in effect from the habit naturally acquired. In a series of good actions he says, by which a habit to good is acquired, the acts can be accepted alone, without the habit; in the same way, an act can be accepted by God without an infused habit informing it. It is the act, not the habit, that matters for Ockham;[2] Bradwardine, on the other hand, regards the habit as always coming before the act; it is the means by which the act is achieved, and so it is the precondition for any act. This is the role of grace; without it there can be no good act:[3] Ockham's view has the effect of making a habit accidental to the act; it is, for him, in no way the essential constituent (without which there would be no act) which it is for Bradwardine.

Such a view Bradwardine condemned as Pelagian. Those, he says, who regard grace as formally, but not actually, producing good acts, as whiteness informs something white, make grace an indirect and accidental form. As such it has no immediate bearing upon what it informs, and this is the error of the Pelagians.[4] The wording of Bradwardine's strictures here again bears a resemblance to that frequently used by Ockham in referring to charity

gloriam et ad poenam; sed negantes has esse ad aliquos certos gradus' (*De causa Dei*, p. 427).

[1] 'Et habet corollarium quod omnes gradus gratiarum, meritorum, prosperitatum, aduersitatum, gloriae siue poenae, in praesenti et in futuro similiter sunt praedestinati a deo aeternaliter et distincte' (*ibid.*).

[2] 'Item ex actibus meritoriis generatur habitus inclinans ad consimiles actus, igitur sicut potest acceptare secundum actum elicitum mediante habitu: ita primum et per consequens potest acceptare actum sine habitu naturalem sine actu infuso' (Sentences, bk III, qu. 5 1).

[3] 'Item gratia est quidam habitus, et diligere Deum super omnia gratuito propter ipsum proprius actus eius; actus autem est finis, et perfectio habitus. . . . Quare habitus est propter actum non e contra' (*De causa Dei*, p. 336).

[4] 'Alii aestimant quod gratia facit actus bonos, non effectiue, sed tantum formaliter sicut albedo facit album, et anima animatum, et quaelibet forma suum formatum: sed ista possunt refelli. . . .
'Item gratia quae est habitus infusus, non est forma naturalis essentialis actus volendi ipsius grati, sicut nec aliquis habitus sui actus; est enim actus actualior habitu, nec subiectum habitus naturale. . . . Si quis autem dixerit, quod gratia est forma improprie et accidentalis quodammodo actus . . . boni quia videlicet informat voluntatem illum agentem incidit in pelagus Pelagii supra dictum' (p. 367).

and grace. Just as no one, says Ockham, has whiteness unless he is white, so having charity makes a man dear; but this in no way means that to be in charity is to be worthy of eternal life. The one does not follow from the other.[1] Thus Ockham will go no further than giving grace a formal status; if infused, it must inform goodness, but this does not mean that this leads to the acceptance of its acts by God. Its role is accidental to anything He does.

Bradwardine regards such a confining of grace to an accident as Pelagian. Yet it is interesting to see that this very refusal on Ockham's part to make a formal cause also an essential cause is his defence against such a charge. That anyone, he says, can be accepted by God without a supernatural form, and conversely, that to be supernaturally informed does not necessarily lead to glory, comes about because God is free. Nothing can necessitate His actions: neither a supernatural habit nor the lack of a supernatural habit. In both cases God is not bound to act in a constant and conditional way. This, he says, is very much the opposite of Pelagianism; for Pelagius postulated that a good act by a man made it necessary for God to reward him: if God did not, then He would have acted unjustly. Thus Ockham's God is free from His own determinism as well as from Pelagianism.[2] In this sense it would be more precise to say that it is not man so much as God who is free from grace: because His acts are not made conditional upon it, neither are His creatures'. It is for this reason that supernatural forms are left out of Ockham's reckoning.

[1] '. . . sicut quod aliquis [non] habeat albedinem nisi sit albus, dico quod bene denominatur talis habens charitatem carus: sicut albedinem albus . . . sed non necessario sit carus quod sit dignus vita eterna: et tamen carus est deo' (Sentences, bk. III, qu. 5 o).

[2] 'Ideo dico . . . quod aliquis potest esse deo acceptus et carus sine omni forma supernaturali inherente . . . quicunque potest habere actum meritorium sine tali forma supernaturali inherente, potest esse acceptus deo sine tali forma supernaturali inherente . . . ex puris naturalibus nemo possit mereri vitam eternam, nec etiam ex quibuscunque donis collatis a deo, nisi quia deus contingenter et libere et misericorditer ordinavit, quod habens talia dona possit mereri vitam eternam, ut deus per nullam rem possit necessitari ad conferendum cuicunque vitam eternam; et sic ista propria opinio maxime recedit ab errore Pelagii. Item errorem Pelagius posuit quod si aliquis habet actum bonum ex genere: deus necessitatur ad conferendum sibi vitam eternam, et non mere ex gratia sua, ita quod necessario foret iniustus si sibi non tribueret vitam eternam. . . . Ego autem pono quod nulla forma nec naturalis nec supernaturalis potest deum sic necessitare . . .' (bk. I, dist. 17, qu. I I and M).

FREE WILL

The place of the human powers is the second aspect of this dispute. It is at once clear that their importance will correspond to the importance given to supernatural habits. A lack of determinism upon God's part cannot help but confer greater freedom upon men; the supernatural element in their actions will be less pervading, because God's direction is less defined. Where, on the other hand, God's hand is in all things, even the smallest details will be informed by the supernatural. Ockham, then, binds human powers far less closely than Bradwardine. While he never specifies the extent of these powers, since this would also impinge upon God, he never gives them a rigid limit; that is, from God's absolute power they are capable of accomplishing anything that God wills for them. Because Ockham is not concerned with maintaining a constant place for the supernatural virtues, he gives human acts a much greater significance. It is the act which will gain merit, not the habit. Ockham's principle of economy is at work here, too; God rewards acts, not habits; therefore, the latter may be ignored as superfluous in discussing which are meritorious and which not. Consequently, Ockham, in looking for the cause of an act, turns away from the habit as accidental, and towards the human will. As we have already seen, in the first question condemned by the *magistri* at Avignon,[1] only that act which comes from free will is pleasing to God and accepted by Him. God, says Ockham, rewards a man for a good act; this act must, therefore, come freely from his own will, above all. Only that which is in us, and within our power, is meritorious; and so our wills are more important than any habit.[2]

The first cause, then, of any reward from God lies in the human will; this, and not the supernatural habit, is the starting-point of a meritorious act. It is this autonomy and initiative that Ockham gives to free will which Bradwardine considers the greatest

[1] Above, p. 189.

[2] 'Praeterea nihil est meritorium nisi quia voluntarium et hoc nisi quia libere elicitum vel factum, quia nihil est meritorium, nisi quod est in nobis, hoc est in nostra potestate. Sed nihil est in nostra potestate, ut possimus agere et non agere: nisi quia a voluntate tanquam a principio movente et non ab habitu, quia cum habitus sit causa naturalis, nihil est indifferens propter habitum, ergo meritum principaliter consistit penes voluntatem quod ipsa libere elicit' (Sentences, bk. 1, dist. 17, qu. 2 c).

menace of the times, as his introduction to *De causa Dei*[1] has shown. Only, he says, with grace acting upon it, can free will achieve good actions; grace comes before the will, in contrast to Ockham's view, where it is not only secondary but superfluous.[2]

What then, for Ockham, is the relationship between the human will and God's will and of what is it capable? God can accept a natural action from a man as worthy of eternal life without any supernatural habit. This acceptance by God, he says, is what the Lombard truly described as the work of the Holy Spirit which guides the human will and is a partial cause in its action. Thus it may be said that, while created charity is not necessary for the will's natural action, uncreated charity, as the Holy Spirit, is the means by which God in His absolute power accepts it.[3]

Once more, what is striking about this view is the almost word for word rejoinder that Bradwardine gives to it. There are many friends of the Pelagians, he says, who all agree on one thing: that created grace is not the true cause of good acts; others say that, while created grace and charity have in no way any effect upon good actions, uncreated grace and charity, as God and the Holy Spirit, do so.[4]

[1] Above, pp. 13–15.

[2] 'Ostenso quidem quod gratia cum voluntate efficit bonos actus. . . . Puto autem quod gratia gratis infusa prius naturaliter voluntate faciat actus bonos' (*De causa Dei*, p. 371).

'Corollarium quod tam Deus, quam gratia eius creata efficit proprie, prius naturaliter quemlibet actum bonum creaturae rationalis quam ipsa . . .' (*ibid*. p. 373).

[3] 'Deus potest aliquem acceptare in puris naturalibus tanquam dignum vita eterna sine omne habitu charitatis . . . et si hec sit opinio magistri sententiarum: tunc verum dicit, scilicet quod charitas potest de potentia dei absoluta non esse aliud quam spiritus sanctus coexistens acceptans actum naturalem et impellens voluntatem per hunc modum sicut causa partialis ad actum illum eliciendum: sed non opportet necessario quod sit aliquod accidens inherens anime' (Sentences, bk. III, qu. 8 c).

[4] 'Hic autem multi Pelagianorum amici conantur multipliciter respondere, qui tamen omnes in hoc uno concordant, quod gratia virtus creata seu charitas non vere et proprie efficit actus bonos, secundum substantiam actuum sed vel omnino non efficit, vel tantum aliquo modo improprie et transumpto. Aliqui namque dicunt quod gratia seu charitas virtus creata nullo modo efficit actus bonos, sed gratia et charitas increata quae est Deus et Spiritus Sanctus Dei. . . Sed isti possent utcunque subterfugere isto modo quasdam auctoritates praemissas, rationes tamen non possunt. Quisquis etiam catholicus Autoritates huiusmodi quasdam in superficie literae, quasdam vero parum interius sanis occulis intuetur, statim potest percipere alium intellectum, de gratia scilicet et charitate creata' (*De causa Dei*, p. 366).

This need only be noted here as an example of the very wide meaning Bradwardine gives to Pelagianism; to deny the efficacy of created grace, even while acknowledging that of uncreated, is, for him, to be implicated in Pelagianism. More significant, from the point of view of Ockham's outlook, is the essential part that the created will plays in any good act accepted by God: its initial impulsion is the *sine qua non* for its acceptance. Human activity is, therefore, the starting-point for any further development, either to good or to bad. This is the pre-condition of all merit and reprobation: the human will must act before God will accept it. But because the act alone counts, its nature is neutral; it is for God to decide whether it should be rewarded with glory or punished with damnation. His will alone makes one deed good and another bad: of themselves they are neither, merely acts. This is where Ockham differs from Bradwardine: only God's will, by His absolute power, makes an act meritorious; alone, all the habits in the world could not give it supernatural reward. Consequently, God's will and the wills of His creatures are the only two elements in merit: on the one side, there must be the act freely produced by a creature, of itself worth nothing; on the other, is the value which God's will alone imparts.[1] This separation of activity and value flows from Ockham's view of the divine will. As the measure for all things, all standards reside in its decree; and because, in its absolute power, God's will is infinitely free, what is worthy in one case can be unworthy in another.

Now the same view of God's will, as the source of everything created, leads to quite a different effect in Bradwardine's case. This is due, firstly to the hierarchy of faculties which reside in God's being and which make the divine will the expression of the

---

[1] '. . . nullus actus esset intrinsece et necessario virtuosus; sed solum contingenter extrinsece' (Sentences, bk. III, qu. 13 E).

'Item quicunque potest habere actum meritorium simpliciter potest cum tali actu acceptari sine omni habitu: sed viator potest habere actum meritorium sine omni caritate, igitur etc, maior patet: quia ideo dicitur actus meritorius: quia acceptatur a deo, minor probatur: quia quando sunt duo actus boni ex genere quorum neuter ex se est meritorius: nec dignus vita eterna si unus potest acceptari a deo et alius, patet de se: quia uterque est indifferens ex se ad acceptationem divinam: sed actus naturalis delectationis et actus elicitus a voluntate sunt huiusmodi patet de se, igitur potest deus acceptare actum naturalem sine omni charitate' (*ibid.* qu. 5 I).

divine essence and not of its ruler. The second reason is that, by Bradwardine's principle of divine participation, God's will is the senior mover in everything created; and so everything, as the extension of His will, bears the same constant and intrinsic values that His will bears. Thus the great gulf between the two views arises from their differences in approach. Ockham will go no farther than postulating God's will, on the one hand, and His creatures on the other; their connexion lies not in any ordered hierarchy, but in the infinite freedom of the divine will to enable them to do anything. In consequence everything is possible, particular things are probable and nothing is certain. Bradwardine, by starting with God and making His will the primary mover in everything outside His essence, introduces the *rationale* of divine causality into everything; in his case, everything, since it is what is, must be what is, and will so remain for ever. While Ockham regards voluntarism as disengaging God from His creatures, Bradwardine sees it as the rule of His will: hence the contrast in their outlooks.

Because Ockham makes an act of free will the first condition for its acceptance by God, its natural powers suffice to reach Him. This is the heart of his Pelagianism as viewed by his contemporaries.[1] It is God who, from His absolute power, decides what is to be rewarded with glory, just as He decides what should be punished. This leaves men capable of carrying out any act, such as loving Him above all, or obeying His commands, for, in each case, they only act: they do not merit.[2]

Thus, while for Ockham the starting-point of merit lies in an

---

[1] '. . . deus potest aliquem acceptare in puris naturalibus tanquam dignum vita eterna sine omni habitu caritatis' (*ibid.* qu. 8 c).

'Deo ergo largiente invenimus gratiam eius ad salvandum hominem cum libero arbitrio concordare; ita ut gratia sola possit hominem salvare nihil eius libero arbitrio agente' (*De causa Dei*, p. 330).

[2] '. . . diligere deum super omnia est actus acceptus deo et magis habet rationem acceptabilis ex natura sua quam habitus . . . ergo post actum etiam si nullus habitus remaneret posset talis acceptari a deo et propter actum bonum preteritum posset remunerari a deo vita eterna' (Sentences, bk. 1, dist. 17, qu. 1 E).

'Praeterea, omnis actus qui cum aliqua circumstantia que non est de se laudabilis est meritorius potest de potentia dei absoluta esse meritorius sine illa circumstantia, sed actus diligendi deum super omnia cum caritate que non est de se laudabilis est meritorius, ergo sine ea potest esse meritorius' (*ibid.* qu. 2 c).

act of free will, without value in itself, for Bradwardine it is grace.[1]

Their concepts differ towards both God and man. Ockham, by enabling man, of himself, to carry out actions which can be made meritorious by God, has cut through Bradwardine's order of priorities. Small wonder that Bradwardine characterizes this as one of the features of the *Pelagiani moderni*.[2] Free will, for Ockham, has, through God's absolute power, a far more exalted status than for Bradwardine. In the first place, the will is virtually the first mover in any act of merit; it has first to perform an action before God will accept it and reward it. Only free will, therefore, can create the necessary conditions for God's acceptance. In the second place, free will is independent of all supernatural habits; an act which came from charity as the first cause would not, in Ockham's eyes, be an act of free will at all.[3] In the third place, free will is capable of every action which God can accept and reward; a man can love God above all, obey His commands, desire to be good of his own powers, uninformed by any habit from God. He can do so, first, because God has no need of intermediary causes in anything that He can do: thus He does not need created habits. Second, because a man can alone perform an act worthy of merit, since only God makes such an act, indifferent in itself, good. Third, because it is the act which

---

[1] 'Cum ergo nullus ex puris naturalibus diligat Deum gratuito super omnia propter seipsum, sed propter aliquem alium finem, habitus ex talibus multiplicatis delectationibus generatus tantummodo inclinabit ad Deum similiter, et non aliter diligendum' (*De causa Dei*, p. 326).

[2] 'Adhuc autem Pelagiani quidem moderni respondent, dicendo, quod homo ex naturalibus puris potest diligere Deum super omnia gratis, propter seipsum secundum substantiam ipsam actus, non tamen meritorie, vel saltem non meritorie de condigno, licet forsan de congruo, sine gratia concomitante' (*ibid.* p. 335).
'. . . ubi recitantur 13 errores Pelagii; duo huius proferantur, non esse liberum arbitrium si Dei indigeret auxilio, quoniam in propria voluntate habet unusquisque facere aliquid, aut non facere' (*ibid.* p. 472).

[3] 'Praeterea nihil est meritorium nisi quod est in nostra potestate, sed illa caritas non est in nostra potestate ergo actus non est meritorius principaliter propter illam gratiam, sed propter voluntatem libere causantem, ergo posset Deus talem actum elicitum a voluntate acceptare sine gratia' (*Quodlibeta*, VI, qu. 1).
'. . . si actus caritatis esset a caritate et non a voluntate, non esset actus voluntarius' (Sentences, bk. I, dist. 17, qu. 2 E).

counts and this must come freely from the will and not from any
habit.[1]

Free will for Ockham, then, is an active and self-directing
agent, capable of good deeds of its own and free from the need for
grace or any other supernatural habit. The importance of this
view can be seen if we examine more closely its relation to merit.

MERIT

In a sense the whole of Ockham's views, as expressed so far,
build up to a view that men can merit *de congruo*; that is, through
their own actions, uninformed by habitual grace, they can gain
God's consideration and reward. Even though any such acceptance by God will be freely from Him, and in no way conditional
upon the justice of doing so, men have a very definite part to play.
They are responsible, as we have seen, for the first movement in
this process, by acting at all and acting freely. God, therefore,
responds to their actions and does not, as Bradwardine held, act
unconditionally, unilaterally and constantly. An act of merit, for
Ockham, then, is inseparable from an act of free will by men.[2]

Since by God's absolute power habits are unnecessary, the
Holy Spirit can accept the natural act of a created will and so
actions of hope and faith themselves can be natural and yet gain
supernatural reward.[3]

This acceptance by God of natural acts is the foundation of

[1] 'Sed omnes actus dilectionis respectu dei possunt esse naturales, igitur
habitus: quia deus potest ita acceptare actum naturalis dilectionis sicut
quemcumque alium actum elicitum mediante caritate' (bk. III, qu. 5 E).

'Quicquid deus potest facere mediante secunda causa in genere cause
efficientis vel finis, potest immediate per se, sed caritas creata si sit causa sive
efficiens sive disposita . . . erit causa secunda . . . ergo sine ea deus potest
dare alicui vitam eternam' (*Quodlibeta*, VI, qu. 1).

[2] '. . . et ideo requiritur ad bonitatem actus quod sit in potestate voluntatis
habentis talem actum . . . et tamen nullus ponit quod bonitas prima actus est
a fine vel a tempore, sed solum actus voluntatis' (Sentences, bk. III, qu.
10 R).

[3] 'Et eodem modo potest acceptare actum sperandi et credendi naturaliter
sine omni habitu supernaturali infuso' (*ibid.* bk. III, qu. 8 C).

'Ideo dico: quod non includit contradictionem aliquem actum esse
meritorium sine omni tali habitu supernaturali formaliter inherente . . . deus
voluntarie et libere acceptat motum voluntatis tanquam meritorium' (bk. I,
dist. 17, qu. 2 C).

Ockham's Pelagianism. It means that a man, by acting, can gain from God, and that natural deeds carry a very rich potential worth. It lies, therefore, in men's own hands to gain glory, even though God is the arbiter.

Merit is made by Ockham a *sine qua non* for reward and grace.[1] Thus, by God's *potentia absoluta*, merit is the joint product of the human will and the divine will. Grace and nature meet and mingle; each has a part to play. This general view of merit Bradwardine attacks as openly Pelagian. To say that a man, not in grace, can either love or obey God in the same way as he who is in grace is Pelagius's error.[2] It makes grace senseless and superfluous.[3] There is thus no point of contact between the mutual activity of God and man, in Ockham's case, and the uncaused unilateral grace of God, in Bradwardine's.

So far Ockham has been dealing with merit under God's absolute power; but he also discusses its place from the point of God's ordained power. In the latter case the ordinary conditions have to be observed and supernatural habits have their accepted traditional place. Yet here, too, merit *de congruo* shows leanings towards the Pelagian views that Bradwardine has attacked. Free will, says Ockham, prevents any man from being beyond salvation. If one loves God above all else, God can, from His ordained power, infuse grace into him. Similarly, an adult, who has the use of his free will, can only have his sins remitted by contrition. The act of hating sin alone suffices for its expulsion and the infusion of grace, because, from God's ordained power, it is worthy of merit *de congruo*; God, by His ordained power, cannot refuse to reward such an act with His grace.[4] God, then, is under

[1] Sed meritum non est nisi causa sine qua non respectu premii et gratie' (bk. IV, qu. I E).

[2] 'Si non gratus posset diligere et facere quodlibet dilectione et factione eiusdem speciei cum grato, possit sine gratia similiter implere omnia mandata sicut gratus, quod est error Pelagii' (*De causa Dei*, p. 369).

[3] 'Si ergo possent sine gratia ita sic facere, sufficeret Deo, et illis; imo nulla ratio, nulla causa, nulla utilitas Deo nec homini videretur, quare haec fieri debeant in gratia cum possent equaliter fieri sine ipsa, sed potius videretur quantum ad omnem actionem, superflua, penitus et inanis, sicut quantum ad omnem significationem citra cum fuerit ultima figura. . .' (*ibid*. p. 336).

[4] '. . . sed nullus habens usum rationis potest poni extra statum salutis, igitur si iste diligat deum super omnia deus de potentia ordinata sibi infundit gratiam (M). Et ideo dico sine omni preiudicio aliorum quod per nullum

compulsion, by His own ordinance, to award grace for actions which are meritorious *de congruo*. Nor, says Ockham, does grace already have to inform the act before God can reward it; for, by His ordained power, grace is conferred simultaneously with the good act and not before it in time.[1] Because acts such as these are uninformed by grace, they cannot merit *de condigno* but only *de congruo*; from which Ockham concludes that many are the acts *de congruo*.[2]

This is indeed the case: Ockham has made free will a compelling agent in gaining God's grace either through His ordained or His absolute power. Either way, the human will plays an all-important part; and, without it, there would be no merit. Where grace is superfluous free will is indispensable, whether in God's acceptance of a natural act by His *potentia ordinata* as *de congruo*, or by His *potentia absoluta* as worthy of eternal glory. In neither situation is grace needed, but the act of free will is the prerequisite in each. Thus Ockham reaches the same point by both methods. In one case God's will is so free that He can reward man's natural act with merit; in the other He has so ordained it that He cannot refuse to do so. Merit *de congruo* is, therefore, as Ockham implies, the general rule; and merit *de condigno*, as first requiring God's grace, the exception.

No wonder that Bradwardine called the use of merit *de congruo* the most specious and notorious aspect of the new

sacramentum potest remitti peccatum mortale sine omni contritione in generali vel in speciali, et hoc dico de eo qui potest uti libero arbitrio . . . adulto autem qui habet usum liberi arbitrii non remittitur sine motu bono proprie voluntatis (Q). . . Tertio dico . . . quod possibile est aliquem actum detestandi sufficere ad deletionem culpae et infusionem gratie, quia ille actus quo aliquis detestatur peccatum propter deum quia est deo offensum circumscripto omni alio sufficit (U). . . . Si queras an ille actus detestandi sufficiat ad expulsionem culpe et infusionem gratie. Respondeo ille actus est solus sufficiens ad meritum de congruo, nam habito isto actu deus statim infundit gratiam et *de potentia Dei ordinata non potest non infundere* (Y)' (Sentences, bk. IV, qu. 8 and 9).

[1] 'Si dicas quod nullus actus potest esse meritorius de potentia dei ordinata sine gratia, et per consequens presupponit gratiam et expulsionem culpae, igitur propter eum non expellitur culpa. Respondeo quod propter istum actum confertur gratia non prius tempore sed simul, et dico quod rĕctĭ gratie nullus actus est meritorius de condigno nisi ille qui est rĕctŭm eterne beatudinis' (bk. IV, qu. 9 Y).

[2] 'Et sic patet quod multi sunt actus meritorii de congruo et non de condigno' (*ibid.*).

Pelagianism.[1] It has given an indispensable place to works and makes them, in effect, a *sine qua non* for grace and reward. The first grace is within the reach of any man's natural powers, if God so wills. That is the centre of Ockham's position;[2] and, for Bradwardine, it was the essence of the Pelagianism against which *De causa Dei* was directed. In the first place, it exalts human powers to an importance and value of their own. In the second place, it makes them independent of the necessity of grace and puts the kingdom of God within their own natural reach. In the third place, it makes merit dependent upon human actions, while able to dispense with grace. Thus men themselves participate in the divine, and without their deeds there would be no reward.[3]

PREDESTINATION

The same divergence between Ockham and Bradwardine is to be found in their views on predestination. Apart from being the one remaining area of dispute in which there is clear evidence that Ockham's view is regarded by Bradwardine as Pelagian, it also shows how differently they regard God. Bradwardine, as we have seen throughout the first part of this work, regards God as having immutably ordained all that comes about, with His will as the instrument in attaining His decrees. This, in effect, makes everything outside God the extension of His will and allows no room for the interplay of secondary causes. It results in the denial of any autonomy or self-direction to men and their complete dependence upon God. We have already discussed how this contrasts with the views of Ockham, in the case of supernatural habits, free will and merit; in the case of predestination it remains to show that this difference is no less marked.

In contrast to the unilateral, uncaused nature of Bradwardine's view of predestination, Ockham sees a double aspect. In

---

[1] See p. 75 above.

[2] 'Ad argumentum dico quod aliquis de congruo potest mereri gratiam ex puris naturalibus, sic aliquis diligens deum super omnia naturaliter secundum rectam rationem et alias circumstantias requisitas ad actum meritorium meretur primam infusionem caritatis' (Sentences, dubitationes (prima), bk. IV).

[3] 'Est error Pelagianorum damnabilis participare fidem aut gratiam, scilicet eius initium et augmentum, unum scilicet dando Deo, alterum vero nobis, totum enim est totaliter dandum Deo' (*De causa Dei*, p. 433).

spite, he says, of the greater doubt as to its cause, compared with reprobation, predestination is twofold: on the one hand it has a cause and a reason; on the other hand, it has none. The reason in the first case is that a man can be saved only on account of his merits; and if he has not merited he will not be saved. In the second case, no reason for predestination is required because it comes about from God's special grace. He ordains those who are to be given eternal life, and they are endowed from eternity in a way that the first class is not.[1] In both cases the reason lies in God's will.[2] There is thus a clear division between the elect, made up of the saints, and the unpredestined. The first are God's chosen, preordained from eternity, and without condition, to eternal life; they are prevented from sinning. The second are saved on account of their merits; they can only gain eternal life by right doing. The choice and the conditions of their glory rest largely, but not entirely, with God: although any final reward must come from Him, He bases His decision upon what He foresees. To those who He knows will make good use of their powers and will persevere in His ways to the end, He gives glory. In this case beatitude appears as a consequence of merit, as damnation of demerit.

Once more, then, for the mass of mankind, free choice and independent action play a large and indispensable part in their destiny; they have much of their future in their own hands by using

[1] 'Sed de predestinatione videtur esse magis dubium. Et quantum ad hoc potest dici (sine preiudicio et assertione) quod alicuius predestinationis est aliqua causa et ratio, et alicuius non est talis ratio vel causa. Huius ratio est quia aliqui propter merita salvabuntur . . . Aliqui autem solum ex gratia speciali sunt ordinati ad vitam eternam, ita quod sibi ipsis non sunt derelicti sicut alii, sed preveniuntur ne possint ponere obicem, ne perdant vitam eternam, sicut fuit de beata virgine . . .' (Sentences, bk. I, dist. 41, qu. 1 B).

[2] Predestinationis primorum videtur esse alia ratio, quia sicut damnandi ideo reprobantur quia previdentur peccaturi finaliter, cum deus non prius est ultor quam aliquis sit peccator. Ita est de quibusdam predestinatis predestinantur quia previdentur finaliter perseverare in charitate, et quod deus non conferet eis vitam eternam nisi prius mererentur vitam eternam.

'Secundorum non videtur esse ratio quare predestinantur, nisi quia deus vult ita quod quicquid eius dat ut consequantur vitam eternam, nec permittit eis aliquid inesse quod potest eos impedire a vita eterna. Causa autem quare ipsos predestinat sine omni ratione: et alios propter rationem non est nisi divina voluntas, sicut causa quare beatus paulus fuit percussus a deo et conversus sine meritis quibuscumque praeviis, et alius non sic non est nisi divina voluntas' (ibid.).

their own resources to good effect. Good works help to prepare for God's grace and lead to predestination.[1] They do not, however, impose a necessity upon God to reward them. As ever, Ockham does not commit himself to the human will as the unqualified cause; all reward can only be given by God acting freely and of His own untrammelled volition. Were God's will to refuse, there would be neither merit nor grounds for expecting it. Thus, Ockham is, as usual, careful to make the divine will the final arbiter and so to bolt the door against charges of Pelagianism.

Yet this use of God's will did not prevent Bradwardine from making that very assertion. In Ockham's conception of predestination there are at least four Pelagian aspects which Bradwardine denounces in *De causa Dei*. First, there is the broad division made between the unconditional grace of the elect and conditions imposed upon the rest of mankind. This Bradwardine calls Cassian's solution,[2] the same view having been propounded by John Cassian in the fourth century; and Bradwardine, true to his habit of describing modern heresies by ancient terms, applied it to Ockham's opinion. It struck at the heart of Bradwardine's outlook. Secondly, Ockham, for all his invoking of God's will, allows that men can reach beatitude, even though not elected, and that their own merits are the means to grace and glory. This is, for Bradwardine, the simple resurrection of Pelagius himself; he does not even deign to discuss Ockham's qualification that God must be willing; to his eyes this is quite plainly to say that God predestines, not by His own will unconditionally and eternally, but through foreseeing the right use to which certain men will put their own powers. He rewards because of their merits and not

---

[1] 'Opera bona ex genere facta in peccato mortale sunt aliquo modo causa quare deus dat alicui gratiam . . . aliquo modo quamvis non sufficienter nec simpliciter meritorie talia opera bona disponunt ad gratiam, et per consequens ad effectum predestinationis. . . . Licet quicquid in homine ordinans ipsum ad salutem tanquam quo posito est dignus vita eterna comprehendatur sub effectu predestinationis, non tamen omne quocunque modo ordinans, scilicet disponendo vel impedimentum amovendo, comprehenditur sub effectu predestinationis, et huiusmodi est ipsa preparatio ad gratiam quae non sub effectu predestinationis cadit. . . . Nihil positivum potest fieri nisi per auxilium divinum et tamen non quodlibet tale est effectus predestinationis' (bk. I, dist. 41, qu. I B).

[2] 'Contra Cassianum mediantem, dicendo, Deum dare quibusdam gratiam suam gratis absque merito praecedenti, quibusdam vero non nisi prius ipsam recipere mereantur . . .' (cor. to cap. 35, *De causa Dei*, p. 313).

of His own forewilling.[1] Thirdly, Ockham, even accepting his plea that it is God who wills to glory or reprobation, makes merit a partial cause in reward. Though the decision lies with God the ground for it rests with man. He has, therefore, exposed himself at each turn to the many prongs of Bradwardine's attack: he makes man instrumental in gaining his own salvation; he makes God's predestination conditional, dependent upon human actions; he makes man's actions a partial and indispensable cause in his own glory.[2]

Finally, with Ockham as we have seen,[3] predestination cannot be called the original cause of all that the predestined do. The principle *non est prius deus ultor quam aliquis sit peccator* applies as much to glory as to sin. Only in its larger meaning, as including the reward God gives to his creatures, can predestination be said to include men's actions. It is, therefore, as much an effect as a cause. This, too, Bradwardine calls Pelagian.[4]

As in their differences over supernatural habits, the power of free will, and its place in merit, so in those over predestination, Ockham and Bradwardine tread along conflicting paths, constantly colliding and encumbering their respective ways. The reason for this lies in their different points of approach and their quite opposite interpretations of the supremacy of God's will. For Ockham its infinite freedom permeates God's creatures so that they, and men in particular, enjoy a largesse of fortune which may take them straight to God. Bradwardine's view of God's will

[1] 'Item iste fuit unus de erroribus Pelagii haeretici, dicere scilicet Deum praedestinare propter merita future praescita' (*ibid.* p. 424).

'Ex his quoque apparet, quod omnes Doctores catholici, et concilia, imo et Ecclesia tota Dei condemnantes haereticos errores Pelagii, ponentes gratiam secundum merita nostra dari, et praedestinari quoscumque propter merita sua futura, intelligunt modo dicto; Quare constat illam assertionem esse haereticam, quae asserit merita causam sine qua non, causam scilicet partialem mouentem, seu excitantem Deum ad praedestinandum quemcumque, vel ad gratiam alicui conferendam' (*ibid.* p. 426).

[2] 'Unde et nec minus clare potest retundi error quidam Pelagianus ficturus forsitan et dicturus, quod Deus non dat gratiam homini propter aliquod meritum antecedens, sed propter merita praeuisa ab eo' (*ibid.* p. 363).

[3] See p. 207 above.

[4] '. . . sic in ista materia fuit Pelagius, ponendo causam originalem Praedestinationis et Reprobationis, non ex parte Dei Praedestinantis et Reprobantis, sed ex parte Praedestinatorum et Reprobatorum, aptitudinem scilicet atque actum' (*De causa Dei*, p. 436).

P

is rather like that of a powerful searchlight, which, in its sweep and power, robs every other ray of the smallest gleam: there is nothing which can stand with it. Ockham, on the other hand, leaves man his own torch, lighted though it is from God. Their conflict throughout turns on their disparate views of God's will and the powers which it gives to men; and this likewise determines their approach. Ockham, by making God's will possibility, has little more to say about Him; he is free to concentrate on the powers this freedom gives to men. Theology, therefore, plays little part in his system, for God Himself is virtually outside it. Bradwardine, on the other hand, has left nothing undefined as springing from the Godhead; his outlook becomes above all an essay in clarifying God's relations to His creatures. In his case, this means virtually their annihilation in God's cause. Thus what contact there is between such discordant systems can only be in their conflict, as we have amply seen.

CHAPTER XII

ASPECTS OF SCEPTICISM

To turn from Durandus of St Pourçain and William of Ockham to Robert Holcot, Thomas Buckingham and Adam of Woodham is to see how far-reaching the new disputes were. In Aureole's case interest centres over God's knowledge of future contingents and the questions of logic raised. The other thinkers, however, all extend the positions of Durandus and Ockham: they not only cross the Rubicon but they burn their boats irrevocably behind them. With Holcot, Buckingham and Woodham the full import of Bradwardine's outlook emerges: they each answer to the more extreme charges he brings against the modern Pelagians. God's *potentia absoluta* seems to swallow up the whole discussion, and even the limited certainty allowed by Ockham to natural actions is sacrificed to the limitless possibilities of God's absolute will. As a result, the positions adopted become more extreme until none of the traditional landmarks remain, and, with future contingents in particular, come to involve the foundations of belief itself.

PIERRE AUREOLE[1]

It is only on the question of future contingents that Aureole collides with Bradwardine. P. Vignaux[2] has shown how contrary Aureole's views were to Ockham's on the questions of supernatural habits and grace; there is no trace of the Pelagian about him. Nor does Bradwardine ever describe his views as being so: his case is far more that of being indirectly on the side of Bradwardine's opponents by refusing to acknowledge God as Bradwardine sees Him. No suggestion, therefore, is made here that Aureole was one of Bradwardine's *Pelagiani moderni* in the

---

[1] I am indebted for most of this section on Aureole to Appendix V in K. Michalski's *Le Problème de la volonté à Oxford et à Paris au XIVe siècle*. He has here anticipated me in collating the relevant texts, and I can do little more than occasionally dot the i's and cross the t's.

[2] P. Vignaux, *Justification et prédestination chez Duns Scot, Guillaume d'Ockham, Pierre Aureole, Grégoire de Rimini*.

complete sense. His importance rests upon his being one of the leading members in the dispute about divine knowledge and contingency.

The problem of God's future knowledge is, for Aureole, that of reconciling certainty with contingency; that is to say, if God knows everything that will come about, how can this knowledge be contingent? The fact of God's knowing that something is to be means that it will be, and, in that case, it cannot not be; far from being contingent, therefore, it will be eternally determined by God's knowledge. Thus it would appear that divine foreknowledge means divine determinism, and annihilation of freedom and contingency. The alternative is to refuse God eternal knowledge on the ground that, for a thing to be contingent, it cannot already exist; and therefore God cannot actually know it. This is the course that Durandus takes, and so, too, does Aureole, though by a different method. In answering the question whether a proposition about a future contingent can be true or false, he quotes Aristotle that, if it is to be known with certainty, it cannot be contingent but already determined. Aureole supports this verdict of the Philosopher's and concludes, first, that knowledge of a future contingent can be either true or false. To say, for instance, that Socrates will run is a neutral proposition since the truth cannot exist until the act of which it is part exists; that is, until Socrates has run. Were the proposition about Socrates to be true, says Aureole, it would be inevitable and so could not be contingent; and Socrates would then be predetermined to run. Secondly, therefore, God's knowledge of future contingents must similarly be neutral; for, unless they are neither true nor false, His knowing would determine what is not and thus destroy its contingency. God's knowledge does not precede the truth that He knows; if it did, were it even to be an instant before the event, the future would be determined and not contingent. Thirdly, Aureole makes the general inference that divine knowledge in no way deals with future contingents except in their actuality.[1]

[1] 'An propositio singularis de futuro contingenti sit determinate vera vel falsa in utraque parte contradictionis. Fuit vera mens Aristotelis opposita, sicut patet I Peri hermeneias et arguit ad hoc, quia si singularis de futuro contingenti sit vera determinate, iam non determinatum quid fiet et ita impossibile est non fieri et per consequens tollitur omnis solicitudo, quia sive solicitemur sive consiliemur sive negotiemur vel non; id quod deter-

It is clear from this, as Michalski points out,[1] that Aureole
bases his denial of future knowledge to God on three-value logic:
that is, he asserts that a thing, in addition to being true or false,
can be either. There is a neutral value between them. Now this
via media in which a thing can be equally possible or impossible
is, in a sense, the pivot of fourteenth-century scepticism: it is implicit in Ockham's whole discussion of supernatural habits in the
last chapter. It is no less evident in his own discussion on God's

minatum est, fiet. Restat ergo nunc dicere, quod videtur sub triplice pro-
positione. Prima quidem, quod sententia Philosophi est penitus conclusio
demonstrata ita, quod nulla propositio singularis formari potest de futuro
contingenti, de qua concedi possit, quod sit vera eius opposita falsa vel e
converso. Sed quaelibet est nec vera nec falsa. Unde quamvis verum sit,
quod Sortes erit vel non erit, formando propositionem disiunctivam, tamen
categorice dicendo: "Sortes currit (=curret)" propositio nec vera vel falsa
est; similiter nec opposita "Sortes non currit (=curret)." Et tota ratio, quia
sequitur demonstrative, quod omne contingens inevitabiliter eveniet; in-
evitabilitas autem tollit omnem solicitudinem, negotium et consultationem;
quod negare est negare per se notum et ponere oppositum principiorum
moralis philosophiae et humanae naturae experientiae, cui inditum est, quod
negotietur et consilietur circa futura. Quod ergo sequatur immutabilitas
futurorum, si conceditur, quod propositio de futuro, illud exprimens sit
vera vel falsa, potest evidenter demonstrari ex duabus propositionibus.
Prima quidem, quod si talis propositio vera est, illa immutabiliter et inevitabiliter erit vero. Secunda vero, quod ex illa inevitabiliter et necessario
sequitur, quod tale futurum ponetur in esse. Primum ergo assumptum patet
ex multis, scilicet quod si haec propositio vera est "antichristus erit" immutabiliter est vera' (Aureole, Sentences, bk. I, dist. 38, art 3, p. 883).

'Secunda vero propositio est, quod notitia divina, quam de affirmativa
praecise vel negativa praecise formata de futuro sit vera vel falsa. Immo re-
linquit utramque nec veram nec falsam, nulla enim notitia dat propositioni
de futuro veritatem vel falsitatem nisi illa, quae tendit in futurum ut distans
per modum notitiae exspectativae. Et ratio huius est quia notitia, quae dat
determinationem alicui pro aliquo instanti, debet coexistere illi instanti. Si
ergo dat determinationem pro instantibus praecedentibus actualitatem,
necessario debet illa notitia praecedere actualitatem et eam aspicere ut
potiorem et distantem et per consequens notitia exspectativa. Sed declaratum
est supra, quod notitia Dei non est exspectativa futuri, nec tendit in ipsum
tanquam in distans; unde non praecedit actualitatem futuri, ergo non dabit
determinationem illi actualitati pro aliquo instanti praecedenti et per consequens nec propositio formanda habebit a divina notitia, quod sit vera vel
falsa. . .' (*ibid.* p. 886).

'Tertia quoque propositio est tenenda in hac materia pro regula generali,
quod divina notitia non dat aliquid futuro contingenti in futurum, nisi
quantum actualitas posita dedit toti tempori praecedenti. Hoc autem sequitur
ex praedictis' (*ibid.* p. 889).

[1] *Le Problème de la volonté*, p. 317. Ph. Boehner, in Ockham's *Tractatus de
praedestinatione*, pp. 43 *et seq.*, has denied this, but this is the effect of
Aureole's position.

knowledge of the future; yet in this connexion Ockham puts it to a different use from Aureole. He only asserts that it cannot be proved by reason that God knows future contingents; he does not deny that God knows them:[1] thus Ockham cannot be accused of denying that God can know the future; he denies that this can be established logically. There is all the difference between this view and that of Aureole's; for the latter uses Ockham's scepticism to support assertion, where Ockham never went beyond scepticism. I cannot, therefore, agree with Michalski when he sees Ockham as hand in glove with Aureole in his denial that God can know future contingents. More significant, it would seem, is that on the basis of their common method Aureole makes a challenge to God's omniscience. It is one further aspect of the conflict in which Bradwardine engages for the defence of God's power. The same issues are involved: to accept as basic the theological truths of divine power and to view everything else from their heights as Bradwardine does; or to refuse to move beyond the scope of logic and proof, even when it means, on occasions, running counter to God, and when it always means doubt and neutrality instead of belief. Thus the whole concept of three-value logic is abhorrent to Bradwardine's outlook; once accept it, and God Himself is in danger and His powers impaired. His reply to Aureole is not to argue in Aureole's own terms of logic, but to invoke God's omnicausality as applied throughout *De causa Dei*.

We have already noticed in Part I[2] Bradwardine's reply to the charge that divine foreknowledge means divine determinism. It is the same as that of Duns Scotus: that is, if the first cause is free then every secondary cause will also be free. God is free; therefore, says Bradwardine, His knowledge, far from destroying contingents, creates them. In this way none of Aureole's difficulties or contradictions have to be met. More specifically, the great interest of Bradwardine's reply lies in his references to Aureole

---

[1] 'Ideo dico ad questionem quod indubitanter est tenendum quod deus certitudinaliter et evidenter scit omnia futura contingentia, sed hoc evidenter declarare, et modum quo scit omnia futura contingentia exprimere est impossibile omni intellectui pro statu isto. . . . Ista tamen ratione [philosophi] non obstante tenendum est quod deus evidenter cognoscit omnia futura contingentia sed modum exprimere nescio' (Sentences, bk. 1, dist. 38, qu. 1 L and M).   [2] Above, p. 100.

under the sixth opinion which he opposes in his discussion on
future contingents. In this Bradwardine talks of a famous
philosopher from Toulouse holding this opinion, whom he
heard engage in public disputation at Avignon. Both the personal
reference and the content of his opponent's argument fit Aureole
closely: although Toulouse is now disputed as his birthplace, he
was commonly associated with the town through his teaching at
the Franciscan house there;[1] moreover it is Aureole's view, which
is quoted in the sixth opinion, that no simple proposition about
future contingents is true or false, as Aristotle stated in *Peri
hermeneias*. This, says Bradwardine, amounts to saying that
nothing is future contingently, but only from absolute necessity,
which he has already refuted. If anyone denies this to be the consequence of Aureole's position, he goes against the Philosopher's
principle of contradiction: that if one thing is false its opposite
must be true. To accept a neutral value would be to make everything, God included, both future and not future at the same time,
all future knowledge thus being removed. This, says Bradwardine, amounts to Cicero's denial that God knows nothing that
will come into being freely. It, therefore, removes all freedom of
movement; for by holding that nothing in contingents is future
this opinion rejects movement and change. No proposition about
the future would be true unless it were so of necessity; and this
Bradwardine denies not only in his own name but in that of truth
and authority.[2]

---

[1] *Dict. théol. cath.* XII, cols. 1811–12.

[2] 'Opinio sexta fingit, quod aliquod est futurum ad utrumlibet vel non
futurum in sensu composito, non autem in sensu diviso, quam sic astruere
moliuntur. Nulla propositio simplex de futuro in materia contingente aequaliter est vera vel falsa, Philosopho I peri hermenias ult. attestante: quare nec
aliquid est futurum ad utrumlibet, vel non futurum diuisim. Hanc autem
opinionem audiui in Curia Romana a quodam famoso Philosopho Tolosano in
quadam disputatione solenni de contingentia futurorum, secundum eam
totaliter publice respondente, quam et Oxoniae similiter audiebam. Sed
haec faciliter conuincetur: nam secundum eam nihil est futurum ad utrumlibet contingenter, sed omnia quae euenient, euenient de necessitate penitus
absoluta, quod 12 huius damnat.

'Praeterea si utramque illarum negaueris, concedes inter contradictoria
medium reperiri, quod omnes sophistae, logici, philosophi, et theologi de-
testantur: quod et philosophus 4. Metaphys. 27 multipliciter reprobat et
condemnat; qui et 29 scilicet ult. Est, inquit, necesse contradictionis partem
alteram esse veram; ubi et immediate subiungit, Amplius si omne aut dicere
aut negare esse necesse, utraque falsa esse impossibile est. Item Antichristus

Bradwardine in opposing Aureole's view is as concerned to rebut his method as what he says. He clearly sets himself against the modern scepticism and stands by the traditional logic that a thing is either true or false but cannot be both. It provides an added indication that Bradwardine was fighting on a front far wider than that of a specific heresy; he was fighting scepticism in all its expressions as it affected belief in God. Although it is true to say that the most dangerous sector concerns human powers, it was no less vital for Bradwardine to prevent assaults upon God's attributes. The two stand or fall together and as such they are indivisible. His controversy therefore with Aureole has a very real importance; and its meaning helps us to place Bradwardine more surely.

ROBERT HOLCOT

Robert Holcot well illustrates how fruitfully Ockham provided for his followers along the path to scepticism. He takes up many of the same positions that Ockham held; and he also extends them. Despite his fulsome qualifications to everything, it is not hard to discern the same trait of doubt that moulded Ockham's views. With room for everything, there is hardly room for God; possibility once again dissolves the stable order that Bradwardine proclaims; and men can do all that God can will. Thus, on the one hand, there is divine causality; on the other divine indeterminacy. Holcot's view represents the application to which the latter

erit vel non erit: ergo Antichristus erit vel non erit; ergo est disiunctiva vera, ergo et altera partium. Item tunc nec Deus, nec Angelus aut Propheta sciret Antichristum, nec quicquam possibilium contingenter esse futurum diuisim vel non futurum, sed tantum esse futurum vel non futurum coniunctim, sicut et scit quilibet idiota; quare et omnis praescientia penitus tolleretur, sicque haec opinio coincidit in secundam 13 huius destructam.

'Item haec opinio tollit omnem motionem et actionem liberam, et meritoriam successiuam. Nam secundum eam in contingentibus talibus nihil est futurum; ergo nullus terminus ad quem motus, nec aliquid mutatum esse. . . Amplius autem secundum istam sententiam, nulla propositio de futuro esset vera aut esse posset, nisi propositio necessaria; quod Logica, philosophia, Theologia, et omnis vera scientia reputat esse falsum. . .' (De causa Dei, pp. 692–3).

Also: 'Alia est opinio Ciceronis, scilicet quod multa euenient libere, sed Deus illa non praescit. . . . Nesciuit enim videre quomodo esset certa praescientia omnium futurorum, nisi et esset absoluta necessitas omniquaque, sicque libertas omnimodo tolleretur. Credidit enim, quod praescientia futurorum et libertas eorum necessario repugnarent. . .' (ibid. p. 689).

outlook can be put. As the almost exact contemporary of Brad-wardine[1] he indicates the attitude against which Bradwardine had to contend, and the effect of Ockham's teaching upon think-ers of his generation.

The setting for Holcot's views on grace, supernatural habits and human powers is, as in Ockham's case, provided by his use of God's *potentia absoluta*. This supplies the freedom for his Pelagian-sounding assertions since, as we have seen, everything is postulated as being freely willed by God and not obtained by men. Thus in the case of grace Holcot follows a similar path to Ockham's. There is, he says, no definite order between grace and glory, sin and reprobation. God can give grace to one and yet not reward him; while He can bestow eternal life upon a mortal sinner. God's love is clearly greater for the sinner to whom He has given beatitude than for him who was given grace. This, says Holcot, shows that God's grace and His love bear no relation to each other; the one does not necessarily imply the other.[2] As with Ockham, Holcot reaches the position that grace, or any super-natural habit, is not a necessary step *en route* to glory. God's will can dispense with it, as He can dispense with everything; He can thus accept natural actions uninformed by a supernatural virtue.[3]

---

[1] They were both born *c*.1290 and both died in the Black Death, 1349.

[2] 'Ad primum quando arguitur contra primam conclusionem ... dico quod ista consequentia non valet: deus infundit charitatem isti: vel auget vel conservat in isto scilicet *a* charitatem: et non *b*: ergo magis diliget *a* quam *b*: quia capio unum praescitum ad mortem eternam existentem in gratia: et alium praedestinatum existentem in peccato mortali: istum plus diligit manifestum est: quia isti vult maius bonum scilicet vitam eternam: et tamen nullam charitatem sibi dat. Similiter et non sequitur formaliter: sed ut nunc tantum: iste caret charitate: ergo si decedat damnabitur, nam non includit contradictionem quod deus hominem sine charitate beatificet. ... Secundo dico quod consequens non est inconveniens, videlicet quod minus diligens deum plus diligatur a deo: nam de facto verum est in exemplo posito de prescito existente in gratia et praedestinato existente in peccato mortali' (Sentences, bk. I, qu. 4, art. 3 H).

[3] 'Dico tunc istam conclusionem: quod deus potest acceptare ad vitam eternam omnes actus naturales alicuius hominis: et facere omnes actus liberos atque indifferentes aut non meritorios. ... Praeterea deus libere acceptat actum voluntatis: ergo non necessitatur ad acceptandum eum nec a se nec a creatura, ergo si sibi placeret: posset acceptare actus naturales ... ergo non est contradictio: dicendo quod actus naturalis sit meritorius si deo placet: et hoc quia eque libere posset illum acceptare ad vitam eternam' (*ibid*. qu. I, art. 4 D).

Once again this view of the supernatural virtues gives an added importance to natural actions. Because grace and charity are not a *sine qua non* for merit and reward, natural actions, God willing, can fulfil their role unaided.

This, in Holcot's system, has three consequences. First, that natural powers can alone suffice for a number of worthy actions such as loving God.[1] The human intellect can, by its own powers, believe that God is the highest good and want to love Him above all; but, as so often happens with Holcot, he qualifies this by saying that, as at present ordained, a man cannot, by himself, obey a command to love God above all things else. It is hard to see that this qualification means more than maintaining respect for God's *potentia ordinata*; so, however much Holcot allows to men, he does not exalt them at the expense of what God has ordained.[2] Secondly, in Holcot's view of human powers, human inclinations are worthy of grace. A disposition to good, even though not followed by a good action, can be accepted by God as worthy of reward.[3] In the same way, a good action through the proper use of free will can gain grace. Thus Holcot concludes that men have grace in their own power albeit indirectly and imperfectly.[4]

[1] 'Circa primam difficultatem quae est an homo ex suis naturalibus sine habitu supernaturali possit diligere deum super omnia: id est sine gratia vel charitate: et in isto articulo dico duas conclusiones. Prima est affirmativa talis, homo potest ex suis solis naturalibus diligere deum super omnia. Hanc conclusionem probo sic, omne illud quod intellectus humanus ex suis naturalibus potest credere est summe diligendum: potest ex suis naturalibus summe diligere . . . nec opportet quod aliquem habitum sibi deus infundat, ergo potest eum diligere super omnia sine habitu. Secundo arguo sub hac forma. Homo potest per sola naturalia diligere deum plusquam istam rem. . . . Tertio arguo sic, homo potest ex solis naturalibus velle deum esse deum: et non aliud a deo esse deum. . . . Quarto quia homo errans potest diligere creaturam super omnia: et frui creatura ex suis naturalibus: ergo pari ratione frui deo' (bk. I, qu. 4, art. 3 F).

[2] 'Secunda conclusio est ista: nullus homo potest libere implere preceptum de dilectione dei super omnia per sola naturalia stante lege que nunc est' (*ibid.*).

[3] 'Dicendum est quod talis meretur non quia credit, nec quia vult credere precise: sed quia vult credere: et deus acceptat actum suum credendi tam dignum praemio' (bk. I, qu. I, art. 5 G).

[4] 'Potest igitur homo in aliquam operationem per usum bonum liberi arbitrii: qua dispositione existente in homine deus infundit sibi gratiam, et sic aliquo modo habemus gratiam in nostra potestate: videlicet dispositive et incomplete: non tamen perfecte et effective' (bk. I, qu. 4, art. 3 K).

Thus far Holcot has followed Ockham's position in awarding to natural powers both capacity to do good and power to influence God's grace. It is hardly necessary to add that Bradwardine regards such views as Pelagian to the full; and we have seen, in the last chapter, how harshly he pilloried them. There is a third aspect of Holcot's view on free will, however, which differs from Ockham's and, in a sense, betrays an even greater scepticism. One of the capital features in Ockham's treatment of free will and natural powers was their importance in any act of merit; time and again we noted how indispensable a part men played in gaining grace. Though supernatural habits could be set aside, the act of free will never. Holcot even eliminates this constant factor: God's will can do everything without the human will needing to move. An act of merit, he says, depends upon its conforming with God's will; a man merits if God wills it, just as God wills his demerit. No power rests with the created will at all; God could treat men like the beasts and allow them to act without laws or precepts.[1] Now while Ockham would not have denied God this complete power, he yet never allowed it full and unilateral play in awarding merit. Thus, though the two thinkers started from a common attitude, they differ in emphasis. With Holcot there is even less order than with Ockham.[2] In the case of loving God, too, Holcot says that one man, by loving Him less than another man does, can gain the greater reward. Thus the less a man loves God the more he may be loved by Him: a further sign that free will can be discounted.[3] Holcot, although not

---

[1] 'De secundo articulo: videlicet utrum sit in potestate hominis quod actus suus sit meritorius vel demeritorius dico istam conclusionem quod non est in potestate hominis quod actus suus sit meritorius alicuius boni vel demeritorius ut ei correspondeat aliqua poena. Hec conclusio sic apparet: omne meritum vel demeritum est ex hoc quod actus creature est conformis vel difformis legi divine: ideo enim homo meretur quia facit sicut deus vult eum facere . . . et ideo demeretur quia facit contrarium legi divine, sed non est in potestate voluntatis creature quod sibi aliqua lex a deo ponatur, posset enim deus permittere hominem sine lege sibi data et sine preceptis vel consiliis sicut permittet bestias: si voluntati sue placeret' (bk. I, qu. I, art. 2 D).

[2] 'Actus naturalis sit meritorius si deo placeret . . . sicut sub ista lege acceptat de facto usum liberi arbitrii, et isto modo videtur deus acceptasse mortem innocentium: in quibus nullus fuit usus liberi arbitrii' (bk. I, qu. I, art. 4 D).

[3] 'Secundo dico quod consequens non est inconveniens, videlicet quod minus diligens deum plus diligatur a deo; nam de facto verum est in

departing from Ockham's path, strays farther along it, and seems more concerned with what he finds there than nearer home. In none of these suppositions would Ockham have disagreed, but he gives less emphasis than Holcot to the way in which God can dispense with the part played by free will. Holcot seems absorbed by the infinite resources that God can employ in creating paradox. He could, he says, order a man to do something and then refuse to reward him for having obeyed. Thus, like Ockham, he refuses intrinsic merit to any action, even obeying God's commands.[1] In Holcot's view, the primary consideration of God's freedom of will virtually excludes everything else, even rational actions on His part; for as we have seen, God can reward for sin, if He so wills. Nevertheless, in this process, men have emerged with a similar freedom and independence which Ockham awarded them. The agreement in their outlooks is greater than the differences, and, in each case, free will and natural powers triumph over the supernatural virtues. In this, each stands equally branded as Pelagian by Bradwardine.

In Holcot's views on merit there is the same mingling of God's absolute and ordained powers as with Ockham; that is to say, men can merit by their own powers if God so decides to accept their actions by His *potentia absoluta*, and they can also merit from His *potentia ordinata* by obeying His decrees.

In the case of God's absolute power, as we have already seen, a man can gain glory by his own powers, just as he could be consigned to the flames if God so willed.[2]

Most striking is Holcot's view that a man can merit by false faith if God so wills. This is one more illustration of the paradoxes of which God is capable when His will is the sole criterion

exemplo posito de prescito existente in gratia et predestinato existente in peccato mortali' (bk. I, qu. 4, art. 3 F).

[1] '. . . nec esset meritum facere divina precepta: nec demeritum facere prohibitum, cuius probatio est: quia pro nullo actu quo sit precipitur: merces foret debita ipsi facienti, posset enim deus precipere homini quod faceret aliquid: et tamen nihil velit sibi dare seu promittere si suum preceptum impletur et eodem modo prohibere ne aliquid faceret: et tamen transgredientem in nullo punire' (bk. I, qu.I, art. 6 H).

[2] 'Deus tamen posset multipliciter ordinare sicut sibi placeret: vel annihilando ipsum: vel conservando sibi vitam eternam sine meritis. . . igitur homo posset mereri coelum ex puris naturalibus. . .' (bk. II, qu. I, I).

of conduct. Unlike Bradwardine and the traditional thinkers, Ockham and his school eschew all proof and definition in discussing God: He is, for them, omnipotent first and last; His attributes and qualities are beyond our ken. They are, therefore, in no way pledged to observe His perfection and goodness as separate qualities in the way that Bradwardine is. Anything that God wills is enough. Holcot expresses this when he replies to the charge that to by-pass the supernatural virtues is to make them superfluous. God's will, he says, by willing makes a thing necessary: it needs no other justification.[1]

God, therefore, can deceive and lie without impairing His perfection in any way; rather, it is additional proof of His freedom. An act is meritorious only if it conforms to the divine will; similarly it is unworthy if it does not. Beyond that there is no good or bad. Thus Holcot, while paying due respect to authority, asserts that God can deceive.[2]

From this it follows that a man can merit by false faith in wanting to believe what God has commanded him to believe. Merit, says Holcot, is not concerned with truth or falsity; it comes from following God's will:[3] in this view, we have reached the limits of indeterminacy; nothing is guaranteed: one thing is as possible or impossible as another; the good can equally be bad; the false is as valid as the truth. God, as Holcot sees Him, is capable of anything; while always paying court to God's law as ordained

---

[1] 'Ad tertium quando arguitur quod tunc potest homo etc. Dico quod hoc non includit contradictionem, et quando arguitur igitur frustra datur gratia negatur consequentia, nam placet deo: et ideo non est frustra, alioquin omnia forent frustra. Nam ideo sunt quecumque sunt: quia deo solummodo placent ut sint: et si aliquid esset quod deo non placeret: frustra esset' (bk. I, qu. 4, art. 3 E).

[2] 'Ad secundum inconveniens quod aufert in eodem argumento: quod deus posset fallere et decipere, dico quod non habendo respectum ad auctoritatem: sed respiciendo ad virtutem voluntatis concedo quod deus potest fallere et decipere, id est voluntarie causare errorem in mente hominis: et facere eum credere aliter quam res se habet' (bk. I, qu. I, R).

[3] 'Ad quintum principale quando infertur pro inconvenienti quod homo possit mereri per fidem falsam: consequens est contra Anselmum II cur deus homo c.XVI . . . sed ponderando propositionem que infertur pro inconvenienti videlicet quod homo posset mereri per fidem falsam: concedo eam, homo enim volendo credere certam propositionem que precipitur esse credenda: et est falsa: potest mereri: nec pertinet ad meritum fidei utrum sit vera an falsa. . . . Posse autem deum precipere aliquem falsum credi non est dubium' (*ibid.*).

in this world, he is not confined by it. Holcot is ever seeking the farthest realms of possibility, removed from all earthly limits. In making God deceive and reward for false faith he has found them.

To turn to Holcot's view of merit under God's *potentia ordinata* is to return to more familiar surroundings, albeit not wholly orthodox. A sinner, says Holcot, can merit *de congruo* justification by contrition. This merits a minimum amount of grace.[1]

Thus an action by the human will, small though it is, is worthy of reward. The act of contrition, moreover, is more deserving of merit than any other action which may be afterwards carried out, even though informed by charity.[2] Consequently, in certain circumstances, God may be man's debtor; for, if He ordained that an act should be done and, when carried out, He refused to recompense its author, God would in a certain way be in his debt. But this would only be the case by His ordained power; by His absolute power God is only what He wills.[3]

The combined effect of Holcot's use of God's two kinds of power is to give natural powers full scope to gain reward on their own and to make it their due in certain circumstances. As we have so often seen, either case tends towards Pelagianism in Bradwardine's eyes; his condemnations apply, therefore, as much

[1] 'Nam peccator meretur de congruo iustificationem per motum contritionis. Unde potest concedi quod est dare minimum actum meritorium qui potest per se subsistere: et illi correspondet una gratia minima que datur pro meritis praedictis. . .' (bk. IV, qu. I, art. 8 CC).

[2] 'Ad secundum argumentum principale quid tendit ad probandum hanc conclusionem: quod homo per primum actum meritorium vite eterne plus meretur quam etc., et similiter quod plus meretur per actum contritionis: quam per actum martyrii vel per ingressum religionis: vel per quemcumque bonum actum elicitum postea ab eodem existenti in charitate: concedo conclusionem pro nunc' (bk. I, qu. I o).

[3] 'Ad tertium quando arguitur quod similiter homo posset mereri tempore. Dico quod aliquem esse debitorem est dupliciter. Uno modo obligatur ad reddendum mercedem operanti ex certo valore absolute, et sic non est possibile quod homo faciat deum debitorem ad dandam vitam eternam. Alio modo potest homo facere debitorem aliquem extensive ex conventione et acceptatione alterius volentis sibi obligari, et sic est possibile quod homo est debitor hominis: quia sic statuit cum homine: quod si servaverit legem suam: reddet sibi vitam eternam. Et tunc ulterius arguendo: aut potest deus premium reddere isti: aut non potest. Dico quod de potentia dei absoluta potest non reddere isti: qui non est debitor hominis nisi quia vult esse debitor' (Determinatio, qu. 2, x).

to Holcot's ideas as to Ockham's, except in the case of God's deceit. This, however, will be dealt with more fully when we discuss
Holcot's attitude to future contingents. So far as merit and grace
and natural powers are concerned, Holcot's position is fundamentally that of Ockham. First, supernatural habits can be dispensed with by God's absolute powers. Second, free will and
natural powers can gain God's acceptance of themselves, though,
equally, God can dispense with them as well as with supernatural virtues. Thirdly, neither merit nor good deeds are dependent upon any supernatural or intrinsic worth, but God's will
alone. Holcot says, too, that it is possible for a man already in
grace to merit its infinite increase, though he does not hold firmly
to this as a positive assertion. More than anything else, it is in-
dicative of his extreme scepticism, which allows anything to be
possible.[1]

This whole outlook of doubt is so contrary to the positive dogmatism of Bradwardine, where the lines restricting men and
creatures are so tightly drawn, that, for them to be relaxed, God
would first have to change the world and, indeed, Himself. Bradwardine regards everything ordained not only as having been
eternally so, but as being the very best that God's infinite capacity could achieve: not because He could not do better, but
because He does everything to infinite perfection. Holcot regards
the divine will's freedom as meaning that its possibilities are
infinite; nothing, therefore, has ever been done to an infinite
degree of perfection since this would curb God's freedom. Thus
we have two different concepts of God's omnipotence: in the
first, as upheld by Bradwardine, everything that is is because of
God's infinite perfection; there is thus no question that it could
not be, without also throwing God's will into question. In Holcot's case this lack of order is the measure of God's freedom.
Hence his assertion that God could have made the world better
than it is and that He can never do so well as He could: each pre-
supposes that there is no limit to God's powers.[2]

---

[1] 'Prima est: quod viator conservatus a deo in statu viatoris ultra quid-
cumque tempus finitum; potest ultra quemcunque gradum finitum augere
meritum suum. Secunda: possibile est quod viator sic conservatus a deo in
statu viatoris: ultra quemcumque gradum finitum augeat meritum suum. . .'
(*ibid*. qu. 2, D).

[2] 'Quibus suppositis dico tria. Primum, quod deus potest facere mundum

The very definition of God, then, is reversed between Bradwardine and Holcot. For Bradwardine it is the identity between
essence and existence that distinguishes Him from everything
else; for it signifies that His being is completely realized and thus
without potentiality. Holcot, on the other hand, attributes to
God alone the faculty of being able to attain what He has not yet
reached; it is this very element of incompleteness and potentiality that makes Him infinite. It is not hard to see why Bradwardine called his treatise *De causa Dei*: God's very nature was
involved; and it was this initial difference in attitude towards
Him that led to these disputes.

Holcot's answer to the question whether God can know future
contingents is remarkable for extending it to revelation. In this it
differs markedly from the previous views discussed here, and it
transfers the argument to quite a different plane, making the issue
not simply one of logic but one between the alternatives of
omniscience or revelation: Holcot, Buckingham and Woodham
each implied that these, in their traditional aspects, were no
longer compatible and that one must be taken in preference to the
other. Buckingham and Woodham chose omniscience, Holcot
revelation; and the whole of his discussion on future contingents
was directed to preserving the infallibility of revelation, even
though at the expense of God's omniscience.

Holcot begins by defining the verb 'to know'. It has, he says,
three possible meanings: firstly, the most general sense involving
only an understanding of true and false; secondly, a more specific
sense derived from experience in which we can generalize without
having immediately to experience what we discuss. Thus we say
that the sun will rise tomorrow without needing to witness the
event. Thirdly, there is the strict sense in which there must be
complete correlation of what we say with what we experience, as
in the case of knowing that the sun is shining at midday, involving
facts not inherent in the general statement. That the sun rises
does not mean that it will shine at noon; its shining is contingent,

aliud ab isto: perfectiorem isto: et eiusdem speciei cum eo: solum numerum
differentem ab isto. Secundo quod potest facere alium perfectiorem alterius
speciei. Tertio quod non potest facere optimum quid potest facere: et ideo
non potest facere mundum ita bonum sicut potest facere: ideo solus Deus est
qui non potest facere optimum quid potest' (Sentences, bk. II, qu. 2, art. 6 R).

as liable as not to take place.[1] God knows all things by the first mode, that is, whether they are true or false. By the second, He knows future contingents: that is, that such a thing will be. But by the third mode, He does not know the future at all; because it represents truths that need never be.[2] If God knew contingents immediately it would mean that He could make what is false and unnecessary appear to be true; for He could reveal contingents to the angels and men and yet they would only be contingents. In this way everything in the Scriptures, such as the day of judgement, could be contingent, equally as liable not to be as to be, and thus they could be false. It would then be possible for, say, Abraham, to merit by false faith. Thus such truths as the day of judgement cannot be contingent, for this would render them liable to be false; they must be necessary and so must God's knowledge of them.

There is, says Holcot, a double aspect in discussing truths, uncreated and created: from the uncreated it is possible to say that Christ could intend to deceive Peter and make him believe falsely, because God's knowledge does not govern the way in which contingents work themselves out. But from the created intention this could never be; for in actual time such an intention is only contingent and will not come to pass.[3] Holcot has reached

[1] 'Restat ponere distinctiones et expositiones terminorum: quarum prima est: quod iste terminus scire tripliciter accipitur. Primo modo largissime: et sic convertitur cum cognoscere et est verorum et falsorum complexorum et incomplexorum. Secundo modo magis stricte pro notitia evidente assensiva alicui vero: qua homo assentit quod ita est in re sicut per illud verum denotatur sine formidine: et sic possum scire istam paries est albus: vel istam sol orietur cras. Tertio strictissime pro notitia evidente assensiva alicui primo: qua homo assentit quod ita est in re sicut per illum verum denotatur: et quid non potest se aliter habere' (*ibid*. art. 8 BB).

[2] 'Primo modo deus scit omnia apprehensibilia a creatura: vera et falsa . . . secundo modo deus scit futura contingentia. Tertio modo non: quia tales propositiones sic sunt vere quod possunt nunquam fuisse vere . . .' (*ibid*.).

[3] 'Ad octavum principale cum dicitur: si deus sciret contingentia: posset ea revelare angelo et homini: sic quod post revelationem manerent contingentia. concedo et cum arguitur: tunc quicquid est revelatum futurum in sacra scriptura: sicut de die iudicii: resurrectione et homini: posset esse contingens: et per consequens scriptura posset esse falsa: concedo: et concedo quod haec est possibilis Abraam meruit in fide falsa: et quod hoc potest mereri per fidem falsam ita bene sicut per fidem veram: quia non ideo meretur homo credendo: quia creditum ab eo est verum vel falsum. . . et ideo potest concedi quod haec modo est necessaria: anima christi asseruit istam propositionem dies iudicii erit, et non dependet ab aliquo futuro plusquam

a position which, in one way, amounts to that taken by Aureole: God can only know necessarily, for, if He knew contingently, either the truths He revealed would be contingent and liable to be as false as true; or there could not be contingency. In the first case God would be the author of His lies: in the second, He would make everything determined by Him. Yet, unlike Aureole, Holcot does not stop there: he explicitly makes truth conditional upon God's inability to know contingently, employing, for the first time, revelation in his support. Thus, for Holcot, revelation is the sign that God cannot know future contingents: in his desire to prevent God's word from being fallible he has chosen the other alternative of limiting His knowledge. Although he has preserved its certainty he has done so at the expense of its scope. As a result revelation has been transformed: it is now no longer the eternal sign of God's foreknowledge, but of its limitations.

Bradwardine, in keeping with tradition, employed revelation to demonstrate the very opposite, namely, that it is evidence of God's knowledge of all future contingents. Yet he reaches this conclusion by denying, as we have seen, that the future is in any way different from the past; and, in that sense, there is not the same problem for him as for Holcot. Accordingly, their conflict derives from their different answers to opinion 33: Holcot sees the future as undetermined and mutable; Bradwardine as eternally fore-ordained.

From his rejection of Holcot's view, Bradwardine proceeds to demonstrate that revelation is the guarantee of God's omniscience. Chapters 33–49 of book III are taken up with showing how, by revelation and the immutability of the Word, God knows all future contingents. First, he says, God's revealed truth is free from falsity either in what it expresses or as it appears.[1] Secondly, it is the cause of all revelation in the future,[2] and without it the created will could in no way cause its own effects. Thirdly, if God

ista Petrus asseruit, et concedendum est quod haec est contingens: anima christi fuit decepta. . . . Eodem modo dico de intentione in christo qua est duplex: creata et increata. Si ergo loquamur de intentione increata: concedo quod christus potuit facere Petrum credere falsum: nec tamen hoc est contingens. Si loquamur de intentione creata: haec fuit impossibile medio tempore illo christus intendens decipere Petrum: sed haec fuit contingens Christus intendebat intentione creata facere Petrum credere falsum' (bk. II, qu. 2, art. 8 EE).

[1] *De causa Dei*, p. 761.   [2] *Ibid.* p. 768.

could not reveal the future to all that is outside Him, this would be a sign of His impotence, which is impossible.[1] Since, therefore, God's revelation is true, and the cause of all future knowledge, it is blasphemous to deny it, or to aver that Christ could have deceived or not have believed truly.[2] Bradwardine devotes four chapters[3] to refuting the suggestion that Christ could have deceived; and he regards the scepticism, of the kind that Holcot displays over God's ability to deceive, as unthinkable.

Thus it is apparent that Bradwardine, in asserting God's complete knowledge of the future, was waging a struggle far beyond its immediate limits. The issue turned on belief itself. Bradwardine was fighting for the whole foundation on which God's power rested: the choice was either scepticism or authority. The lengths to which the doubt of Ockham and his followers led them is the measure of Bradwardine's dogmatism. Unless he defended every outpost of God's territory, the corrosive of his opponents' solution would seep in and lay it waste. Seen in this light, Bradwardine's defence of God's future knowledge was an integral part of his counter-offensive against the scepticism of his day. Both Aureole and Holcot, though differing in so much of their outlook, shared the same scepticism towards God; and they portrayed it most fully in their attitudes to future contingents. It was lack of a working faith which placed them together in the same camp and in the opposite one to Bradwardine.

THOMAS BUCKINGHAM[4]

Thomas Buckingham shares in the same flight from the thirteenth century as the other Pelagians. His concern, like theirs,

---

[1] *Ibid.* p. 770.   [2] *Ibid.* pp. 785–7.   [3] Cap. 42, 43, 44, 45.

[4] Born *c.*1290, died 1351. Throughout this section on Buckingham I have only referred to his 'Commentary on the Sentences'. This differs so greatly from his later '88 Questiones' (New College MS.134) that to have drawn from the latter in this connexion would have distorted his views there. His '88 Questiones' are those of a man severely chastened after his earlier views; they lack the tone of scepticism which pervades the Sentences; and though in certain cases Buckingham holds to his earlier opinions, he scarcely makes a mention of God's *potentia absoluta* or of the consequences which he drew from its use in his Sentences. (See pp. 260–1 below.) I have taken the extracts below from the printed edition of 1505 and MS. F.L. 16,400, Bib. Nat., Paris, which are very similar.

was to disengage God from His creatures and, by the use of His *potentia absoluta*, to release them both from immutable ties. As with them, freedom for both God and men was the object of his quest, together with the consequences which spring from God's unbounded omnipotence. Within this broad area of common ground with the rest of Bradwardine's opponents, Buckingham has his own traits: his scepticism seems even more pronounced than that of Holcot; frequently he discusses an opinion *gratia disputandi*, for its own sake rather than for his beliefs. Moreover, he has reined his own chariot so firmly to God's will that more often than not he is carried away by a force beyond his own control: whatever he might believe, God could do otherwise. Thus, in the final analysis, Buckingham's own views must defer to the possibilities of God's will, however much he may think one course preferable to another and no matter how flagrantly God's will could confound tradition. Finally, as we shall see in the case of future contingents, Buckingham adopts a solution different from any that we have discussed so far, and one which displays the conflict between Bradwardine and his opponents in a yet clearer light.

Buckingham shows less concern than even Holcot to establish any relationship between free will, grace and merit; indeed he scarcely mentions merit at all. At his hands the place of the supernatural virtues is quite as insecure as it is with the other Pelagians; and while he reaches the same broad conclusions he has his own means for doing so. This is to establish a neutral state between grace and sin in which the absence of one does not compel the existence of the other. The foundation for Buckingham's venture is God's *potentia absoluta*; for without it he would be helpless to defend himself against charges of heresy or to manœuvre his arguments in his support. He, too, makes freedom of God's will the justification for exalting men. For this reason lack of grace does not necessarily mean to be in sin; if it did, God's absolute power would be unable to create a man in his natural state without either: a check to God's power, not men's resources.[1] God's

---

[1] 'Et res vera videtur mihi mirabile quod deus non potest de potentia sua absoluta facere creaturam rationalem nisi sit digna clare dei visione vel sit in peccato mortali' (*Sentences*, qu. 6).

freedom, therefore, is the issue, and His infinite freedom is made the guarantee for a *medius status* between grace and sin. Buckingham thus follows Bradwardine's opponents, in making God's omnipotence the first consideration; it comes before any others. Questions of right and wrong, of tradition and authority, become secondary, and almost irrelevant, in the face of God's will.[1] It is from these premises that Buckingham makes his attack on supernatural habits, denying the inherent need for grace or charity.

In the first place, he holds that there is a natural justice in man which enables him to be righteous and good without being informed by a *habitus*.[2] This can be shown in the case of the first angels and man before the fall; they were not in grace and yet they were without sin.[3] This view of human nature is at the farthest extreme from Bradwardine's; for him there could be no distinction between natural and supernatural qualities; nothing worthwhile inhered in men which was not of supernatural origin. Everything good, therefore, for Bradwardine depended upon a *habitus*. Buckingham's *medius status*, like Durandus's distinction between the moral and divine, allowed exactly for human goodness in its own right. By giving to men a measure of natural justice, sufficient for natural needs, it freed them from constant dependence on God. Thus it removed any call for created grace, since men can live this life supported by their own resources. Buckingham, indeed, goes so far as to concede that it is possible that Adam was without habitual grace and was, nevertheless, rewarded with eternal life; for this reward natural justice could suffice. There is no need to infer that only habitual grace is

[1] 'Utrum si deus crearet creaturam rationalem cum privatione gratie gratum facientis sine demerito ipsius vel alicuius alterius nunquid talis privatio esset culpa mortalis eodem modo si iam creatura dicto modo aufert gratiam. . . .

'Ad idem arguo per rationes sic. Si carere gratia in creatura rationali semper foret peccatum et culpa mortalis, sequeretur quod deus de potentia sua absoluta non posset creaturam facere esse in puris naturalibus sine peccato et sine gratia gratum faciente quod esset quidam habitus additus suis naturalibus. Consequens est falsum, quid sic multipliciter probo' (*ibid.*).

[2] 'Concedo preter tamen charitatem est una naturalis iustitia qua creatura rationalis potest esse iusta et recta sine charitate' (*ibid.*).

[3] 'Ad idem arguitur sic: primi angeli et parentes in statu innocentiae erant sine gratia gratum faciente et sine peccato et culpa mortali et veniali, et per consequens inter peccatum et gratiam est medius status possibilis, antecedens probo per auctoritatem' (*ibid.*).

rewarded with glory any more than that to be without it means eternal reprobation.[1] Similarly, free will, as distinct from appetite, can of its own resources choose or reject sin and can avoid everything sinful; though, without habitual grace, it will not usually succeed in resisting temptation.[2] In every case, Buckingham clearly recognizes moral qualities in free will and regards them as playing an important part to good in human affairs.

The second consequence of Buckingham's view of grace is to make created grace superfluous: since, he says, there can be a middle status between grace and sin, grace itself is neutral.[3] To possess it in no way involves God's love or acceptance. A man can remain the same with it as without it; neither justification nor reward is needed for God to give a man glory. If a supernatural habit were necessary this would put God under an obligation; but, in fact, God is quite free to love one in mortal sin and to reject another in grace. Hence, the value of created grace is non-existent: God could as well infuse charity into an ass as render a man worthy of eternal life by its medium.[4]

---

[1] 'Ad tertium argumentum dico quod posito quod adam in statu innocentie fuisset sine gratia gratum faciente ut videtur esse communis opinio doctorum. Nescio tamen an ista fuit vel non. Sed scio quod est possibile quod non et in utroque statu potuit mori et eternaliter vivere et nego istam consequentiam: ergo fuit in gratia gratum faciente quia fuit dignus regno ut supra dixi . . . quia per iustitiam originalem potuit fuisse principaliter iustus, et similiter nego hanc conclusionem, fuit dignus ex illo non habere regnum celorum, igitur est in peccato mortali . . .' (qu. 6).

[2] 'Ad octavum argumentum dico quod stante quacunque temptatione inclinante ad peccatum est in libera potestate voluntatis existentis in puris naturalibus velle vel nolle cadere vel non cadere in peccatum dico quod voluntas sine gratia gratum faciente solum donis nature vitare potest omne peccatum forte tamen non est possibile quod sine gratia resistat vel sic vitet peccata et ad istum sensum capio auctoritates' (*ibid.*).

[3] 'Primo deus mediante gratia vel infusa naturalibus acceptat creaturam ad vitam eternam, et non nisi secundum acceptationem et institutionem divinam et non ratione habitus in se, igitur sicut acceptat mediante gratia posset acceptare mediantibus naturalibus vel per aliam rem a caritate vel gratia, et per consequens potest creatura rationalis esse sine peccato et sine gratia creata. Similiter deus potest seipsum rectificare et iustificare creaturam sine omni habitu infuso, et secundum multos de facto sic facit . . .' (*ibid.*).

[4] 'Si deus non potest de potentia absoluta facere creaturam rationalem esse sine gratia creata et sine peccato mortali, hoc principaliter esset propter effectum gratie sue que est per quam creatura sit grata deo et digna vita eterna, quia gratia secundum illud quod est potest deus ponere in asino vel in aliquo existente in peccato mortali; sed non ad eundem effectum ad quem nunc ponitur, quia non redderet illum deo dignum vita eterna. Et per con-

Buckingham, like Ockham and Holcot, arrives at the same rejection of natural grace. For each of them this comes from their refusal to bind God, as any set scheme would destroy His freedom. Divine acceptance needs no prompting or order to which it must work; God's will is the only law. As we have so often remarked, the superfluity of grace is the direct result of God's omnipotence; it is, first and foremost, the expression of His infinite resources and only secondarily has it any connexion with free will as such. Thus, although human freedom is the greatest beneficiary of voluntarism, it does not in itself provide the *raison d'être* for Buckingham's rejection of created grace. A supernatural habit, by this view, is like a reservoir; it can only store, but not create: hence in itself it is not essential, for other channels can be found. God's goodness is none the less potent for dispensing with created grace, just as rain without tanks still waters; but in God's case, whatever He does is its own justification.

Buckingham, in the third place, having dispensed with created grace, distinguishes uncreated charity as the only valid supernatural virtue. This, he says, is another way of regarding the Holy Spirit,[1] who alone constitutes uncreated grace and charity. In company with Ockham, Holcot and, as we shall see, Woodham, Buckingham makes acceptance by the Holy Spirit alone necessary for salvation. Now this distinction between created and uncreated grace is, in effect, the same distinction which the Pelagians constantly make between a habit and God's will; and in rejecting the former for the latter they are only denying everything other than His will. Bradwardine clearly realized this, for, as we have seen, he castigated those making this distinction as Pelagian.[2] Moreover, it is hard to think that Buckingham and his

---

sequens potest ponere in existente in puris naturalibus non ad vitam eternam. Talis creatura non est digna vita eterna nec in peccato mortali, igitur potest creatura rationalis esse sine gratia et effectu gratie et peccato mortali. Ad idem sic potest deus facere in creatura rationali sine hoc quod gratificet eam' (*ibid.*).

[1] 'Idem patet per magistrum in primo sententiarum dist. 17 videtur ponere quod spiritus sanctus est charitas qua diligimus deum et christum, nec secundum eum est aliqua charitas creata ad minus necessario requisita et per consequens creaturam rationalem in puris naturalibus potest deus rectificare et instituere sine quocumque dono infuso et potest in ea esse charitas increata sine charitate creata per quam esset digna vita eterna' (*ibid.*).

[2] See p. 199 above.

confrères were doing any more than give a flavour of orthodoxy to their innovations. Even if their reference to the Lombard,[1] where this distinction is explicitly stated, is to be taken at face value, the fact remains that uncreated grace is made one of their justifications for dismissing created grace. As with their use of God's *potentia absoluta* to override His *potentia ordinata*, the use of uncreated grace is an important means of dispensing with created habits. In each case, the invocation of God's will is used to undermine traditional ordinances.

The fourth inference that Buckingham makes in support of a *medius status* is that grace and sin can stand together; for, since each can be absent in any one person, the presence of one does not contradict the presence of the other. Grace can exist and yet not bring love; sin may be present and yet glory can result.[2] Any order is destroyed and God's *potentia absoluta* rules supreme. It is always to His absolute power that final appeal is made: Buckingham, like Holcot and Ockham, combines logic with the appeal to God's omnipotence: if, they argue, privation of grace, for example, were to involve sin, and a man could not be in both states at once, this would reflect upon God's power and His will could be impeded.[3] In a sense, then, just as Bradwardine's final appeal rests upon faith and authority, that of his opponents rests upon God's absolute power: in each case they are not prepared to argue from a purely metaphysical basis. They differ, of course, in their different conceptions of God's role; but there is a similarity in their methods. This can be seen plainly in the present case: not only is grace not vitiated by sin, but a man who sins may

---

[1] Sentences, bk. I, dist. 17.

[2] 'Dico quod charitas et peccatum nunc de facto et de lege currente sunt contraria sed non formaliter' (qu. 6).
And: 'Ad idem sic potest deus facere in creatura rationali gratiam sine quod hoc gratificet eam, faciat deus sic et quero an talis creatura est in peccato mortali vel non. Si non tunc est medium inter peccatum mortale et dignum vita eterna sine peccato mortali. Contra est in gratia, igitur si iste sit in peccato mortali et in gratia tunc ista non formaliter repugnarent, et per consequens nec opposita eorum. Assumptum patet quia potest facere in lapide vel in consimili. Similiter non obstante quod hic peccet potest deus conservare illam rem que est gratia, et tunc est gratia et non gratificabit' (*ibid.*).

[3] E.g. 'Ad idem si privatio gratie quam deus auferret et foret peccatum vel foret equale cum originale vel maius vel minus, consequens est falsum quia sequitur quod deus non posset facere de potentia sua absoluta aliquam creaturam modicam iustam sicut talis est iustus' (*ibid.*).

receive eternal glory. By God's absolute power it is not impossible that a man may be without grace, and in mortal sin, during his life and yet be saved; and, conversely, that in death he is in a state of mortal sin from which he was free while alive.[1] The result of this overturning of any fixed order is to give a place to merit *de congruo*. For, since neither grace is a guarantee to glory, nor sin the source of reprobation, a man in mortal sin could act in such a way that it were meet for God to reward him.[2]

This is Buckingham's sole reference to merit *de congruo*, but it is enough to show whither his outlook leads. By means of God's *potentia absoluta* Buckingham has reached a position from which all order and value have flown. Firstly, he makes possibility his yardstick so that its logic constantly overrules authority. Secondly, sin and grace lose any separate identity and, in effect, have no meaning of their own. There is no criterion of good and bad; everything, other than God's will, takes on a neutral colour, devoid of intrinsic qualities or defects. God Himself, in the larger sense of possessing attributes, is likewise bereft of a constant nature. His nature becomes as indeterminate as the possibilities of His will. Finally, the mediation of supernatural habits having been rendered unnecessary, the only forces ultimately concerned with reward and punishment are the divine and human wills. Thus, *ipso facto*, free will has an important part to play as the object of God's actions: it is regarded for its own sake, whether for good or ill, and hence is not the cipher that Bradwardine would have it. Moreover, Buckingham in rejecting both sin and grace as essential cannot but make human resources self-sufficient; his *medius status* is independent of external states, and, in the case of the first man, was supported by the natural justice of his own nature. Each of these consequences leads to what Bradwardine regarded as Pelagianism for it makes God and

---

[1] 'Ad idem arguo sic: non est inconveniens quod aliquis per totam vitam suam fuit in peccato mortali et sine gratia et nunquam in gratia et tamen in instanti mortis est sine peccato et salvatus . . .' (*ibid.*).

'Ad argumenta iam facta respondeo et teneo responsionem quam prius. Et dico quod in casu isto in *a* instanti primo est dare peccatum et est primo peccatum et si sortes tunc sit primo mortuus dico quod ipse est in peccato mortali secundum animam et dignus vita eterna, tamen in tota vita sua fuit bonus, iustus et in gratia et nunquam in peccato mortali' (*ibid.*).

[2] 'Ad aliud concedo quod aliquis in peccato mortali potest aliquid facere unde sit congruum deum dare tali gratiam et perseverantiam' (qu. 3, art. 2).

men independent of any ordinance. Grace, therefore, is not the condition for merit, but man alone; for, passive or active, good or bad, he is the object of God's reward.

Buckingham's Pelagianism, then, comes closer to Holcot's than to Ockham's, in placing such emphasis on God's will that the human will does not have to follow any particular course to glory; reward can come to sin as well as to goodness. Nevertheless, the final balance is in favour of human powers; men, by Buckingham's system, are freed from dependence upon supernatural habits; they have it in their power to avoid sin; they are free to be carried direct to God and no natural impediment stands in their way to salvation. Together with Ockham and Holcot, Buckingham must answer to Bradwardine for such Pelagianism.

It is with future contingents that Buckingham's scepticism reaches fullest expression. He, more than any other of the Pelagians, reveals how closely the question engages the full range of the divine and human wills. In essence the problem is how to reconcile God's eternal knowledge of everything with men's freedom to act contingently; that is, if God knows all from eternity how can men act freely without either making His knowledge mutable or their actions determined? It is a problem which arises only when there is a break between God's will and its operations in this world; with no hierarchy between God and men, there can, in the circumstances, be only two alternatives, if freedom for future events is to be preserved: either God, while knowing the general shape of things to come, forgoes, in the interests of freedom, any foreknowledge of their details; or His knowledge of these particulars must be contingent, as subject to change as they themselves are. Holcot, together with Durandus and Aureole, took the first course, each in his own way: they denied to God such detailed knowledge in the interests of free futures. Buckingham, however, chooses the second way and makes God's knowledge of the future as contingent as the contingents He knows. This is the great interest of his discussion on the problem, and his conclusions constitute the very opinions that Bradwardine attacked.[1] Moreover, there is in this connex-

---

[1] See pp. 107-9 above.

ion another clue to identifying Buckingham as one of Bradwardine's opponents. Although Bradwardine never mentioned by name Buckingham or any other contemporary, there is a reference to a dispute between them by Thomas of Cracow,[1] in which he says that the author of *De causa Dei* engaged in public disputation with Buckingham on future contingents at Paris. Thus in Buckingham's case we have at least circumstantial evidence of a conflict between him and Bradwardine.

Buckingham's argument on future contingents falls into two clear divisions: one deals with the nature of anything future; the other with its effects upon God's Word, Christ's Word and revelation. If the first part establishes the fundamentals, the second is no less important for the conclusions drawn.

Buckingham first turns to the nature of the future. This is inseparable from the relationship between the divine and created wills. The problem, says Buckingham, is to know how anything can be done without God's participation.[2] The answer is twofold: on the one hand, God's will gives a rational creature power to act or not to act,[3] but, on the other, it is in the power of free will to be able to choose to do so or not to do so.[4] Thus, in effect, God's will, although not a direct cause in the actions of free will, is the *sine qua non*. Without Him there would be no freedom for a rational being.[5] Buckingham expresses the relationship between the divine will and free will in seven conclusions. These may be summarized as follows: first, that God's will is the first and principal cause of anything created; second,

---

[1] MS. F.L. 15,409. f. 23; Bibliothèque Nationale, Paris.

[2] 'In isto modo videtur tota difficultas materie questionis esse quomodo est quod aliquid potest fieri nisi deo principaliter volente et concurrente, seu coagente; et deum coagere vel velle nullo modo cadit sub possibilitate seu libertate creature' (Sentences, qu. 3, art. 2).

[3] 'Ad omnia argumenta facta respondeo sic quod deus dat creature rationali posse producere actum vel non producere. Et ista volitio dei est causa precedens et sufficiens unde creatura procedat ad actum, et ista causa non est in potestate creature nec ex ista sequitur necessario effectum produci' (*ibid.*).

[4] 'Et si non possim velle aliquid vel facere sine deo coagente, et deum coagere non est in potestate mea, facere tamen illum effectum est in libera possibilitate et potentia mea et stat in me potentia et possibilitas sufficiens ad faciendum illum actum . . .' (*ibid.*).

[5] 'Nec est ista volitio qua deus vult rem produci nec causa quare res producitur inesse vel non producitur, nisi causa sine qua non' (*ibid.*).

that His willing does not constitute irrevocable (antecedent)[1]
necessity for anything secondary. Third, that the human will,
thus free, produces its own effects freely and that its actions, good
or bad, are not in conflict with God's will. Fourth, not everything
future is so of necessity.[2] From these it can be seen that while

---

[1] Buckingham distinguishes between two kinds of necessity: antecedent
and consequent. The first is either simple or conditional. As simple, it is the
active cause of every effect, allowing of no alternative; it cannot, therefore,
apply to the future for it has already been decided in the present. It is conditional when there is potentially an alternative, e.g. in the case of the sun
rising. Here, while there is still no free alternative, there is an element of the
future: the sun must rise tomorrow though it sets for tonight; a flower must
eventually fade though it is now in full bloom.

Consequent necessity is not the cause of something but an effect inherent
in it: it is absolute when the cause is irrevocable, such as that God is innocent
or that the world was willed by Him; it is conditional when the effect is contingent, such as that the antichrist will come: his coming is not inherent in his
nature but the product of God's knowledge, and therefore contingent:

'Necessitas antecedens est duplex: scilicet simpliciter et secundum quid.
Necessitas simpliciter est causa activa respectu alicuius effectus qua posita
non stat possibilitas et potentia ad oppositum. Et isto modo loquendi respectu nullius futuri est necessitas, quia respectu cuiuslibet in deo est possibilitas et potentia ad oppositum. Alio modo dicitur necessitas secundum quid
et est quando in aliquo est potentia et possibilitas ad oppositum . . . ut est
necessitas qua dicitur quod solem oriri cras, et corruptibile de necessitate
corrumpetur. In deo tamen est possibilitas et potentia ad oppositum: in
sole etiam corruptibili necessitas ad corruptionem et ortum . . .' (qu. 3, art. 2).

'Necessitas consequens . . . est que facit esse rei et ipsa non est causa rei,
sed ipsa facit potentiam rei necesse de ipsa. Ista necessitate dicimus necesse
est deum non esse iniustum, necesse est deum esse innocentiam, necesse esse
mundum fuisse. . . . Adhuc necessitas consequens est duplex. Quedam est
simpliciter et absolute qua dicimus mundum fuisse et similia, quia nihil
potest facere quod mundum non fuerit et quod sit immortalis et sic de
consimilibus. Alio modo dicitur necessitas consequens, que non simpliciter et
absolute est necessitas, sed magis conditionata. Isto modo dicitur necessitas,
quia aliquod est positum inesse, sicut verbi gratia sic deus velit antichristum
fore voluntas vel prescientia est posita. Ex qua sequitur necessario antichristum fore, sed hec necessitas denotat magis necessitatem in dicto quam
in re . . .' (ibid.).

[2] 'Ex hoc respondeo ponendo septem conclusiones quibus declaratis patet
quid sit respondendum ad questionem et argumentum. Prima conclusio est
quod cuiuslibet entis creati voluntas eterna est prima et principalis causa
efficiens. Secunda conclusio volitio divina non est cuiuslibet effectus sui
necessitas antecedens. Tertia conclusio omnis et solus actus voluntatis est
liber a necessitate antecedentis. Quarta conclusio voluntas creata omnem
suum effectum producit libere et contingenter. Quinta conclusio est quod
nec per se nec per accidens meritum nec demeritum repugnat necessitati
consequenti. Sexta conclusio est quod de necessitate antecedente factum sit
per accidens meritum vel demeritum. Septima conclusio. Non omne futurum
est necesse esse futurum' (ibid.).

God has over-all control, free will is not subject to the necessity of His will; it has it in its own power to act either for good or for bad; it can produce its own actions freely and without constraint.

Now, in discussing these conclusions, Buckingham shows quite clearly that he was reacting against the Greco-Arab determinism of the thirteenth century. He quotes the 1277 Paris condemnations by Bishop Tempier to reject the view that everything is eternally preordained or that God represents antecedent necessity; in either case he says all freedom would be destroyed.[1] Because everything is not from necessity, two important consequences follow: first, that a rational creature is free to act of his own, even if this should be contrary to God's desire; and secondly that the undetermined character of free will to do or not to do is the source of contingency. In the first case, just as God is free to act or not, so is a creature.[2] Consequently, it is in the nature of free will for Peter, say, to commit a certain act, even against God's will; he has it in his own power to do so independently of God's support and aid.[3] This is not a let to God's will, but rather the result of a course freely willed by Him: He, as the free and first cause of the human will, endowed it with the very ability to choose between alternatives and the power always to take either course. God, then, as infinitely free, has granted to man a similar liberty to create his own effects. Thus human freedom is a remote reflexion of God's unrestricted liberty: the infinite possibility of His will finds an echo in the freedom of choice in the

---

[1] 'Similiter esset falsum ponere omnia preordinata a principio quod est error Parisius. Similiter secundum istud humani actus non regerentur divina providentia' (*ibid.*).

'Secundam conclusionem probo videlicet quod volitio divina non est cuiuslibet effectus sui necessitas antecedens. Et arguo quod si foret tunc cum omne quod sit, sit a voluntate divina, ut dicit prima conclusio, sequitur quod omnia eveniunt de necessitate antecedente, quod est contra Anselm, 2. "cur deus homo", cap. 17' (*ibid.*).

[2] 'Similiter deus nihil ad extra dicitur producere ex necessitate et nihil faciet quin potest illud non facere, ergo de creatura consimiliter erit, quia in libera potestate creature est facere vel non facere. Talis ergo creatura illum effectum non necessitatur facere' (*ibid.*).

[3] 'Respondeo et concedo quod stante volitione divina qua deus vult petrum non producere *a* actum, est in libera possibilitate et potestate petri producere *a* actum . . . tamen et si deus non coagat nec velit coagere adhuc habet petrus possibilitatem et potestatem ad producendum *a* actum' (*ibid.*).

human will.[1] It is the measure of Buckingham's system that God
plays so indirect a part in the created world; He is virtually excluded from any active influence, or indeed from any real place at
all. Buckingham comes perilously near to this when he gives the
reason for the created will's conforming to the divine will: it is
less in the nature of free will, which is sufficient in itself to act
alone, but rather because not to do so would go against God's
nature.[2] This is virtually saying that God's direction could be
dispensed with in this world. Although the cause for this lies in
divine omnipotence, and the opposite state of affairs could always
exist,[3] Buckingham has nevertheless reached the other extreme
from Bradwardine: there is all the room in the world for free
will to act alone, whereas Bradwardine will not release man from
God's control by the minutest degree.

The second conclusion follows from this, that any act of free
will, because it is undetermined, must be contingent.[4] Any act
not yet accomplished by free will need not take place; hence the
future differs from the present and the past in that it may never
happen: this is in the very nature of free will. It need hardly be
recalled that Bradwardine[5] took the contrary view: he refused
to distinguish the future on the grounds that, if it were changeable, then God's will, too, would be subject to change. These
opposed views spring from their differences over free will; in
each case it is from the nature of free will that their outlook on
future contingents derives: because, for Buckingham, it is free
and undetermined, the future must be equally free and mutable;

[1] 'Et ideo cum tali volitione qua deus vult rem fieri, licet non sit impedibilis
stant possibilitas et potentia ad oppositum' (qu. 3, art. 2).

[2] 'Sed causa quare requiritur deum coagere non est quia creatura per se
non sufficit cum illis donis que habet a deo, sed quia repugnat nature divine
quod aliquid producatur in esse nisi specialiter producente. Credo enim
quod tantum sit in potestate creature rationalis producere actum suum sicut
esset si deus nullo modo coageret et si creatura per se sola ageret' (ibid.).

[3] 'Si tamen illam rem que est voluntas deus necessitaret, ille actus non
esset voluntarius nec liber. . . . Si deus velit voluntatem necessitari ad actum,
vult tunc deus voluntatem illam pro tunc non habere possibilitatem et
potentiam ad oppositum et tunc necessitatur voluntas illa' (ibid.).

[4] 'Sed si loquatur de necessitate vel impossibilitate quoad deum credo
quod respectu nullius futuri est necessitas vel impossibilitas, sed mere contingentia, quia quodcunque futurum potest deus producere et non producere
indifferenter' (ibid.).

[5] See pp. 107–9 above.

similarly, since Bradwardine regards free will as an extension of divine will and eternally ordained, there can be no genuine contingency in future events.

Now that we have traced the cause of Buckingham's and Bradwardine's conflicts over future contingents, we are in a better position to see the direction they take over the effect.

In the first place Buckingham, as we have noted, makes God's knowledge of the future contingent; God knows all things future and wills them to be contingent.[1] Hence all His knowledge of the future is contingent since it is knowledge of contingents. Secondly, this means that all revelation becomes contingent; for it refers to what will happen and this may never take place.[2] Thus both Christ and the elect only know the Word contingently: it does not communicate to them eternal verities. At one sweep, the whole foundation of their lives becomes suspect;[3] they are no longer acting from immutable ordinances. Even when a truth has been revealed in the Word it may never happen. The coming of the antichrist, for example, may have been announced to Peter and yet he may never appear.[4] This raises, in the third place, the capital question of whether God and Christ can deceive. Buckingham, having made God's future knowledge contingent, is faced with the alarming consequence that for everything that God reveals in the Word its opposite may take place. If this is so, God could mislead and deceive Christ and the elect; and they, in turn, could be the means of asserting falsehoods. Buckingham's reply is one which, while recognizing these implications, tries to adjust the burden of responsibility: on the one hand, he says, if

---

[1] 'Ideo respondeo alio modo sic. Quod omnia futura contingentia deus novit ab eterno: et sicut sunt futura deus novit illa esse futura: et vult illa esse futura' (Sentences, qu. 3, art. 1).

[2] 'Et sic quando aliquis in verbo videt aliqua esse futura vel quando deus revelat in verbo aliqua futura, adhuc hec est contingens quod illa futura sunt revelata vel visa in verbo: ymo stat quod non sint visa sed opposita sint visa' (ibid.).

[3] 'Et eodem modo si deus promittat aliqua contingenter promittit et contingenter iurat. Et eodem modo dico de beatis qui vident futura contingentia in verbo, et maxime de christo qui fuit deus et homo quod scivit in verbo contingentia et contingenter sciunt illa et scivit contingenter sciunt; sic contingenter voluit ita et ea esse futura asseruit' (ibid.).

[4] 'Ad istud respondeo et dico quod facta revelatione in verbo adhuc est possibile antichristum non fore etsi ita sit nunquam fuit revelatum' (ibid.).

Peter is deceived about the antichrist, he deceives himself.[1] On the other hand, although it is possible for God to deceive, this would not be His main intention, but, rather, inherent in contingency.[2] In effect, then, Buckingham, while not making God wilfully deceive, is prepared to recognize that He could do so. Similarly Christ could be deceived and misled, since what is revealed to Him in the Word need not come to pass.[3] These are the ultimate conclusions to which Buckingham's arguments lead, and, despite the qualifications, it is clear that he appreciates them and accepts them.

It is not hard to see that Buckingham's arguments represent most of Bradwardine's main targets. We saw with Holcot[4] the counts of Bradwardine's charges; they answer Buckingham's assertions in almost every respect. These were that God's knowledge of the future is immutable; that revelation is free from all falsity or uncertainty; that God's will is alone its cause; that neither God nor Christ could have deceived or misled. For each of these it is only necessary to insert 'not' to reach Buckingham's positions: they are diametrically opposed.

This conflict on future contingents between Buckingham and Bradwardine crystallizes their differences. It springs first and foremost from their contrary ways of regarding God. For Buckingham, none of the uncertainties which inhere in the future is a sign of God's limitations; they rather express the freedom of His own will and the freedom which He has bestowed on free will. There is no question, in Buckingham's eyes, but that God *could* urge and compel men as easily as Bradwardine allows Him to do; but then there would no longer be free will. On the contrary, it is the existence of free will which causes the problem to arise, and so we may say that with Buckingham, as with Holcot and Aureole, their views on the future spring from their aim to safeguard free

---

[1] '. . . et erit petrus in casu deceptus, si credat hoc cognitione in proprio genere. Nec tamen deus decepit ipsum sed ipse seipsum' (qu. 3, art. 1).

[2] 'Credo tamen quod est possibile quod deus aliquem decipiat, non tamen principaliter intendit decipere, seu deceptionem' (*ibid.*).

[3] 'Et si obiiciatur sic. Necesse est quod christus dixit antichristum fore et potest esse quod antichristus non erit, ergo possibile est quod christus dixit falsum. Respondeo et concedo quod possibile est quod christus dixit falsum, et quod necesse est quod christus dixit illa verba. Sed non est necesse quod christus asseruit illam. Sed hoc est futurum contingens' (*ibid.*).

[4] See pp. 226–7 above.

will. Bradwardine, on the other hand, has his first concern with God's will. Each side accordingly has started from the opposite extreme: Buckingham, Holcot and Aureole from the world of men, making free will the primary objective; Bradwardine from God, seeking to preserve His attributes. Each is prepared to sacrifice what for him is the lesser to the greater: with Buckingham and the others, God's knowledge is made mutable so that the future may be free; Bradwardine denies the future any separate identity in God's interests. With such diverse objectives their views could never be reconcilable. God and men have a different meaning and importance for each.

ADAM OF WOODHAM[1]

Adam of Woodham is yet a further example of the scepticism which derives from Ockham. He shows at once marked affinities with, and differences from, his master, whose avowed disciple he was.[2] On the one hand, in addition to constant reference to Ockham, he emphasizes, with him, the role human actions and powers play in merit; on the other hand, he comes closer to Holcot and Buckingham when he rejects any order whatever in the interests of God's *potentia absoluta*. In a sense, then, Adam stands between the two trends, if the variations between these thinkers can be so described; and he never seems quite able to follow one in preference to the other. He therefore leaves behind a hint of uncertainty in his approach. In the cases both of the supernatural habits and of future contingents, although assigning a definite part to free will, he seems then to neglect it for the possibilities of God's absolute power, so that the final effect is confused: it is hard to see where the one meets the other; rather they tend to overlap. This seems to be most easily explained by seeing Adam as trying to ride two horses at once: although they follow the same road and tread a parallel course, their individual rhythms are hard to combine: Ockham's emphasis on the role of

---

[1] So far no printed edition of Adam's Commentary on the Sentences exists. That printed at Paris in 1512 consists of the Abbreviations of Henry d'Oyta. I have taken the extracts given below from MSS. F.L.15,892, Bibliothèque Nationale, Paris, and 915, Bibliothèque Mazarine, Paris. Those from the former are marked (*a*), and from the latter (*b*).

[2] See A. Pelzer in *Revue d'histoire ecclésiastique* (1922), p. 248 note.

R

free will does not quite blend with the later Pelagians' whole-hearted submission to God's *potentia absoluta*. We are left trying to make the connexion and, as if to say that there is none, Adam reaches conclusions so startling (even for the Pelagians) that no final balance is possible.

This dualism between the claims of God's will and free will is apparent in Adam's treatment of supernatural habits. Although his conclusions are substantially those of the other Pelagians, and put him on the opposite side to Bradwardine, there is a lack of cohesion in his arguments. Free will has a definite part assigned to it only to be left aside, ultimately, in face of the overwhelming possibilities of God's will. There is no guiding thread around which everything is arranged, and a jump has to be made from one position to the other.

Adam, like Ockham and the Pelagians, denies a place to the supernatural virtues on two main grounds: that they contain in themselves no independent worth which God cannot communicate directly; and that there is no constant order between grace and glory, sin and damnation, which makes them necessary. These reasons turn upon God's *potentia absoluta*, for Adam is careful to distinguish the different consequences which flow from God's two kinds of power. Indeed, in this he is more directly explicit than any of the other Pelagians. In a remarkable passage he states that the *raison d'être* for God's *potentia absoluta* is that it enables God to do otherwise than by His ordained power. It would, he says, be vain to distinguish between them were He not free to do by His absolute power what He could not do by His ordained.[1] Clearly, then, freedom for God's will is the main consideration and the only constant yardstick; everything else, authority and revelation included, is at best transitory. With God's will as the sole law, contingency alone becomes absolute. This is the root of the Pelagians' attack on supernatural virtues, and it can be seen clearly in Adam's case.

In the first place, he undermines the status of created grace by making uncreated grace alone necessary. As we have already re-

---

[1] '. . . frustra videtur mihi distinguerent doctores de potentia dei ordinata et absoluta nisi aliter posset facere et disponere de rebus quam disposuit de facto' (*b*) (Sentences, bk. I, dist. 17, qu. 3).

marked,[1] this is another way of asserting the primacy of God's will; for it makes reward dependent only upon acceptance by the Holy Spirit. By this means, there is no need for any mediating agency between God's will and the soul He rewards.[2] Created grace is thus by-passed and rendered superfluous in the face of God's absolute power.

In the second place, like Ockham, Adam denies any intrinsic quality to grace. No form of itself is good or bad, but only as God wills it.[3] Grace does not necessarily gratify nor is sin in itself detestable. A man can be in grace and yet not dear to God: conversely, he can be dear to Him without grace.[4] God, by His absolute power, can accept one for glory *ex puris naturalibus* without any supernatural habit first informing him. It is enough that God wills to accept him; created grace neither helps nor hinders Him in His object.[5] This, as Adam is careful to point out, is only by God's *potentia absoluta*; by His ordained power a supernatural habit is required.[6] In the same way as he dispenses with the need for a form leading to good, Adam rejects sin as inherently bad. Of

---

[1] See pp. 199, 231 above.

[2] 'Sed intelligendo questionem hypothetice, id est si debebat pertingi ad salutem utrum gratia ad hec requiritur, dico quod sic loquendo de gratia increata, que est divina acceptio et preordinatio huius ad salutem, quia beatitudo finalis que hic vocatur salus, ut suppono, sine divina acceptione immediata eius actione in aliquo causari non possit. Secundo dico quod gratia creata que debeat animam informare non requiritur necessario necessitate absoluta si pertingeretur ad salutem . . . hoc probatur quia nuda substantia anime est finalis beatitudinis sufficiens susceptum et deus ipse est sufficiens ipsum productum. Tertio dico quod gratia data non est necessaria ad salutem secundum quid, quia nulla gratia nec habitus vel quelibet pertingens est vera . . . a potentia absoluta igitur creata gratia non necessario ad hoc requiritur. . . . Quarto dico et ultimo quod si quis salvari debeat de communi lege secundum eandem legem necessario requiritur gratia creata que animam informet' (a) (bk. I, dist. 17, qu. 1).

[3] 'Respondeo quod rectitudo est quod vult et rationale est omnino quod fiat sibi' (a) (*ibid.*).

[4] '. . . cuius oppositum plane dico vel opportet dicere quod non omnis habens talem rectitudinem habet eam per gratiam sine qua non est salus et que sola in sanctis sufficit . . . et ita non omnis rectitudo per se servata includit gratiam' (a) (*ibid.*).

[5] 'Respondeo quod nulla repugnantia quod aliquis sit carus deo sine gratia informante sed quod sine caritate et gratia acceptus esset' (a) (*ibid.*).

[6] 'Sed quamvis de facto et de potentia ordinata nullus de peccatore fiat non peccatore sine infusione gratie . . . tamen quando de potentia dei absoluta aliter fieri valeat, non video sed talis posset esse carus et acceptus deo sine infusione alicuius doni supernaturalis' (a) (*ibid.*).

its own nature, original sin, he says, is not detestable: God's hate renders it odious.[1] Adam has reached the same position as Ockham and the other Pelagians in removing all intrinsic value from created forms. Only God's will confers worth, and by His absolute will He works to no pattern: good and bad, deeds or habits, as such, have no meaning apart from the value with which His will invests them.

This leads, in the third place, to the disruption of all order between deeds and rewards. The infinite freedom of God's will has destroyed any constant relation of cause and effect between them; it leads to a world of exceptions, not rules. For everything a man does God could will the contrary; He could destroy what a person had created and will him to want something which He, God, did not Himself want.[2] As a result there is no defined status either for the elect or for the sinner. For the elect, glory not grace is the ultimate end, and, following the Aristotelian axiom that the first in intention is the last in execution, Adam is able to show that one is not dependent on the other. God can reach the end without any set means; therefore, He can give glory to one without his ever having previously been in grace.[3] For the sinner, the same indeterminacy prevails: as to be in grace does not in itself mean final glory, so to be in sin does not preclude election. One can die in sin and yet have been predestined by God to everlasting life.[4]

---

[1] 'Quia videtur si aliquis possit esse oditus non propter aliquid detestabilem actum inherens ei . . . Praeterea natus in peccato originali non habet aliquam formam necessario detestabilem deo et tamen est oditus' (a) (bk. 1, dist. 17, qu. 2).

[2] 'Ad istud dico quod concedendum est quod nihil absolutum potest voluntas in se producere libere nec velle aliquid quin deus posset illud destruere nunc et cum probatur quod non per anselmum, dicendum quod deus volens posset secundum potentiam suam auferre rectitudinem istam. Et ad probationem concedo quod loquendo de virtute sermonis quod deus potest voluntatem velle non velle illud quod vult eam velle' (a) (ibid. qu. 1).

[3] 'Item sicut doctor subtilis quod ultimum in executione est primum in intentione et ideo secundum eum beatitudo est primum volitum . . . ergo non per gratiam acceptatur ad gloriam, sed e contrario, quia deus predestinavit eum ad gloriam ideo dat sibi gratiam, ideo cum gloria non dependeat a gratia informante in aliquo genere cause . . . non videtur quod ad hoc quod deus prius conferat non beato beatitudinem quod omnino optet precedere gratiam' (a) (ibid. qu. 2).

[4] 'Prima conclusio quod dei potentia ordinata sola gratia seu caritas increata non potest sufficere viatori ad salutem. Hoc patet in questione precedenti: secundo teneo cum scoto et okam in presenti distinctione pro secunda conclusione quod de potentia dei absoluta potest deus naturam

That the greatest penalty in this world (death) can go with the greatest glory in the next is shown by Christ's passion; similarly with other men, a corresponding punishment could lead to a like measure of glory.[1] God, by His absolute power, can accept and reward any sinner.[2]

A striking effect of this absence of order between deeds and rewards is Adam's conclusion that his future damnation could be revealed to an angel or to one in grace.[3] He here discloses an extremism greater than we yet have found in any of the other Pelagians; and, by it, the final outcome of their use of God's *potentia absoluta* is made abundantly clear. Their views contrast so fiercely with Bradwardine's that, like two men in a sinking boat, while one bails out the water, the other makes new holes for it to enter.

Finally, Adam, having denied a *habitus* any efficacy or place, simply takes the final step when he allows grace and sin to stand together. In this case, too, he goes farther than the other Pelagians in extending this to include mortal sin.[4] Neither, he says,

beatificam existentem in puris naturalibus sine omni forma sibi supernaturaliter inherente ad vitam eternam acceptare et per consequens sibi carum et acceptibilem habere. Praeterea . . . potest deus quemcunque preparare et prius ea vitam eternam sibi conferre sine tali habitu previo . . . quia deus de potentia sua absoluta potest alicui conferre vitam eternam qui nunquam habuit talem habitum et per consequens erat in tali statu quod non habebat aliquid repugnans vite eterne et poterat deus istum preparare ad vitam eternam posita quod nunquam habeat talem habitum' (a) (ibid.).

[1] '. . . et ideo si deus actum bonum ex genere istius qui immediate ante sic fuit in culpa mortali acceptet sicut potest de potentia absoluta, et forte de ordinata, tunc remittit sibi culpam istam vel omnino vel partim . . . tunc non video quin sicut anima christi habuit de dei potentia vitam eternam tunc maximam penam, ita posset unus actus per totum tempus futurum et per consequens de dei potentia esse dignus tali premio beatifico et habere sine termino penam sensus' (a) (ibid. art. 2).

[2] '. . . sic ergo patet quod non est absolute necessarium quod ille de peccatore fiat acceptus vel recipiat donum supernaturale licet aliter non fiat de potentia dei ordinata' (a) (ibid.).

[3] 'Hic dico primo duas conclusiones quarum prima est quod existenti in caritate potest deus dampnationem revelare et patet ex superioribus. Secunda quod de potentia absoluta posset etiam existenti in caritate qui secundum veritatem est casurus in peccato mortali in eo finaliter permansurus et sibi revelare, quia non est hoc impossibile secundum potentiam absolutam quam quod petro existenti in caritate revelaverit de facto negationem suam que secundum auctoritatem augustini . . . erat culpa mortalis in petro' (a) (bk. III, qu. 6).

[4] 'Ad istud respondeo quod non dixi quod aliquis habens gratiam

formally contradicts the other, and though a man could not be in both states at once, it is possible for grace and mortal sin to co-exist. The importance of such an attitude cannot be over-stressed: it is to destroy the traditional order by which God moves and men are moved; it devaluates all hitherto accepted stand-ards of good and evil; and it removes any constant criteria by which anything may be judged. As a result, men are left with nothing to follow and God becomes the source of disorder and uncertainty instead of their guide and stay. This is whither the arguments of Adam and the Pelagians must lead: the whole tra-ditional relationship between God and His creatures is ruptured; and men triumph from the destruction which is wrought.

As with all the Pelagians, Adam's rejection of created grace and charity reduces the relationship between God and men to the direct impact of their respective wills. They become the only two constant factors with the elimination of all intermediaries. Such a situation cannot but give a greater impetus to free will both in its own right and through God's will. On the one hand, free will, if rewarded, is rewarded for its own sake and not for any *habitus*. On the other, the infinite possibility of God's will gives a corres-pondingly unlimited scope to free will, since He could do any-thing for it that He desired. Thus free will is the gainer in each case: all the onus for reward shifts to God and all glory accrues to men.

Adam regards men as capable of good in their own right; they are far from the worthless creatures that Bradwardine considers them to be. This can be seen in several particulars. Firstly, the human will can conform to the dictates of reason from the intel-lect, as, for example, when the intellect rightly sees God and knows that He should be loved above all. The human will can carry out this duty by its own volition, and without need for help

increatam secundum quam deus secundum presentem iustitiam acceptat ad vitam eternam, possit cum hoc esse in culpa mortali de dei potentia absoluta sed dictum est quod gratia informans non habet formalem repugnantiam ex natura sua ad culpam mortalem . . . et ideo dicendum quod non starent simul hec duo: iste habet gratiam et iste peccat mortaliter, nec huic repugnat hec quod dixi, scilicet quod gratia creata non repugnat ex natura sua culpe mortali vel quod potest simul stare de dei potentia absoluta cum culpa mortali' (*a*) (bk. 1, dist. 17, qu. 3).

beyond the guidance of reason in man.[1] Secondly, from this it follows that in the case of, say, loving God above all, men can do this by their own resources, independently of grace.[2] They have it, therefore, within them to reach God directly and independently, a view that was heresy to Bradwardine.[3] Thirdly, this, in turn, means that men could equally fulfil God's mandates alone: God could command that, even without charity, He should be loved above all, and, since everything from God is reasonable, this would be possible.[4] Adam is quick to point out, however, that this does not mean that men can fulfil all precepts and avoid all sins, for this would lead to Pelagius's error of putting merit within their power, not God's. He is, rather, prepared to grant that men can avoid many sins though not all.[5] Finally, then, men are not weak vessels, unable to do anything but sin; they are strong enough both to know good and to do good.

Adam, in discussing merit, is careful to distinguish between an act, on the one side, and its value, on the other.[6] He is constantly

[1] 'Prima conclusio sit hec: quod in via stante congregatione viatoris enigmatica in universali vel particulari voluntas potest in se causare active dilectionem dei super omnia et propter se sine fruitione dei, quia voluntas potest se conformare recto dictamini intellectus, sed intellectus potest ratione dictare quod deus sit cognitus, sit super omnia diligendus et bonus, ergo multo fortius si clare videtur, quia non minus potest voluntas in obiectum perfectius cognitum quam minus perfectius cognitum. Item omnis potentia libera potest habere aliquem actum circa deum sic cognitum et etiam circa deum clare visum multo fortius et non necessario deordinatum, ergo ex puris naturalibus potuerit habere ordinatum actum circa deum, licet non meritorium sed bonum ex genere et natura actus' (a) (bk. I, dist. I, qu. 10).

[2] 'Ad primum istorum concedendum est mihi videtur quod sine infusione supernaturali posset voluntas viatoris, mediante dictamine possibile haberi de deo in via libere causari in se dilectionem dei super omnia . . .' (ibid.).

[3] De causa Dei, preface; see p. 15 above.

[4] 'Praeterea precepta non viderentur rationabilia si ponerentur impossibilia. Deum autem etiam si charitatem infundere vellet [=nollet] rationabiliter posset precipere amorem sui super omnia, ymo adhuc teneretur instinctu nature, igitur talem actum ex naturalibus elicere posset qualis caderet sub precepto potest' (b) (bk. I, dist. I, qu. 10).

[5] '. . . et cum dicit quod tunc possem ex puris naturalibus implere precepta omissionis, dico quod non sequitur tamen quia non est in potestate nostra aliquid facere ex huius precepto. . . . Concedo tamen quod multa peccata mortalia et etiam venialia vitare potest homo sine caritate infusa nec propter hoc erravit pelagius, sed quia dixit quidem omnia et quod mereri etiam potest ex puris naturalibus, ut estimo, et hoc falsum est, quia non sit in potestate nostra quod deus illos acceptat ad vitam eternam' (ibid.).

[6] 'Licet non meritorium sed bonum ex genere et natura actus' (a) (bk. I, dist. 17, qu. 1).

aware that something may be good in itself but still not meritorious. This is because God alone can confer merit, and His will
alone is the arbiter. Adam is so obsessed with God's will as the
source of all ultimate value that, having given human powers
their own worth, he is not able to form a direct link between them
and reward. However good they may be, only God rewards
them; merit could never come by their own qualities alone. This
is shown in Adam's preference for an act to a habit. Because an
act of loving God can come freely from the will, it is far more
acceptable to God than any habit.[1] Ockham used this argument
to make an act of free will the only condition for God's acceptance: what a man began God completed.[2] Adam, however, stops
short of this and does not move beyond asserting the superiority
of the act. He seeks no full union between an act and God's merit:
each, therefore, merely confronts the other. It would seem that
Adam, while following Ockham in his rejection of a habit, cannot, in face of God's unlimited freedom, bring himself to make
an act play a direct part in God's decisions. As a result, Adam
only uses the primacy of act over habit to assert the superfluity of
the latter.

The effects of his view of merit may be summed up as follows.
In the first place, it makes both act and habit neutral, incapable
of reward in themselves, but dependent on God's acceptance.
Thus, by God's will, an act of loving God and one's neighbour,
though uninformed by a habit, can be accepted as worthy of
everlasting life.[3] In the second place, this, in effect, exalts the act

[1] 'Ad secundum dicit okam quod non est necesse quod deus diligit ex
aliquo inductivo, sed mere libere diligit quem vult . . . adhuc non necesse
esset quod sic diligeret quod daret vitam eternam' (a) (bk. I, dist. 17, qu. 2.).
   And: 'Item actus diligendi deum sic omnino libere causatus habet magis
rationem acceptabilis ex natura sua quam quilibet habitus viatoris, ergo
possit deus aliquem acceptare ad vitam eternam' (a) (ibid.).
   '. . . multo magis potuerit vel eque de potentia dei absoluta acceptare
aliquem propter solum actum diligendi deum super omnia nullam habentem
circunstantiam malam' (b) (ibid.).
[2] See pp. 189, 198 above.
[3] 'Tertia conclusio principalis quod actum dilectionis dei et proximi
circumstantionatum circumstantiis mere naturalibus a parte voluntatis libere
eum causantis secundum dictamen rectum conscientie naturalis posset deus
de potentia absoluta acceptare tanquam meritorium vite eterne: probatur
quia quando sunt plures actus in potestate alicuius quorum neuter de natura
sua est dignus vita eterna, uterque est bonus simpliciter qualiter potest esse
bonus ex naturalibus qua ratione potest unus illorum esse meritorius vite

at the expense of the habit, for while Adam refuses to see either as *per se* the starting point of merit, it is the act which God transmutes: neutral though it is, God can make it good and indeed does so. Accordingly, while the habit falls by the wayside, of no account in the journey to God, the act is taken up by Him and made the vehicle to glory. In the third place, merit becomes a relationship between free will and divine will. God can accept a man *ex puris naturalibus* and this frees him from the need for grace.[1] Man's own nature is enough to make him dear to God, were he even in sin.[2]

Adam reaches the same goal as the other Pelagians, though the steps appear less defined. He has effected the same triumph of natural resources over supernatural habits and man has emerged the stronger, and virtually independent. Once again, merit *de congruo*, as an act rewarded for itself and not for the grace which informs it, becomes the main source of reward. Grace is submerged between the forces of free will and God's will. Man, in fact, has been taken into partnership with God; he has to answer to nothing else. With these views, Adam must take his place as one of the upholders of the damnable heresy of Bradwardine's.

On the question of future contingents, too, Adam gives further evidence of his position. As we have already seen with Durandus, Aureole, Holcot and Buckingham, this problem has its roots in the conflict between God's authority and free will. Whatever the aspect, whether of logic (Aureole) or the effect of God's knowledge on revelation (Holcot and Buckingham), the problem

eterne et reliquus de potentia absoluta, sed actus talis cum tali forma supernaturali et actus diligendi deum super omnia in tali forma quod sic se habent quod neuter ex natura sua est meritorius vite eterne sed quia deus contingit acceptare sicut patebit post, ergo qua ratione potest unus istorum esse meritorius et acceptus de potentia dei absoluta' (*a*) (Sentences, bk. 1, dist. 17, qu. 2).

[1] 'Item caritas non sit necessaria videtur quia ceteris paribus quanto voluntas cum gratia eliceret actum bonum volendi tanto esset magis meritorius, quia tanto plus accresceret actus bonus voluntatis et maiorem conatum apponeret, ergo ut videtur tantum conatum potest apponere quod etiam si totaliter deesset caritas adhuc esset actus meritorius' (*a*) (*ibid.*).

[2] 'Ad sextum licet non sit in potestate hominis in puris naturalibus vitare omne peccatum, cuius oppositum dicit pelagius . . . tamen in potestate dei est hominem in puris naturalibus acceptare, nec plus includit peccatum nisi quod peccatum privat gratiam, sed hec absolute remitti posset per dei potentiam absolutam sine infusione gratie' (*b*) (*ibid.* qu. 3).

remains the same: How to maintain God's will and knowledge unimpaired and yet not impede free will. Each of the different solutions we have discussed has had to make a sacrifice somewhere. Bradwardine refused to recognize the future as anything different from the past or present, thereby viewing time from God and, in effect, denying contingency. The Pelagians started from the created nature of time and so ultimately made God share in contingency (Buckingham) or else withdraw in its interests (Aureole and Holcot). In either case they had to uphold one aspect in preference to the other. Adam, as befits a Pelagian, follows Bradwardine's opponents in asserting the contingency of the future. Moreover, he follows Buckingham's path in allowing that God knows everything, thus knowing the future contingently. This leads him to substantially the same conclusions as Buckingham, but with two marked differences. First, he does not base the existence of future contingents primarily upon free will, as Buckingham did; but on God's *potentia absoluta*. Second, this leads to his discussing the future in far more speculative terms than even Buckingham: the justification for the consequences lies in what God, in His absolute power, *could* do, rather than from the scope which is due to free will. Thus Adam again betrays the same lack of correlation between the divine and free wills: although each is free, it is left to God's will to account for whatever may result.

Adam makes God's omniscience the starting-point of his discussion of future contingents. God knows all things, impossible and possible, past, present and future.[1] Yet, since the future, if free, has yet to be, Adam, like Buckingham, makes God's knowledge of the future equally free and undecided. Unless it were uncertain, it would destroy contingency and subject everything to necessity.[2] God, therefore, because He foresees that a future

---

[1] 'Hec sit ergo prima conclusio quod scientia dei immensa est vel immensum iudicium. Ex hac sequitur quod nullum vere indivisibile latet eum nec etiam possibile est quod quid aliud sit vere indivisibile et non ab eo evidente iudicatum, quia sicut propter immensitatem sue potentie vel essentie nusquam deesse potest ubi aliquid potest esse . . . ergo evidenter et illud certiter novit deus quod bene stant simul quod *a* fore dependeat cum ex contingenti voluntatis libertate sive create sive increate et tunc quod a deo evidenter sciatur *a* fore . . . sicut dei immensitas secundum essentiam non determinat sibi ex natura sua . . .' (*a*) (bk. III, qu. 2).

[2] 'Quarta conclusio sit quod cum hoc quod *a* fore dependeat ex contingenti

act A will come from free will, cannot, in the interests of its freedom, know it certainly. This is the essence of Adam's position, and from it follow his views on revelation and the Word of God and Christ. Though at other times, however, Adam pays court to the more traditional views of God's knowledge, which at first sight would seem to go against his more extreme assertions,[1] these play no real part in moulding his argument. Like his constant references to FitzRalph, one of his main official persecutors,[2] they are there for his own protection.

From Adam's recognition of the future as undetermined it follows that any proposition about it can be true or false, as, for example, that tomorrow a battle will or will not take place. Each for today is as true as the other, since the morrow has yet to come.[3] Thus far Adam has followed through the nature of a future action in general; he now applies to it God's Word in particular, which ultimately leads to God's will's taking control. Since revelation, he says, applies to the future, it deals with events which have yet to take place; this means that, as God does not determine the future, it is concerned with contingents. The nature of the future, as free, is the cause of making God's knowledge of it, through the Word, contingent. In consequence, what is revealed in the Word need never take place.[4] Thus all God's knowledge of

libertate voluntatis create vel increate stat quod deus incerto sciat ipsam fore, quia eo ipso quod deus necessario sciret *a* fore *a* necessario foret, quia oppositum antecedentis repugnat formaliter antecedenti, sed consequens est impossibile quod *a* necessario sit futurum si *a* fore pendet ex contingenti libertate voluntatis create vel increate, ergo antecedens' (*a*) (*ibid.*).

[1] 'Respondeo in quid hybernicus et dico de vera voce quod prescientia dei est causa quando res sunt future' (bk. III, qu. 3).

[2] See A. Gwynn, *English Austin Friars in the time of Wyclif.*

[3] '. . . in illis de presenti omne quod est necesse est esse quando est et omne quod non est necesse non esse quando non est, ita in futuris necesse est disiunctivam ex contradictoriis veram esse, sed tamen neutram partem disiunctive necesse est esse veram navale bellum erit cras . . . ex istis sequitur quod illa disiunctiva est vera' (*a*) (bk. III, qu. 2).

[4] 'Ex hac sequitur quinta conclusio quod verbum dei contingenter scit solummodo *a* fore sit contingens ad utrumlibet et per consequens dependens a voluntate contingenter operativa, quia supponendo quod aliquid sit futurum contingenter vel necessario est futurum, ergo si *a* est futurum cuius fore dependet ex contingente libertate et per consequens non necessario futurum sit *a* solum contingenter est futurum, ergo *a* verbo dei solum contingenter scitur esse futurum' (*a*) (*ibid.*).

'Ex hac sequitur ultima quod nihil necessario scitur a deo esse futurum quod nihil est futurum secundum veritatem fidei quod non dependet ex

the future, as foreseen in the Word, may equally have never been known to Him;[1] it could, moreover, be upset by emergence of events opposite to those which He foresaw.[2] The Word then, far from contradicting contingency, derives from it.[3] Adam now suddenly changes the ground of the argument. God's will, he says, is the cause of all such contingency and this is the reason for it.[4] He proceeds to base the mutability of God's Word upon the absolute freedom of His will. If, he says, revelation were necessary then God Himself would be subject to His knowledge of it. But there is nothing that He cannot refuse to do, whatever its cause: He can, therefore, go against His own knowledge and beliefs.[5] With one exception, Adam draws all the consequences that could follow from the mutability of the Word, from God's *potentia absoluta*. This is that, if revelation were necessary, all the

libertate voluntatis divine, quia deus nihil necessario operabatur, ergo etc.' (*b*) (bk. III, qu. 2).

[1] 'Ex hiis sequitur septima conclusio, scilicet quod omne illud quod deus scit esse futurum potest adhuc nunquam scivisse se esse futurum . . . ergo sequitur conclusio dist. 17, quod *a* quod prescitum a deo fore potest nunquam fuisse scitum a deo fore' (*a*) (*ibid.*).

[2] 'Octava conclusio est de contingenti ad utrumlibet cuius futuritio expendet a libertate voluntatis create, puta a voluntate mea, quia ego possum facere quod deus ab eterno scivit *a* esse futurum et similiter quod in libera potestate mea quod deus sciverit *a* non esse futurum quod nec est nec fuit possum facere quod erit libere et possum facere quod *a* nunquam libere proveniat a voluntate mea. Nona sequitur ex premissis quod illud nunquam prescivit deus fore possum facere quod nunquam prescivit' (*ibid.*).

[3] '. . . eo ipso quo sunt contingenter futura et per consequens contingenter eveniant scientia taliter esse futura, ergo deo verbi scientia non obstat contingentem futurum . . . quia novit futura isto modo debere evenire et evenient et non aliter alioquin deciperetur vel decipi posset quod non est verum et ideo sicut quidem evenient ita prescit quod contingenter evenient et causa est, ut dixi in precedenti questione, quia non ideo quia presciuntur fore erunt, sed quod erunt' (*ibid.* qu. 3).

[4] 'Et est dicendum quod libertas divine voluntatis est prima causa omnis talis contingenter futuri; ipsa et eius libera volitio respectu essentie vel non essentie rerum talium est causa sufficiens rerum' (*a*) (*ibid.*).
'. . . tunc absolute loquendo omnia futura simpliciter necessario evenient quod est erroneum et contra fidem. . . . Item contra hoc est articulum parisiense' (*a*) (*ibid.*).

[5] 'Ad istud dicendum est concedo hanc esse contingentem et post predicationem huius a christo *a* erit vel non erit et hoc similiter quod christum predicat esse futurum non eveniet est contingens sic quod non simpliciter impossibile est . . . tamen nulla principatio absoluta necessitat deum quin possit simpliciter loquendo non implere quod principavit vel fecit credi futurum esse' (*a*) (*ibid.*).

crimes and weaknesses revealed in the Word would be excused
as beyond the control of those who committed them. In consequence, this would exonerate Judas and Pilate, those who cruci-
fied Christ, together with Peter, and all to whom God had revealed their future deeds. None of these could be justly punished
because they were all subject to forces beyond their own free will.[1]

Adam's other consequences of the freedom of revelation, as
coming from God's will, are much more extreme. Firstly, Christ
could have been deceived, though not by God's *potentia ordinata*.[2]
Secondly, God and Christ could deceive since they reveal only
what is contingent.[3] Adam is at pains to distinguish this from wilful deception: for Christ to tell His disciples that *A* will be,
though *A* does not come about, is not to lie. Christ was only
following what He believed to be true, with no intention of misleading His disciples.[4] Nevertheless, the full logic of God's
potentia absoluta asserts itself before long and Adam concedes
that deceit, too, is possible by His absolute will.[5] Even worse,

[1] 'Utrum alicuius contingentis futura absoluta revelatio sequens tollat
contingentiam. . . . Primo ad questionem dico quod non et probat hybernicus
primo pro eo quod conclusio opposita non videtur bene sapere, quia excusat
iudam a peccato et pylatum et iudeos crucificantes et petrum negantem et
omnes alios quorum peccata fuerunt predicta seu revelata a christo, quia
nullus peccat in eo quod vitare non potest . . . praeterea tollit libertatem
respectu cuiuslibet revelati' (*a*) (*ibid*. qu. 5).

[2] 'Dices forte quod anima christi licet verbo unita si non esset ditata gratia
et gloria naturaliter posset dicere et credere aliquod futurum quod tamen non
eveniret et iuxta talem credulitatem producere talem false credidisset . . .
dicendum quod argumentum procedit solum de potentia dei absoluta quod
secundum potentiam dei ordinatam animo christi verbo unita non potest
ignorare se uniri nec potest decipi credendo falsum' (*a*) (*ibid*.).
And: 'Dicendum quod facta revelatione adhuc ista revelata contingenter
evenient et non necessario verum est' (*a*) (*ibid*.).

[3] '. . . concedo sicut in argumento responsum est quod si *a* sit adhuc
futurum, nec est contingens *a* erit et deus vel christus asseruit vel non *a* fore,
quia hec est contingens *a* erit. . . .
'Si autem christus secundum scientiam suam ac voluntatem expresse vult *a*
fore volens absolute dare, intendere et signare sicut verba pretendebant et
quod discipuli sui sic tali dicto fidem adhibent tunc veritatem ut estimo . . .
quod postquam christus predixit discipulis suis futura contingentia fuit hoc
contingens christus assumit falsum' (*a*) (*ibid*.).

[4] '. . . et negat hybernicus et bene istam conclusionem: hec fuit ex tunc
possibilis est mentitus vel dixit mendaciam, quia non sufficit ad mendaciam
sola assentio falsi. Sed requiritur intentio fallendi' (*a*) (*ibid*.).

[5] 'Ad istud concedo quod non fuisset impossibile secundum dei potentiam
absolutam quin sic seduxisset unde . . . christus in quid fuit vere seductor' (*a*)
(*ibid*.).

God, by His *potentia absoluta*, though not a liar, could knowingly mislead, and both He and Christ could sin.[1]

Adam has indeed reached the furthest limits of possibility; he has surpassed all the other Pelagians in the audacious use to which he puts God's absolute power. He has so freed God from every obligation that He has no obligation even to Himself. Good and evil have no more meaning in Him than in themselves. Nothing is so impossible but that God can do it: this is the essence of Adam's Pelagianism. It can have no room for laws or precepts. We can understand the importance that the struggle over the future had for Bradwardine; upon it hung both the nature of God and the power of free will. He and his opponents were each striving to fill the vacuum left by the disruption of the thirteenth-century systems. Neither in the illumination of Bonaventure nor in the Aristotelianism of St Thomas did the problem of God and the future arise in such sharpness. For both these there was a firm and constant contact between God and His creatures; the existence of the latter, in whatever temporal stage, was inconceivable apart from their union with God. For Bradwardine and his contemporaries, however, the bond had gone: though God might still rule as strongly in their hearts, there was not the same means for asserting Him. Thus with the connexion between God and His creatures broken, they tended to fly apart: instead of the ordered relationship, which of its very nature compassed every aspect of their existence together, they were left with two wills, each free, and neither liable to any limitation which might impair its freedom. Accordingly, the struggle over future contingents involved taking sides either for God or men; as such it was inseparable from the rest of fourteenth-century Pelagianism.

---

[1] '. . . et ideo deus non potest ut dicit mentiri quamvis possit vel posset asseverare falsum scitum esse falsum . . . hec sint dicta de deo et de anima christi dicendum est posset mentiri sicut posset peccare' (*a*) (bk. III, qu. 5).

CHAPTER XIII

THE DISPUTES AND AFTER

THE disputes between Bradwardine and the Pelagians show clearly the changed climate of their age. Despite what might, at first sight, appear as arid and obscure, they involved the entire foundation of scholasticism. Far from showing those traits of hair-splitting and logic-chopping for which the period is renowned, the questions involved were matters of substance. They have an unmistakable unity deriving from their preoccupation with the place of the divine in the created. In the stand that each side took over one in preference to the other, scholasticism was split into its component parts of faith and reason.

We may discern three aspects in this breakdown of the traditional systems. The first was the virtual disappearance of metaphysics as a point of contact between the divine and the created. Diverse though previous concepts had been, they all united in seeing a common reality which extended from God to His creatures. Whether in the illumination of the Augustinians, in the analogy of St Thomas or in the univocity of Duns Scotus, there was, common to all, the conception of a link between God and His creatures. Can the same be said of either Bradwardine or the Pelagians? Bradwardine, it is true, accepted the Thomist distinction between necessary and possible being, and also causality: yet these, beyond helping to assert God's existence in conjunction with the diametrically different ontological proof, played little real part in his system. We have already examined the predominantly theological tone of his argument, his dependence upon authority, and the scarcely veiled contempt for the powers of reason to reach the truth. The Pelagians, for their part, from the first ruled out metaphysics as an aid to understanding; their use of God's *potentia absoluta* was testimony to the impossibility of discussing Him in rational terms; their rejection of habits, their denial of intrinsic values, their attitude of doubt towards all but established fact, illustrated their refusal to pass from the individual to the general, from the practical to the speculative, from fact and experience to metaphysics and understanding. Knowledge, in becoming identified with practice, was given no scope to extend to concepts, or, if it did so, it was no longer firmly grounded.

The second aspect was the necessary corollary of the first: the end of the old systems and the rise of the new outlooks which we have examined above. It is clear that once reason was distrusted, on the one hand, and confined, on the other, it had not the resources to discuss matters which lay beyond it. The ability of reason to extend beyond the practical had been the guiding thread of scholasticism. Whatever the definition attempted, no view of scholasticism can be complete without including the very special relationship of faith to reason. Unlike pure faith, more was involved than the simple assertion of dogma; reason was there to translate its truths, bringing knowledge and, where possible, fact to its support. Similarly with reason: it did not remain restricted to the tangible, but, like the propositions in geometry, dealt with the truths that lay beyond it, relating its knowledge to the wider scheme of things. Accordingly each supplemented the other in their efforts to come nearer to God.

Such a position could not be upheld in the different circumstances of the fourteenth century, and there was a marked change in direction. We have already noticed the new questions, the eclecticism and the different ways of viewing the role of reason. Their importance need hardly be stressed: for in the process many of the traditional topics were excluded and those examined treated in a novel manner. Both the sceptics and Bradwardine bear witness to this.

As we have already suggested, God's *potentia absoluta* introduced another dimension into thought. Far more than the exercise of critical logic it transformed the entire discussion. In the name of possibility it became a destructive agent on a cosmological scale. With God's omnipotence as its spearhead it was an irresistible force subject to no laws. Its effect was twofold: firstly, God's own nature disintegrated into an indefinable, uncircumscribed power governed only by the dictates of His will. All values and principles lost meaning both in Him and among His creatures. He could only be associated with infinite possibility, ever able to do differently than He did, and constantly free to amend His own decrees. God, in fact, lost all the traditional attributes of creator; He became the source of uncertainty instead of eternal light. Secondly, in this role, God lost any real place in the created world and man became the centre of reason's attention. The final balance struck by God's *potentia absoluta* was in man's favour; his ways, not God's, were the starting-point, and God in His absolute power was the justification for virtually no God at all. Theology and faith had to concede to natural standards or be banished into the realm of dogma; there was room only for reason.

Bradwardine's reply was to deny all independent existence to man or to reason. He filled the Pelagian-created vacuum of divine absence with divine participation. Where they had consigned God to the margins, he asserted Him to the exclusion of His creatures; where they had discussed God in natural terms Bradwardine made them share His law; while the Pelagians denied man nothing in God's name, Bradwardine vindicated His cause in the ashes of human achievement. He answered their one-dimensional outlook of the natural by the equally single dimension of the divine. In answer to their use of God's *potentia absoluta* Bradwardine countered with God's *potentia ordinata*; his system was an essay in applying revealed truth to every question. Authority, not reason, assertion, not speculation, was his reply. In this sense, then, the conflict between the two sides may be seen as that over God's two different powers; although it was never thus expressed, it, in fact, involved pitting authority against scepticism. These rival claims governed the whole discussion, making it radically different from the previous epoch.

This led to the third aspect, the main issues of the time. Traditionally the first half of the fourteenth century is regarded as the second phase of the struggle between realism and nominalism, with Duns Scotus and William of Ockham as its leading figures. Yet there are considerable difficulties in accepting this view. The first is over the nature of the terms themselves. Far from being the direct continuators of the line of William of Champeaux and Roscelin, Duns and Ockham were faced with quite different circumstances. The disputes of the twelfth century had largely

S

centred around the place of the universal in the individual: resurrected in Porphyry's *Isagogue*,[1] the discussion had, at that time, four aspects: the independent existence of the universal in reality and not as a purely mental concept; whether it was corporeal or incorporeal; whether it was separate from or part of sensible things; and (Abelard's question) whether it had meaning apart from the individual. These all involved relating the mind's understanding to external reality and in this sense never went beyond logic, epistemology, and metaphysics, with the meaning of the terms 'genus' and 'species', the way in which the mind grasped them, and their source, the primary concern. While it is true that extreme realists would see the latter in God, whereas the nominalists would not, this was not then at issue.

When we turn to the controversies waged by Ockham against Duns it must be asked whether these sprang from the same circumstances, covered the same area or bore a similar emphasis. As to the first, we have already noticed the circumstances in which both Duns and Ockham lived: they were very different from those of Abelard and William of Champeaux: where in the twelfth there were only the beginnings of dialectic and the great syntheses had yet to come, the late thirteenth and early fourteenth centuries were in their aftermath. The disputes of the twelfth century had comparatively little bearing upon matters of faith, and whichever way the argument went it would not have altered the standing of theology; for the latter was too supreme and independent. The same could not be said of the fourteenth century: the rise of reason to an autonomous discipline meant that it could challenge theology, as Averroism had shown, if set loose. This was the great difference between the two periods: had Duns and Ockham even wished to take over the exact questions of their predecessors these would still have had different implications in the changed circumstances; in fact they did not.

This brings us to the second point: although it is true that both adopted positions over universals corresponding to those of nominalism and realism, these do not suffice to explain their outlooks. Duns's *distinctio formalis* made the universal a reality in itself and the individual simply its most immediate expression, the particular thisness (*haecceitas*) from the general thatness, but

[1] See Brandt (ed.), *In Isagogen Porphyrii*, p. 159.

his outlook was not confined to these concepts. Ockham's theory of knowledge had the effect of denying the universal any independent reality, but it had theological implications extending far beyond it, as we have seen in this study. Thus the terms, however just, lack the necessary precision to compass these thinkers. Moreover, in a certain sense, they apply to every thinker of any age, and while they may help to place him over the particular issue of genera and individuals they do not *per se* explain his wider outlook or his circumstances and aims.

In the third place, with both Duns and Ockham, their realism and nominalism were not complete in themselves, as with their forerunners. Duns's view of universals was essentially part of his refusal to start with the effect rather than the cause: knowledge, for him, was not derived by separating the form from the matter in which it was embodied, despite his use of St Thomas's method of abstraction: the universal form of being came before any genus or individual: *equinitas est equinitas tantum*. Ockham, similarly, rejected the universal, *en route* to his aim of freeing reason from what was beyond its ken; but he did not stop there. *Pluralitas non est ponenda sine necessitate* cut quite as sharply at theology and with much more telling effect. Thus we have to ask whether it is correct to regard Duns and Ockham as diametrically opposed: true, they started from opposite poles, but this very opposition brought them together. They were both in agreement over the incompatibility of reason to discuss matters of faith; they both made the infinite freedom of God's will beyond human calculation; they both, though with differing emphasis, used God's *potentia absoluta* to show how contingent His decrees were; they both turned their backs with such vigour upon the syntheses of the thirteenth century that the divine and the created lost contact. Despite Ockham's polemics against Duns, and their different methods, they arrived at fundamentally the same destinations.

If this is true for Duns and Ockham how far does it apply to their contemporaries and successors? At the present stage of our knowledge it is not possible to make any final judgement; but, so far as the thinkers examined here are concerned, we can say that their division did not arise over the problem of universals. While, as we have suggested, this would be implicit in whatever view they adopted, it was not the main issue, and neither Bradwardine nor his opponents was primarily concerned with it. It was, for them, authority versus scepticism in which reason was made to doubt the validity of faith, and faith, in turn, denied the efficacy of reason. Both Bradwardine and the later sceptics made the relation of the divine and created wills their central preoccupation. Far from the rival standpoints of Duns and Ockham over universals dominating the discussion, they gave little or no attention to their differences, and Adam of Woodham went so far as frequently to couple their names together in support of his own views. If nominalism versus realism was the main issue of the early fourteenth century it is not to be found in the thinkers examined here.

It is not, then, too much to say that we have to look away from the traditional categories in viewing Bradwardine and the Pelagians. Even if their chosen topics were peculiar to themselves —and this has yet to be proved—the new positions they took up cannot be ignored. For them, at least, the discussion did not centre around nominalism or realism, Augustinianism or Thomism, but over the rival claims of scepticism and authority.

What, then, was the importance of this struggle? We have already shown how it cut at the foundation of scholasticism; but did it have a more positive effect? This is a question which offers no satisfactory answer in the present state of our knowledge. It gives rise to two separate considerations: the immediate effects and the long-term effects. So far as the immediate repercussions were concerned we are still confronted with uncertainty at every turn. Bradwardine's name itself is strangely absent from the greater part of the treatises known, and even where his influence is recognizable, as with some of Jean de Mirecourt's propositions, [1] it does not build up to a common attitude. To date, two tangible signs are in evidence: Buckingham's *88 Questiones* and Wyclif's *Summa de ente*; different though they are they both give clear indications of the existence of an anti-Pelagian counter-attack during the fourteenth century. Buckingham's *Questiones* [2] are

[1] See K. Michalski, *Le Problème de la volonté à Oxford et à Paris*, Appendix 7, pp. 352–8.

[2] We have already referred to them in the note on p. 227 above. That they came later than the 'Commentary on the Sentences' can be established, firstly, by Buckingham's references to his Commentary in them (fo. 368 a); and

chiefly remarkable, not so much for what they say as for their difference in tone compared with his 'Commentary on the Sentences'. The incipit[1] states expressly that they are directed against the errors of Pelagius, Cicero and Scotus over predestination and free will, and, in the *Questiones*, practically all trace of his Pelagianism has vanished; God's *potentia absoluta* is rarely mentioned and then not to the same purpose as in his previous work; moreover, there is none of the speculation for speculation's sake; and when he expresses his own opinion it is always profusely qualified with the greatest deference to authority and with an awareness of his own limitations.[2] That Buckingham experienced a change of heart seems likely[3] even though on the question of future contingents he still supports free will, and that he had suffered severe censure at some stage seems apparent from his more than usual hesitance in voicing his own views. Could the effect of Bradwardine's disputation with him, mentioned by Thomas of Cracow,[4] and the denunciations of his views in *De causa Dei*, have had their effect upon him? We can only finally reply with fuller information, but it seems at least probable.

With Wyclif the evidence is much clearer:[5] he himself frequently mentions Bradwardine by name and he largely takes over the latter's views on grace and predestination. Although his argument, unlike Bradwardine's, is founded upon the metaphysics of being, and its modes, it is directed to a similar theological end; and in this sense it can be regarded as heir to the problems which exercised Bradwardine. This is particularly apparent in Wyclif's

secondly because the 'Commentary on the Sentences' was the means of inception for a master of theology and therefore came at the beginning of his career in the theological faculty. It may also be remarked that the '88 Questiones' together with Bradwardine's 'De causa Dei' make up New College MS.134, a possible indication of Buckingham's later standing.

[1] 'Questiones tractate per Thomam de Bukyngham nuper ecclesie exoniensis chancellarium, ostendentes inter errores pelagii Citheronis et scoti catholicum medium invenire predestinationem ... stare cum libera voluntate et merito creature ...' (fo. 324 a).

[2] E.g. 'Ad hoc respondeo semper salvo iudicio meliori' (fo. 345 a); and 'dico semper sub correctione' (fo. 347 d).

[3] 'Ego magis desirans veritatem antiquam quam novam apparentiam vacuam et fallacem ...' (fo. 399 d).

[4] Above, p. 235.

[5] For the following remarks on Wyclif I am indebted mainly to Mr J. A. Robson's unpublished study of his *Summa de ente*.

polemic against Cunningham[1] over future contingents, where he had to combat the same doubts over revelation as those cast earlier by Holcot, Buckingham and Woodham. Thus both of these thinkers bear traces of Bradwardine's influence, or, in Buckingham's case, the influence of views of a similar kind. What is so striking in Wyclif's case is that in the 1360's the same questions of grace and future contingents were exercising him as had exercised Bradwardine in the 1330's.

As to the prevalence of the disputes themselves during the fourteenth century there is again no firm information. Such names as Gregory of Rimini, Richard FitzRalph, Jean de Mirecourt are all associated with questions of grace and free will; but none of them has yet been examined with special reference to the conflict between authority and scepticism. That the use of God's *potentia absoluta* was more than a passing phase is illustrated by Wyclif's reference to it, quoted above, and also by the use to which Uthred of Boldon, a Durham monk, put it.[2] Finally, signs of the awareness of these questions in the literature of the period are to be found in Chaucer's *Canterbury Tales*, already mentioned,[3] and *Piers Plowman*.

So far, then, the immediate evidence of Bradwardine's and the Pelagians' impact is scanty, and this is hardly surprising. There still remains a great deal to be done. Furthermore, and perhaps equally important, Bradwardine's system and the views of his opponents are yet too unfamiliar to modern eyes to expect immediate recognition of their doctrines in others. Only in exceptional cases are they to be found by personal reference. There is no reason why Bradwardine, any more than his contemporaries, should have been exempted from the general habit of anonymous reference.

When we turn to the longer-term effects of these disputes their implications can be more readily grasped. Each side was preparing the way for the new outlooks associated with the Renaissance and the Reformation; medieval men though the contestants remained, syllogistic and technical though their method was, they

[1] *Fasciculi Zizaniorum magistri Johannis Wyclif*, ed. Shirley (London, 1858), pp. 4 *et seq.*
[2] See M. D. Knowles, 'The censured opinions of Uthred of Boldon', in *Proceedings of the British Academy*, XXXVII.
[3] See p. 3 above.

nevertheless were departing from its ways. To compare Brad-wardine's denunciation of reason in the interests of God's power, or the sceptics' denial of the tenets of authority, with St Thomas's attitude to reason, say, or with St Bonaventure's view of God, is to see how far the former had travelled from the latter. They marked a vital stage in the journey which was to lead to the com-plete separation of the two; for this was, in essence, the hall-mark of the two movements that we call the Renaissance and the Re-formation.

The Renaissance made the natural and the human the centre of its attention: Leonardo's drawings, Machiavelli's *Prince* or Galileo's calculations all looked to this world and not beyond it. This new empirical approach is one of the main features of the post-medieval outlook: it dispenses with hierarchy in knowledge, politics, art and science, and springs from an attitude similar to that of Ockham and his followers. It makes the natural self-sufficient. Already there were straws in this new wind at the time of the disputes examined above, such as the scientific ideas of Buridan and Nicholas Oresme, the writings of Petrarch, and together with scepticism they helped to make the change in direction.

Thus the part played by scepticism was of the first importance: it helped to put philosophy, science and secular knowledge upon an empirical footing, with the natural as the only terms of refer-ence. Without this break-up of the close-knit union of faith and reason this could never have become full-fledged.

Bradwardine's contribution to this process was no less far-reaching. By removing faith from reason's sphere, he was making it independent of everything but authority and dogma. Faith was the sole motive force once reason was withdrawn; belief had no use for reason's aid or the knowledge which was from practical experience, for it proceeded independently upon an entirely different plane. This, too, though from the other end, thrust against the medieval hierarchy from grace to nature. Theology became separated from philosophy, politics, and science, neither calling upon the other's aid. Although Bradwardine's doctrine cannot be equated with Luther's *justitia sola fide*, or Calvin's dis-missal of all save the voice of the elect, it was moving unmistak-ably in that direction. His dependence upon Scripture and authority for all argument, his identification of all worth with supernatural goodness, his lack of consideration to man or human works approach their reliance upon Scripture and conscience as the sole guides. Like the Reformers, Bradwardine could find no place for the claims of the created in the divine. His withdrawal of theology from philosophy was no less marked than the sceptics' separation of the two.

Thus it is that we have to regard the activities of the two sides: opposed as they were they contributed to a common result. Though much still remains to be known it is not too much to regard them in a special sense as the destroyers of the old and the precursors of the new.

A NOTE ON THE DATE OF 'DE CAUSA DEI'

T HE central figure amongst Bradwardine's contemporaries is William of Ockham. Between 1318 and 1323 he annotated Peter Lombard's Sentences, wrote the *Quodlibeta* and occupied himself with most of the theological works that he produced. After 1323 he was engaged almost entirely with questions of logic, to which after 1326 were added his political writings against the pope. In 1326 certain of Ockham's views in the Sentences were drawn up into fifty-one articles and condemned before a commission at Avignon; there had previously been a similar condemnation at Oxford by John Luttrell, the chancellor. Now at this time, Bradwardine was proctor of the university; and, although there is no direct evidence of association between him and Luttrell, it is difficult not to think that they knew each other and each other's views. At the very least, Bradwardine's attention must have been drawn to Luttrell's condemnation of Ockham and to the questions involved. The first four articles in the subsequent condemnation at Avignon were all of the kind that Bradwardine was attacking so strongly in *De causa Dei*. It seems highly probable, therefore, that Bradwardine must have been aware of Ockham's opinions when he wrote *De causa Dei*; indeed, it may well have originated in Ockham's condemnations, as the doctrinal prong of the counter-offensive against him.

It would not follow, however, that Bradwardine wrote *De causa Dei* before the commonly accepted date of 1344. Michalski,[1] in an examination of the question, tried to establish 1325–8 as the most probable period of its composition: he gave as his reasons that the word 'perscriptum' on the explicits of three different manuscripts of the work each bore a different date; from this he concluded that 'perscriptum' referred to its transcription, not to its composition, and that each of these manuscripts was of a later date than the original. He also brought forward as a second reason Bradwardine's generally accepted influence upon Jean de

[1] K. Michalski, *Le Problème de la volonté à Oxford et à Paris*, pp. 236–7.

Mirecourt, Nicholas d'Autrecourt and Gregory of Rimini: since their Commentaries are said to have been completed before or about 1344, this date would, Michalski held, rule out Bradwardine's influence upon them.

So far as the question of dating is concerned, an examination of other manuscripts of *De causa Dei* has shown that the date 1344 is given for its composition, and that the word 'perscriptum' used by Michalski as the main evidence cannot be taken exclusively to mean transcription.[1] As for the second argument, that of influence, it would be no less awkward to make *De causa Dei* date from 1325, for then neither Buckingham nor Woodham could be among his opponents. Rather, if we recall Bradwardine's preface[2] we can see that there was a delay between the lectures from which *De causa Dei* sprang and its appearance as a written treatise. Is it not possible that, as so frequently happens, Bradwardine continued to give these lectures over the years, incorporating additional arguments against the Pelagians as they became current?[3] This would account both for Bradwardine's influence upon subsequent thinkers and the width of his net in catching Pelagians so scattered as the six discussed above. Finally, in support of this argument, it should be remembered that, since he was a member of a medieval university, Bradwardine's ideas would have been known to his colleagues, opponents and pupils long before he published them. Although the written word is the main support for historians, for members of the same community, a man's view could be known as well without it; and, in contrast with today, disputation was then one of the main ways of expressing an opinion. Thus we must beware of seeing the genesis of these controversies in the date of their written appearance; for, more often than not, they put into writing what had long been proceeding orally.

[1] I am indebted to Professor E. F. Jacob for this valuable information; he has found that each of the following distinguishes between the date of the copy and that of the original: Lambeth 32 is described as 'perscriptum' at Cambridge but 'editum ab eodem Thoma . . . millesimo trecentisimo quadragesimo quarto'. Merton 71, giving the date of composition as 1344, was 'scriptus anno domini MCCCLXIX'. Corpus Christi, Cambridge, Grub 24, was 'compilatus et editus per reverendum sacre theologie doctorem tunc cancellarium Lond'.

[2] See pp. 14–15 above.

[3] Mr John Saltmarsh first made this suggestion to me.

THE MODERN TERMS AND DIVISIONS OF GRACE[1]

IT is important to distinguish modern theological usage from that of the fourteenth century: otherwise there is a danger of confusing their different meanings. To facilitate this distinction the following summary of the present-day terms and divisions has been appended. It makes no claim to be complete, but is rather the briefest of guides intended to point the differences in expression between the two periods.

GRACE is commonly divided into uncreated and created. *Uncreated* grace is God communicating Himself directly to His creatures. *Created* grace is a gratuitous, supernatural gift, distinct from God, and the effect of His love.

CREATED GRACE can be regarded from the following aspects:

(1) *Its cause* is either the grace of God or the grace of Christ. God's grace is that which is awarded independently of Christ's merits, as, for example, with the angels or Adam before the fall. Christ's grace is that given on account of Christ's merits and includes all grace bestowed upon man in his present fallen state.

(2) *Its mode* is either external or internal. It is *external* when it is outside the subject as in the case of Christ's teachings or the examples of the saints. It is *internal* when it inheres in the subject as an intrinsic attribute.

(3) *Its end*: internal grace is subdivided into (*a*) *gratia gratis data*, given to an individual for the help and salvation of others, as for example the gift of healing; it is not awarded to all Christians and can include sinners; (*b*) *gratia gratum faciens*, given to an individual for his own aid and salvation. It is both habitual and actual: habitual in making a person dear to God; actual as the means of acquiring, or augmenting, habitual grace. It is superior to *gratia gratis data*.

(4) *The subject and effects of grace*: As stated above, *gratia*

[1] Taken from Ad. Tanquerey, *Synopsis theologiae dogmaticae*, vol. III, Paris, 1947.

gratum faciens is divided into habitual and actual grace. *Habitual* grace is a supernatural quality permanently and intrinsically inherent in the soul, and the means by which the soul participates in the divine nature. He who possesses habitual grace is described as being in a state of grace. Habitual grace is by its nature sanctifying and justifying; by its effects it is given the different names of *Amicitia Dei*, in uniting man with God, *Filiatio adoptiva*, *Inhabitatio Spiritus Sancti*.

ACTUAL GRACE is an internal supernatural movement of the will or intellect which comes from God, and enables a man to exceed his natural powers. It is entirely gratuitous. Since it moves the intellect and will, it is internal, unlike those graces (*improprie*), such as those of miracles, which remain outside the soul of the subject. The effects of actual grace are (*a*) to illumine the soul, (*b*) to excite the will to salutary actions.

Species of actual grace. Operating grace is an internal movement of the will or the intellect by God: *in nobis sine nobis*. It is also known as *excitans*, an involuntary movement of the will. *Co-operating grace* is the aid which God bestows upon one already incited by grace that he may do good; it is also called *adjuvans*.

Operating and co-operating grace differ in three respects: (i) while operating grace can exist by itself, co-operating grace, as deriving from it, cannot; (ii) while operating is involuntary, co-operating implies an act of free will; (iii) operating, by itself, is 'sufficient'; co-operating is solely 'efficacious', for it is only given when the will has consented to act. *Sufficient* grace gives merely the power of acting without involving the achievement of a good action. It is immediately sufficient when it gives the power of acting directly; it is remotely sufficient when it gives the proximate power of doing something, or praying for help to do it. *Efficacious* grace enables the will freely, and actually, to consent; accordingly it is always associated with the act to which it gives effect. In the same way, *prevenient* grace precedes the will's desire for good and *subsequent* grace follows from this state; *gratia excitans* excites to good, *gratia adjuvans* helps to achieve good.

Final perseverance unto death constitutes a special efficacious grace, which is also a *magnum donum*. Its greatness distinguishes it from all other graces, but it is not specifically different from them.

SELECT BIBLIOGRAPHY

I ORIGINAL SOURCES

A. Manuscript

Thomas Buckingham, Super Sententias. Bibliothèque Nationale, Paris, F.L.15,888 and 16,400.

Adam of Woodham, Super Sententias. (*a*) Bibliothèque Nationale, Paris, F.L.15,892; (*b*) Bibliothèque Mazarine, 915.

Other manuscripts consulted:

Bibliothèque Nationale, Paris: F.L.14,514, 14,576, 15,409, 15,880, 15,893, 15,894, 15,976 and 15,977.
Bibliothèque Mazarine, Paris: 916.
Bodleian Library, Oxford: New College 134.
Gonville and Caius College, Cambridge: 153/101.

B. Printed

Pierre Aureole, *Commentariorum in primum librum sententiarum pars prima*, Rome, 1596.

Thomas Bradwardine, *De causa Dei* (ed. Savile), London, 1618.

Thomas Buckingham, *Super sententias*, Paris, 1505.

Robert Holcot, *In quattuor libros sententiarum quaestiones . . .*, Lyons, 1518.

Petrus Lombardus, *Libri IV sententiarum, etc.*, Quaracchi, 1916.

William of Ockham, *Questiones super IV libros sententiarum, etc.*, Lyons, 1495.

William of Ockham, *Quodlibeta septem*, Argentine, 1491.

William of Ockham, *Tractatus de praedestinatione et de praescientia dei et futuris contingentibus* (ed. Ph. Boehner), St Bonaventure, New York, 1945.

Durandus of St Pourçain, *Super sententias theologicas Petri Lombardi commentariorum libri quattuor*, Paris, 1550.

II SECONDARY WORKS

Baudry, L. *Guillaume d'Occam: sa vie, ses œuvres, ses idées*, Paris, 1949.
——'Les rapports de G. d'Occam et Walter Burleigh' in *Archives d'histoire littéraire et doctrinale* (1934), IX, pp. 155–73.
——*Le 'Tractatus de principiis theologiae' attribué à G. d'Occam* (Études de philos. méd., XXIII), Paris, 1936.

Becker, H. 'Gottesbegriff und Gottesbeweis bei Wilhelm von Ockham', in *Scholastik*, III (1928), pp. 369–93.

Boehner, Ph. 'The text tradition of Ockham's Ordinatio' in *The New Scholasticism*, XVI (1942), pp. 203–41.

——'The "notitia intuitiva" of non-existents according to William of Ockham with a critical study of the text of Ockham's *Reportatio*' in *Traditio*, I (1943), pp. 223–75.

——*The 'Tractatus de successivis' attributed to William of Ockham* (Franciscan Institute), New York, 1944, vol. I.

——'Scotus' teaching according to Ockham. I. On the univocity of being. II. On the *natura communis*', in *Franciscan Studies*, IV (1946), pp. 100–7, 361–75.

——'Ockham's theory of signification', *ibid.* pp. 163–7.

——'Ockham's theory of supposition and the notion of truth', *ibid.* pp. 261–92.

——'The realistic conceptualism of William of Ockham' in *Traditio*, IV (1946), pp. 307–35.

Bréhier, E. *La Philosophie du moyen âge*, Paris, 1937.

Butterfield, H. *Origins of Modern Science, 1300–1800*, London, 1949.

Callus, Fr. D. A. 'Introduction of Aristotelian learning to Oxford' in *Proceedings of British Academy*, XXIX (1944).

Carlyle, R. W. and A. J. *A History of Medieval Political Theory in the West*, London, 1903.

Carré, M. H. *Phases of Thought in England*, Oxford, 1949.

Chadwick, O. W. *John Cassian: a Study in Primitive Monasticism*, Cambridge, 1950.

Chenu, M. D. *La Théologie comme science au XIIIe siècle* (2nd ed.), Paris, 1943.

——'Le "Quaestiones" de Thomas de Buckingham', in *Studia medievalia in honorem admodum reverendi patris R. J. Martin*. Bruges, 1948; pp. 229–41.

Crombie, A. C. *Robert Grosseteste and the Origins of Experimental Science*, Oxford, 1952.

De Ghellink, *Le Mouvement théologique au XIIe siècle*, Paris, 1914.

De Lagarde, *La Naissance de l'esprit laïque au declin du moyen âge* (6 vols.), Paris, 1943.

Duhem, P. *Le Système du monde*, Paris, 1913–17.

Ehrle, F. *Der Sentenzenkommentar Peters von Candia des Pisaner Papstes Alexander V* (Franziskanische Studien, IX), Münster, 1925.

Elie, H. *Le Complexe significabile*, Paris, 1936.

Garrigou-Lagrange, R. *Dieu: son existence et sa nature*, St Louis and London, 1934.

Giacon, C. *Guglielmo di Occam. Saggio storico-critico sulla formazione et sulla decadenza della scolastica*, Milan, 1941.

Gilson, E. *La Philosophie au moyen âge* (1944 ed.), Paris, 1947.

——*Jean Duns Scot*, Paris, 1952.

——*Reason and Revelation in the Middle Ages*, New York, 1939.

——*The Unity of Philosophical Experience*, London, 1938.

——*L'Esprit de la philosophie médiévale* (2nd ed.), Paris, 1947.

Gilson, E. and Boehner, Ph. *Die Geschichte der christlichen Philosophie*, Paderborn, 1937.

Glorieux, P. *La Littérature quodlibétique*, Kain, 1925.

——*Repertoire des maîtres en théologie de Paris du XIIIe siècle* (Études de philos. méd., XVII, XVIII), Paris, 1933-4.

Grabmann, M. *Die philosophische und theologische Erkenntnislehre des Kardinals Matthaeus von Aquasparta*, Vienna, 1906.

Guelluy, R. *Philosophie et théologie chez Guillaume d'Occam*, Paris, 1947.

Gwynn, A. *English Austin Friars in the time of Wyclif*, London, 1940.

Hahn, S. *Thomas Bradwardinus und seine Lehre von der menschlichen Willensfreiheit* (in Beiträge zur Gesch. derPhilos. des Mittelalters, v), Münster, 1905.

Harnack, A. *History of Dogma* (trans. W. M'Gilchrist), London, 1899.

Haskins, C. H. *Studies in the History of Mediaeval Science*, Cambridge (Mass.), 1924.

Hochstetter, E. *Studien zur Metaphysik und Erkenntnislehre Wilhelms von Ockham*, Berlin-Leipzig, 1927.

Hook, W. *Lives of the Archbishops of Canterbury*, London, 1865.

Klibansky, R. *The Continuity of the Platonic Tradition in the Middle Ages*, London, 1939.

Knowles, M. D. 'The censured opinions of Uthred of Boldon', in *Proceedings of British Academy*, XXXVII (1950).

Koch, J. *Durandus de S. Porciano* (Beiträge zur Gesch. der Philos. des Mittelalters), Münster, 1927.

——'Neue Aktenstücke zu dem gegen Wilhelm Ockham in Avignon gefurten Prozess', in *Recherches de théologie ancienne et médiévale* (1935), pp. 353-80; (1936), pp. 168-97.

Laun, J. F. 'Recherches sur Thomas de Bradwardine, précurseur de Wyclif', in *Revue d'histoire et philosophie religieuses*, IX (1929).

Lechler, G. *De Thoma Bradwardino Commentatio*, Leipzig, 1862.

Little, A. G. and Pelster, F. *Oxford Theology and Theologians*, Oxford Hist. Soc., 1934.

Maier, A. *An der Grenze von Scholastik und Naturwissenschaft*, Essen, 1943.

——*Das Problem der intensiven Grösse in der Scholastik*, Leipzig, 1939.

Mélanges Mandonnet: études d'histoire littéraire et doctrinale du moyen âge (Bibliothèque Thomiste, XIII, XIV), 2 vols. Paris, 1930.

Michalski, K. *Le Problème de la volonté à Oxford et à Paris au XIVe siècle*, Lemberg, 1937.

——'Les courants philosophiques à Oxford et à Paris au XIVe siècle', in *Bulletin de l'Académie polonaise des sciences et des lettres* (1920).

——'Le criticisme et le scepticisme dans la philosophie du XIVe siècle', *ibid*. (1925).

——'Les courants critiques et sceptiques dans la philosophie du XIVe siècle', *ibid*. (1927).

——'Les sources du criticisme et du scepticisme au XIVe siècle', *ibid*. (1928).

——'La physique nouvelle et les différents courants philosophiques au XIVe siècle', *ibid*. (1928).

Milner, Rev. J. *History of the Church of Christ* (revised by Grantham), London, 1847.

Moody, E. A. *The Logic of William of Ockham*, London, 1935.

Paulus, J. 'Sur les origines du nominalisme' in *Revue de philosophie*, XXXVII (1937), pp. 313–30.

——*Henri de Gand. Essai sur les tendances de sa métaphysique* (Études de philosophie médiévale, XXV), Paris, 1938.

Pelzer, A. 'Les 51 Articles de Guillaume Occam censurés en Avignon en 1326',in *Revue d'histoire ecclésiastique*,XVIII (1922),pp. 240–71.

Powicke, F. M. *Medieval Books of Merton College, Oxford*, 1931.

Poole, R. L. *Illustrations of the History of Medieval Thought and Learning*, London, 1920.

Rashdall, H. *Medieval Universities* (ed. Powicke and Emden), Oxford, 1936.

Ross, W. D. (ed.). *Works of Aristotle translated into English*, Oxford, 1926–.

Schwamm, H. *Das göttliche Vorherwissen bei Duns Scotus und seinen erstern Anhängen*, Innsbruck, 1934.

Seeburg, R. *Lehrbuch der Dogmengeschichte*, III, *Die Dogmengeschichte des Mittelalters* (4th ed.), Leipzig, 1930.

Sharp, D. E. *Franciscan Philosophy at Oxford in the XIIIth Century*, Oxford, 1930.

Thomson, S. Harrison. *The Writings of Robert Grosseteste, Bishop of Lincoln 1235–53*, Cambridge, 1940.

Thorndike, L. *A History of Magic and Experimental Science*, London, 1923.

Vignaux, P. Art. 'Nominalisme', in *Dictionnaire de théologie catholique*, XI (1931), cols. 876–89.

Vignaux, P. *Justification et prédestination chez Duns Scot, Guillaume d'Ockham, Pierre Aureole, Grégoire de Rimini*, Paris, 1934.
——*Nominalisme au XIVe siècle*, Paris, 1948.
Werner, K. *Der Augustinismus in der Scholastik des späteren Mittelalters*, Vienna, 1883.
Williams, N. P. *The Grace of God*, London, 1930.
——*The Ideas of the Fall and of Original Sin, a Historical and Critical Study*, London, 1927.
Workman, H. B. *John Wyclif*, 2 vols., Oxford, 1926.
Wulf, M. de. *L'Histoire de la philosophie médiévale*, vol. III, Louvain et Paris, 1947.

III   REFERENCE WORKS

Denifle, H. S. *Chartularium Universitatis Parisiensis*, 4 vols. Paris, 1889–97.
Denzinger, H. and Bannwart, C. *Enchiridion symbolorum etc.* (14th and 15th ed.), Freiburg, 1922.
Dictionnaire d'histoire et de géographie ecclésiastique, Paris, 1937.
The Dictionary of National Biography, London, 1886.
Dictionnaire de théologie catholique, 15 vols. Paris, 1903–50.
Uberweg-Geyer. *Grundriss der Geschichte der Philosophie*, vol. II, Berlin, 1928.
Migne, J. P. *Patrologiae latinae cursus completus*, Paris, 1844–64.

IV   OTHER JOURNALS AND SERIES CONSULTED

Cambridge Historical Journal   *Mélanges de science religieuse*
Church Quarterly   *Moyen Âge*
English Historical Review   *Revue néo-scholastique*
Études Franciscaines   *Revue des sciences religieuses*
Journal of Ecclesiastical History   *Revue Thomiste*
Journal of History of Ideas   *Speculum*
Journal of Theological Studies   *Zeitschrift für katholische Theologie*
Mediaeval Studies   *Zeitschrift für Kirchengeschichte*

INDEX

T*